D0193435

MELTDOWN

MELTDOWN

How Greed and Corruption
Shattered Our Financial System
and How We Can Recover

▼ ▼ ▼

Katrina vanden Heuvel and
the Editors of *The Nation*

INTRODUCTION BY WILLIAM GREIDER

NATION
BOOKS

A Member of the Perseus Books Group

Compilation copyright © 2009 *The Nation*

"Wall Street and Washington" by Steve Fraser first appeared on TomDispatch.com
© 2008 by Steve Fraser. "The Rise of Market Populism" by Thomas Frank was adapted
for *The Nation* from *One Market Under God: Extreme Capitalism, Market Populism,
and the End of Economic Democracy,* © 2000 by Thomas Frank. Used by permission of
Doubleday, a division of Random House, Inc. "Show Me the Money" by Walter Mosley
© 2006 Walter Mosley. All rights reserved. "America Needs a New New Deal" by
Eric Schlosser and Katrina vanden Heuvel was first published in the *Wall Street Journal.*
All other pieces reprinted by kind permission of *The Nation.* All rights reserved.
"The Global Perspective" by Will Hutton © 2008 by Will Hutton. All rights reserved.

Contents

Part Two: Alarm Bells

Part Three:
The Crisis Hits

Part Four:
The Road to Recovery

Preface

THE YEAR 2008 will live in infamy in the annals of American economic history. As mass foreclosures, bank failures and multibillion-dollar government bail-outs rocked the country, the media scrambled to stay on top of the big story of the moment: how the collapsing U.S. financial sector was threatening to take the rest of the economy down with it. As you will see from the articles reprinted in this book, *The Nation* bore witness to the worst economic crisis since the Great Depression with compassion and insight, scrutinizing events like the bank bail-out and the twin crashes of the stock and housing markets with a keen eye to how they affected people's lives far from the centers of power on Wall Street and in Washington.

Well before the Dow's wild swings captured the headlines, *The Nation*, like an early alert warning system, identified the dynamics that would prove so disastrous, using history as a guide and refusing to accede to the "Don't Worry, Be Happy" conventional wisdom. Indeed, flipping back through the pages of the magazine in preceding years, one can track the policy decisions and economic trends that led to the crisis we are facing today. During the heady days of 1999, for example, the magazine editorialized in "Breaking Glass-Steagall" against the "grossly misnamed 'Financial Services Modernization Act,'" which would remove the Depression-era wall between commercial and investment banks and thus pave the way for "future taxpayer bailouts of too-big-to-fail financial institutions." As far back as 1990, Robert Sherrill discerned in the S&L crisis the early signs that something similar might be in store for the banking sector. At that time, Sherrill noted, the chorus calling for deregulation was recklessly demanding the repeal of laws that "protect the banking sector from its worst instincts by insisting that the banks remain banks, and not become gamblers, hucksters and hustlers in other lines as well."

Unfortunately, the bipartisan backers of the deregulatory agenda won out, and banks went on to devise virtually any risky scheme that struck their fancy, shielded from the unwanted gaze of federal regulators. Wall Street's speculative fever culminated in the frenzied trading of toxic mortgage-backed securities in the early 2000s, which allowed investors to get rich off an unsustainable bubble in the housing market. When real estate went south, the house of cards collapsed.

Quite naturally, the architects of this financial disaster would prefer not to get into the question of responsibility; they just want to talk solutions—foxes and henhouses be damned. As this volume went to press, Lawrence Summers, who as Treasury secretary under President Bill Clinton abetted the deregulatory agenda, was on the shortlist for the same post in the Obama administration. But history matters. As we try to find a way out of this mess, shouldn't we listen to the voices that warned of the perils of deregulation; that pointed out there was something seriously awry in the industry of predatory lending; and that saw how rising inequality posed a threat to the health of the whole economy?

As things fell apart in 2008, these voices of reason reasserted themselves. Proposals to tax speculative financial transactions, rein in executive pay and crack down on exploitative lenders—proposals that had languished for years—suddenly gained traction. "Responsible" people in Washington were openly contemplating the partial nationalization of banks; Wall Street executives were forced to answer tough questions—and even repent for certain actions—before Congressional hearings; and a large-scale stimulus package that would advance the transition to a green economy went from top of the wish list of liberal think-thanks to top of the incoming administration's agenda. A lame-duck President Bush even felt compelled to offer a defense of the system of free-market capitalism, as he shoveled taxpayer cash out the door as fast as he could to bail out the people he once called his "base," the rich.

This collection, compiled from articles published in the magazine and on thenation.com, proceeds from the roots of crisis through its early stages to its alarming escalation, and it concludes with a series of pieces that tackle that age-old question, What is to be done? As none other than Milton Friedman, the father of free-market fundamentalism, once wrote, "Only a crisis—actual or perceived—produces real change. When that crisis occurs, the actions that are taken depend on the ideas that are lying around." Friedman was right that ideas are important, but actions depend even more on who controls the levers of power, which segments of society they represent and what kind of pressure can be brought to bear on them from the outside. As the torch is passed from one administration to another, at a moment infused with hope and fear in roughly equal measure, we offer these ideas with a sense of possibility, if not certainty, that action may follow.

The Editors
November 17, 2008
New York City

A Note to Readers: The date on each article reflects the cover date of the issue in which it appeared. Actual press dates are three weeks earlier.

Who Rigged Wall Street?

W HO RIGGED WALL STREET? The question absorbed
people for years after the crash of 1929 and the Great
Depression that followed. Now it is before us again. The financial crisis that has swept away great wealth and important banking firms was not an accident of nature. The ingredients for
disaster were engineered by human architects seeking greater
fortunes and authorized by political actors in both parties. The
wiring for this calamity was complex, involving obscure
changes in how the financial system functions. It will take
months, maybe years, to understand it fully.

But in order to reform the system, the country has to find answers. The economy will not be truly healed until the causes are
identified and the financial system is reconstructed on sound
public principles. The names of key players in both parties
must be identified, not for vengeance but because many of them
still exercise enormous influence and hope to supervise the repair work, protecting their interests and papering over their
past errors. Economic policy makers like Robert Rubin, Lawrence Summers and their protégés arranged Wall Street for inflated profits and ruinous risk-taking and are now hovering
around President Obama. We will not get to the hard truth
about what went wrong and how to fix it if these people are in
charge of investigating themselves.

In the early 1930s, the country had the Pecora hearings and sensational disclosures that stunned Wall Street and public opinion. Formed by the Senate, the commission of inquiry went through three chief counsels before it found one person tough enough to stand up to the titans of banking—an assistant district attorney from New York City named Ferdinand Pecora. His investigators pored over the books of famous Wall Street firms; then Pecora personally grilled the self-righteous bankers. Among many revelations, the commission found that J. P. Morgan Jr. and twenty partners of his firm had paid no income taxes in 1931 or 1932 and only trivial amounts before that. "If the laws are faulty, it is not my problem," Morgan testified.

The Morgan bankers maintained lists of "preferred clients," who were invited to participate in their speculative stock-market schemes. The list of insiders included public figures like FDR's first Treasury secretary. Hoping to discredit the "circus" atmosphere of the hearings, Morgan's men brought with them a person with dwarfism, who sat on Morgan's lap. Their PR stunt backfired. The nation was convulsed in derisive laughter. The securities regulations enacted by the New Deal were grounded in what Pecora revealed.

Our crisis might not get a Pecora investigation, not one that digs out the whole truth, for this reason: This time, the dirty details of who rigged what involve many incumbent politicians, Democrats and Republicans alike, and the deals they worked out with their financial patrons on Wall Street. A close accounting would reveal how both parties collaborated for more than two decades in repealing or gutting the prudent safeguards put in place by the New Deal reformers. Congress still has some bulldog investigators, like Representatives Henry Waxman and John Conyers, but their colleagues will have very little appetite for "naming names" or exploring the money connections between Washington and Wall Street.

To dig out the answers, we must rely on the next best thing—a vigilant free press and tough-minded reporting. If that sounds improbable, some elements of major media are already on the case (perhaps seeking redemption for the Fourth Estate's utter failure during the run up to war in Iraq). For example, Peter Goodman of the *New York Times* produced a devastating account of how the Federal Reserve and the Clinton administration collaborated to block efforts to regulate the credit derivatives that became a critical factor in inducing the present crisis.

Goodman patiently reconstructed how the Commodity Futures Trading Commission's (CFTC) efforts to impose regulatory oversight on derivatives were stymied by Fed chair Alan Greenspan, Treasury Secretary Robert Rubin and SEC chair Arthur Levitt in 1997. Greenspan, Rubin and Levitt very publicly kneecapped commission chair Brooksley Born and effectively drove her from government. They staged a brutal dressing-down and urged Congress to prevent her from acting. Congress complied with a law blocking CFTC action. Lawrence Summers, Rubin's deputy at Treasury and later secretary himself, personally rebuked Born and accused her of threatening a financial crisis.

The opposite proved to be true. By not applying timely regulation, Washington set up the country for the disaster that followed. Given a free hand and virtually no oversight, major banks and investment houses became the leading salespeople for the dubious derivatives, assuring clients these devices protected them against risk on mortgage securities and other high-flying investments. Instead, the derivative contracts became a multitrillion-dollar time bomb threatening the banks themselves.

The history of purposeful rigging includes at least six other pivotal changes that slyly dismantled the old banking system and created a debt casino with extraordinary gambling and outrageous profits. Reporters, for instance, might look into the initial deregulation of banking—enacted by the Democratic Congress and president in 1980—when interest-rate ceilings were repealed and the sin of usury was decriminalized, authorizing the predatory lending and sky-high rates that are now commonplace. Another bipartisan project worth investigating was ably assisted by the Federal Reserve—the repeal, in 1999, of the New Deal's Glass-Steagall Act by the Gramm-Leach-Bliley Act. The latter measure allowed the merger of closely regulated commercial banks with unregulated investment houses and opened numerous trapdoors and escape hatches for bankers to game the differences between the two.

At the time, leading newspapers led cheers for this stuff, but even the *New York Times* editorial page is revising its views. The press lacks subpoena power, but the *Times* financial and business section is a bright, shining beacon for tough reporting, with a dozen or more deeply informed and aggressive reporters, who, led by Gretchen Morgenson, are destroying the old myths of deregulation and Wall Street rectitude. (The *Times* also has a stable of cheerleaders who keep promoting the official happy talk.)

Greenspan, under grilling from Representative Waxman, offered a weasel-worded admission that he had been mistaken about derivatives. Otherwise, none of these guys have acknowledged error, much less apologized to the American people.

Right now, national politics is in the midst of a deep power struggle over who controls the path of reform and recovery. The old order understands viscerally that its domination is threatened, and financial titans in the shrinking Wall Street club are attempting to preempt opposition. The bail-out action so far, with hundreds of billions devoted to preserving what's left of the status quo, suggests they are succeeding. But events are not cooperating, and a deepening recession will keep raising the question: What did the public get for all its money? Bush and Paulson will be gone, but President Obama will have to answer that question.

As president, Barack Obama inherits the awkward straddle the Democratic Party has maintained for many years—trying to serve the financial sector and its interests on one side while satisfying (or appeasing) popular constituencies like labor on the other. But Obama will have to manage this balancing act in much tougher circumstances—an economic contraction swiftly turning darker. As a candidate, he has mostly surrounded himself with Clinton-era economic policy-makers and people implicated in "reforms" that led to financial breakdown. This has caused considerable despair in some left-liberal quarters over the possibility that Obama will repeat the abrupt about-face of

Clinton's first administration, when Clinton dumped his "putting people first" campaign rhetoric and governed instead as an ally of multinational finance and business.

The despair is premature. It grossly underestimates the high skills and distinctive nerve of this very astute politician. Given his Harvard background and cautious manner of calculating positions, Obama is at home among centrist, establishment figures. As an African-American man and a junior senator running for president, Obama needed their respectability and courted them. When he takes office in January, he will be governing in very different circumstances and will have to decide if his presidency can subsist on cautious, small-bore reforms or must govern with a far more ambitious conception of what the country needs. Things are changing rapidly, and none of us know how it will turn out. Obama probably doesn't, either.

A photo op Obama arranged with his economic advisers a few weeks before the election tells the story. Arrayed on either side were policy leaders from the old order. Former Federal Reserve chair Paul Volcker collaborated in the initial deregulation of banking in 1980 and presided over the initial bail-outs of banks deemed "too big to fail." Robert Rubin was the architect of Clinton's center-right economic strategy and is now senior counselor at Citigroup, itself endangered and the recipient of $25 billion in public aid. Lawrence Summers, disgraced as president of Harvard, is now managing partner of D. E. Shaw, a $39 billion private-equity firm and hedge fund that specializes in esoteric mathematical investing strategies. Laura Tyson was chair of Clinton's Council of Economic Advisors and is now a University of California–Berkeley professor who sits on the boards of Morgan Stanley, AT&T and KPMG, the global accounting giant.

None of these people are well equipped to lead fundamental reform of the system they helped create or to speak reliably for the broader interests of society. Volcker, now 81, was a brilliant Fed chair who subdued runaway inflation, but he was no friend of working people. His hard-nosed monetary policy smashed wages, even as he managed the rescue of major banks in the Third World debt crisis, replacing their exposure with public lending from the I.M.F. and World Bank. Rubin is preoccupied with saving his bank from ruin, but Obama's staff is loaded with Rubin acolytes. Nine months ago, Rubin dismissed this crisis as a cyclical hiccup. Summers, on the other hand, seems to be actively running for Treasury secretary or maybe Fed chair. His public pronouncements are taking on a softer edge, and he has dropped his Calvinist devotion to balanced budgets. But now that he works for a celebrated hedge fund and private-equity firm, where does Summers stand on regulating these creatures?

Informed gossip says other leading candidates for Treasury secretary are New York Fed president Timothy Geithner, a Rubin protégé; New Jersey Governor Jon Corzine, a former Rubin colleague at Goldman Sachs; and Jamie Dimon, CEO of JP-Morgan Chase, the bank with the largest vulnerability on dangerous derivatives. Corzine is the only one with a strong record of social concerns. Another long shot is Sheila Bair, a Republican regulator and chair of the FDIC; her aggressive corrective actions have angered some big-name bankers.

Finding a financier without severely conflicting personal interests and with experience enough to manage the massive bailout will be difficult, no matter who would have won the White House. And standing too close to the old order does not seem very promising. Given this country's deformities of power, the president usually needs the establishment's help to prevail or at least avoid open warfare on important matters. Given the extreme circumstances Obama will inherit, he may face a very different calculation. If the old financial order is at the heart of the economic problem, would the president be better off protecting it or trying to disturb its power and cut its institutions down to size? For the first time in many decades, it may be smarter politics to confront the "economic royalties" (as FDR called them in the 1930s) and force major reforms of their behavior. Does Obama have the guts for such a dramatic confrontation? We don't yet know. But we do know it took a lot of nerve for a young African-American man with a different vision of the country to run for president when the reigning elders told him it was not his turn.

The established order, meanwhile, is setting out some "opportunities" for the next president to demonstrate that he is a high-minded, responsible leader. These are really traps that could doom his presidency. Military leaders are insisting on larger Pentagon budgets after withdrawal from Iraq—preempting the social spending that people have been promised. Financial leaders are urging that greater powers be given to the Fed despite the failures of that cloistered institution. This would be a great victory for the Wall Street club, cementing the privileged powers of the corporate state the bail-outs seem to have created. The so-called responsibles are likewise proposing "reform" that will cut benefits for entitlement programs, especially Social Security, as a way to correct the nation's budget deficit. This would constitute another historic swindle of the people—much larger than the bank bail-out.

President Obama would probably gain favor with the public if he rejected all three of these propositions. He would be bolstered further if the people found their voice. This expression can take the form of direct actions, large or small, nonviolent civil disobedience that pushes the new president further than he perhaps intends to go. People can reshape public opinion by showing other citizens they have the power to stop foreclosures in their neighborhood or rally the jobless to demand public employment for all or surround the rescued banks with thousands of their new public "investors," demanding lower credit-card interest rates or relaxed terms for failing mortgages.

The financial crisis continues to spread upheaval in many directions, and we do not yet know how wide or deep the destruction will flow. But strange and sometimes wonderful surprises can happen in unsettled circumstances. In the crisis of the Great Depression, a Mormon Republican banker from Utah showed up in Washington, pushing his heretical understanding of the crisis. Marriner Eccles never graduated from college, but he figured out from his banking experiences the basic economic principles the nation should follow (which later became known as Keynesian economics). Eccles was desperate to share his insights. In February 1933, he managed to testify before the Senate

Finance Committee. In one sitting, he laid out an agenda that encompassed nearly all of the important measures the New Deal subsequently enacted. The left-wing advisers around Roosevelt recognized a kindred spirit, and Eccles was asked to join the White House staff. He drafted the 1935 reform legislation that created the modern Federal Reserve. Then FDR appointed him as Fed chair.

Maybe in our chaotic circumstances, there will be similar odd convergences. One hopes our new president will be open to them—willing to listen to fresh thinking from outside the circle of established opinion-makers and brave enough to act on new ideas. Barack Obama will need all the help he can get.

William Greider
November 2008
Washington, D.C.

MELTDOWN

Part One

Seeds of Disaster

▼ ▼ ▼

Wall Street and Washington: How the Rules of the Game Have Changed

STEVE FRASER

September 19, 2008

W HAT IS WASHINGTON TO DO as the financial system col-
lapses? Clearly, stark differences in approach as well as
in public policy have already emerged. Bail out Bear Stearns
and pump up the brokerage and investment business with new
lines of credit. Nationalize Fannie Mae and Freddie Mac on the
backs of the taxpayer—but let Lehman drown. Tell the financial
community to save itself, after which Bank of America salutes
and buys Merrill Lynch. Then, the Fed gets cold feet and decides it can't let an institution the size of the insurance giant
AIG go under as well. Washington is left staring into the abyss.
The old rules no longer apply.

And that's the point. At moments of crisis since the mid-
1980s, the relationship between Washington and Wall Street has
changed fundamentally, at least when compared to anything
that would have been recognizable in the previous century. As a
result, the road ahead is dark and unknown.

During the nineteenth century, Washington was generally
happy to do favors for Wall Street financiers. Railroad tycoons,
who often used those railroads as vehicles of extravagant specu-

lation, enjoyed subsidies, tax exemptions, loans and a whole smorgasbord of financial fringe benefits supplied by pliable Congressmen and senators (not to mention armadas of state and local officials).

Since the political establishment was committed to laissez-faire, legerdemain by greedy bankers was immune from public scrutiny, which was also useful (for them). But when panic struck, the mighty, as well as the meek, went down with the ship. Washington felt no obligation to rush to the rescue of the reckless. The bracing, if merciless, discipline of the free market did its work and there was blood on the floor.

By early in the twentieth century, however, the savage anarchy of the financial marketplace had been at least partially domesticated under the reign of the greatest financier of them all, J. P. Morgan. Ever since the panic of 1907, the legend of Morgan's heroics in single-handedly stopping a meltdown that threatened to become worldwide, the iron discipline he imposed on more timorous bankers, has been told and retold each time an analogous implosion looms.

Indeed, last week's news carried its fair share of 1907-Morgan stories, trailing in their wake an implicit wistfulness. They all asked, in effect: Where is the old boy when we need him?

Back then, with Morgan performing his role as the nation's unofficial private central banker, Teddy Roosevelt's administration continued to keep its distance from Wall Street, still unready to offer salvation to desperate financial oligarchs. Not normally chummy with Morgan and his crowd, Roosevelt did cheer from the sidelines as the über-banker performed his rescue operation.

As it turned out, though, the days of Washington agnosticism about Wall Street were numbered. The economy had become too complex and delicate a mechanism and, in 1907, had come far too close to meltdown—even Morgan's efforts couldn't prevent several years of recession—to leave financial matters entirely in the hands of the private sector.

First came the Federal Reserve. It was established in 1913 under President Woodrow Wilson as a quasi-public authority meant to regulate the country's credit markets—albeit one heavily influenced by the viewpoints and interests of the country's principal bankers. That worked well enough until the Great Crash of 1929 and the Great Depression that followed and lasted until World War II. The depth of the country's trauma in those long years vastly expanded the scope of Washington's involvement in the financial marketplace.

President Franklin D. Roosevelt's New Deal did, as a start, engage in some bail-out operations. The Reconstruction Finance Corporation, actually created by President Herbert Hoover, continued to rescue major railroads and other key businesses, while some of the New Deal's efforts to help homeowners also rewarded real estate interests. The main emphasis, however, now switched to regulation. The Glass-Steagall Banking Act, the two laws of 1933 and 1934 regulating the stock exchange, the creation of the Securities and Exchange Commission and other similar measures subjected the financial sector to fairly rigorous public supervision.

This lasted for at least two political generations. Wall Street, after all, had been convicted in the court of public opinion of reckless, incompetent, self-interested, even felonious behavior with consequences so devastating for the rest of the country that government was licensed to make sure it didn't happen again.

The undoing of that New Deal regulatory regime and its replacement, largely under Republican administrations (although Glass-Steagall was repealed on Clinton's watch), with what some have called the "socialization of risk" has contributed in a major way to the mess we're in today. Beginning most emphatically with the massive bail-out of the savings and loan industry in the late 1980s, Washington committed itself, at least under conditions of acute crisis, to off-loading the risks taken by major financial institutions, no matter how irrationally speculative and wasteful, onto the backs of the American taxpaying public.

Despite free-market/anti-big-government rhetoric, real-life Washington has tacitly acknowledged the degree to which our national economy has become dependent on the financial sector (Finance, Insurance and Real Estate—or FIRE). It will do whatever it takes to keep it afloat.

This applies not only to particular institutions like Bear Stearns, or even to mortgage mega-firms like Fannie and Freddie, but to finance in general. When it seemed necessary, public monies were indeed funneled in the general direction of the banking/brokerage community to shore up the whole rickety structure. This allowed one burst bubble—the dot-com debacle—to be replaced by another, namely our late, lamented mortgage/collateralized-debt-obligation bonanza, just now dramatically going down the tubes.

Backstopping the present bailout is the ever-credulous, put-upon American public with its presumably inexhaustible resources. Even while Washington was instituting the periodic "socialization" of bad debts, it was systematically abandoning the New Deal's commitment to regulation. That, of course, was in the very period when financial markets became ever more arcane, ever less comprehensible even to their Frankensteinian inventors, and ever more in need of monitoring. So the "socialization of risk" was accompanied by the "privatization of reward," which now is likely to prove a truly deadly combination.

That the crisis has now reached a newly terrifying stage is suggested by Washington's sudden willingness to depart from the new orthodoxy and let the huge investment bank Lehman Brothers go under. Some may see in this a steely return to a laissez-faire faith. More likely, it represents wholesale confusion on the part of Bush administration and Federal Reserve policymakers about what to do, even as all endangered businesses have come to take it for granted that Washington will toss them a life preserver when they need it.

The times call for a new departure. The next administration, which will surely enter office under the greatest economic pressure in memory, must confront reality. The financial system is out of control and has led the economy into a wildly turbulent sea of heavily leveraged speculation.

It's time for a reversal of course. Stringent re-regulation of FIRE is not enough anymore. Washington's mission may, at this late date, be an even greater one than Roosevelt's New Deal faced. The government must figure out how to deploy its power to shift the flow of investment capital out of the minefields of speculative paper transactions and back into productive channels that will help meet the material needs of American society. Real value must be created in place of chimeras. In the meantime, we all have ringside seats—in fact, far too close to the action for comfort—as another gilded age is ending. What comes after is, in part, up to us.

The Looting Decade (Excerpt)*

ROBERT SHERRILL

November 19, 1990

Charles Cheating Jr.

If any one hustler was the living symbol of the underlying rot of the savings and loan industry as created by Congress and Reagan's bureaucracy in the 1980s, it was Charles Keating. He was pious, he was a devoted family man—and he was lawless. He believed the main purpose of politics was to make people like him rich.

Although Keating eventually wound up, by hook or by crook, a very wealthy fellow, it was a failed wealth. Everything

---

*On November 19, 1990, in the wake of the Savings and Loans scandal, *The Nation* devoted an entire issue to Robert Sherrill's article, "The Looting Decade: S&Ls, Big Banks and Other Triumphs of Capitalism." Unfortunately, space doesn't allow us to reproduce the whole article here. What follows are two extracts from this epic piece.

The essay was based largely on these books: *Inside Job: The Looting of* he ever did was, in a way, a failure. Twenty years ago, he got one of President Nixon's most meaningless appointments—to the President's Commission on Obscenity and Pornography. Ten years ago he briefly managed one of the biggest and most costly busts in politics: John Connally's campaign for the presidency. Nine years ago President Reagan tried to make him Ambassador to the Bahamas, but the nomination fell through when the press resurrected a 1979 scandal. It seems that Keating and his boss, Carl Lindner of the multibillion-dollar holding company American Financial Corporation ("A holding company," as Will Rogers once explained, "is a thing where you hand an accomplice the goods while the policeman searches you"), had been charged by the Securities and Exchange Commission with fraud in making millions of dollars of improper loans to insiders and friends. Keating got off by promising he wouldn't do that sort of thing in the future.

Five years ago he and his family were worth $100 million, at least on paper. Today Keating claims to be broke (by which he means he had to sell his yacht and some of his wife's diamonds), but he still lives and travels in high style, followed by a retinue of costly lawyers. Whatever money he has, his reputation is shot. Mother Teresa probably won't be dropping by to give him another crucifix, as she once did (after Keating gave

---

America's Savings and Loans, by Stephen Pizzo, Mary Fricker and Paul Muolo; *The Greatest-Ever Bank Robbery: The Collapse of the Savings and Loan Industry,* by Martin Mayer; *The S&L Insurance Mess: How Did It Happen?* by Edward J. Kane; *Thrifts Under Siege: Restoring Order to American Banking,* by R. Dan Brumbaugh, Jr.; and *Honest Graft: Big Money and the American Political Process,* by Brooks Jackson.

her $1.4 million). Most people would probably agree with the *Chicago Tribune*'s assessment of Keating as "the greediest man in America," and with the Resolution Trust Corporation, which in its $1.1 billion racketeering suit against him said he had "an evil mind."

In 1976 Keating bought American Continental Homes in Phoenix from Lindner and became a highly successful real estate developer, who trained for his later dealings with Congress by contributing as much as $25,000 to a mere city councilman's race. Developers do, after all, sometimes need to get permits from city governments.

When the savings and loan industry was deregulated in the early 1980s, Keating saw a window of opportunity as big and as gloriously brilliant as the stained glass of Sainte-Chapelle. Saying that he was certain that he could "profit immensely," in 1984 he bought for $51 million the old-line Lincoln Savings & Loan of Irvine, California, which had assets of almost $1 billion. Money for the purchase was obtained, naturally, by everyone's favorite junk-bond swindler, Michael Milken of Drexel Burnham Lambert.

How could a guy who only five years earlier was battling the S.E.C.'s fraud charges, which he escaped not by proving his innocence but by promising to behave himself, wind up with a savings and loan? Why would the bank board approve such a purchase? It was one of the blackest marks on Ed Gray's record, hardly lessened by his claim of ignorance: "I had never heard of Charles Keating. Didn't hear of Charles Keating until sometime later. There are a lot of Lincoln Savings in America. That meant nothing to me."

To win bank board approval of his purchase, Keating lied, lied, lied. He said he would keep Lincoln's experienced managers; he said he would continue to concentrate on home mortgages in Southern California. But immediately on taking over he fired the managers and quit making home loans. He began doing what so many of the scoundrels were doing—getting the big brokered funds and investing them in wild schemes.

Apparently the network of federal home loan banks never made follow-up checks to see if the people granted S&L charters kept their word. If the San Francisco home loan bank, which had jurisdiction, had done a follow-up, it would have seen that from the very beginning Keating intended to make Lincoln his personal piggy bank. One of his first gambles was on a hunk of land outside Austin, Texas, a deal in which his old pal John Connally was involved. Connally defaulted, leaving Lincoln (and now the taxpayers) holding a $70 million loss on the land.

Some of the other early loans and joint ventures, a total of $134 million, went to companies owned by Lee Henkel, who had been Keating's friend since they worked together on Connally's campaign. Keating surely must have thought his investment in Henkel would pay off when, in 1986, Keating got Reagan to appoint his buddy to the bank board (in part by getting one of his patsies, Senator Dennis DeConcini, to lobby Don Regan). There, according to Gray, Henkel "proposed a regulation that appeared to us could only benefit Lincoln Savings"—the proposal being made just a few weeks after Lincoln paid Henkel's personal blind trust $3.7 million for 25,000 shares of stock in one of Henkel's companies. (Insisting that his intentions had been completely honorable and misunderstood, Henkel resigned a few months later.)

Much of Lincoln's money was spent through the S&L's parent, American Continental Corporation, which became a developer of grandiose planned communities, resorts and hotels. The most infamous of the planned communities is Estrella, 20,000 acres in the Arizona desert that was supposed to be home to 200,000 tanned and happy residents.

Looking at Lincoln's books, one would have assumed that Estrella was making enormous profits from land sales; what the books did not show, say government examiners, was that Lincoln hired straw buyers and gave them money to buy the land at grossly inflated prices. It was a marvelous bit of abracadabra: the creation of "profits" by giving money away, after which these "profits" launched another wave of borrowing and lending, et cetera. Pure Ponzi. Today you and I own those 20,000 acres, still inhabited only by coyotes and jack rabbits, and we are spending about a million dollars a year just to keep the landscaping in shape.

As mentioned earlier, Keating was a great family man. At least ten members of his immediate kin were on the payroll of American Continental. The Keating family as a whole reaped at least $34 million in salaries, bonuses and stock sales.

Alan Greenspan and the Five Stooges

Keating's biggest troubles with the government began when Gray, in one of his smartest moves, ordered in 1985 a radical reduction in the amount an S&L could invest directly in a project. Lincoln was already $600 million over the maximum set by Gray. Furious and frightened, Keating went to work in his usual style to have Lincoln grandfathered under the new rule.

First he tried to get Gray out of the way by offering him a job at $300,000 a year. When that didn't work, he began calling in political chits. Descending on Washington, Keating went to see Vice President Bush (aides said nothing of importance was discussed).

Then Keating hired Alan Greenspan—whose conduct as a sleazy peddler of endorsements in this affair bodes no good for the future of the Federal Reserve Board, which unfortunately he now chairs—to write letters to Congressmen and to the bank board arguing that Keating's desires should be met because he was a financier of infinitely sound judgment and ethics. Greenspan enclosed with his letter a report by the notorious accounting firm of Arthur Young; the Arthur Young agent who wrote the report later went to work for Keating at a salary of nearly $1 million a year.

Finally, in April 1987 Keating called in his five senatorial stooges: Alan Cranston of California, John McCain (whose wife and father-in-law were partners with Keating in a shopping center) and DeConcini of Arizona (DeConcini's campaign manager's company got loans totaling $68 million, some now delinquent, from Lincoln), John Glenn of Ohio (Keating hired three of Glenn's former staff members as lobbyists and lawyers) and Donald Riegle Jr. of Michigan. Of course they would later deny that the $1.4 million they received from Keating and his associates had anything to do with their actions, but they got plenty rough with Gray: What the hell were he and his regulators doing, harassing this good man? Officials from the San Francisco home loan bank were summoned to Washington one week later to be given a further going-over by the Keating Five.

The West Coast regulators called their bluff. They came to the meeting loaded with evidence that Lincoln should be taken away from Keating because it had become a rogue institution operating in an unsafe and illegal way, stuffing its files with post-dated documents, doing no credit checks on its borrowers and lending money with phony appraisals or with no appraisal at all.

Nevertheless, despite this evidence, Keating was about to win the battle. A couple of months after these encounters, Gray's term as chair ended and he was replaced by Senator Garn's protege, M. Danny Wall, one of the chaps who had written the disastrous Garn–St. Germain bill. The S&L lobby would not have a more dedicated friend. The *Wall Street Journal* later called him "The S&L Looters' Water-Boy."

First he took the Lincoln case away from the San Francisco office and buried it in Washington. Then he killed Gray's direct investment limit and some of the other reforms Gray had proposed. The upshot was that for another two years Keating and his gang at American Continental were allowed to loot Lincoln until it was hardly more than a shell. In April 1989 American Continental declared bankruptcy and the next day the government seized Lincoln. The failure of this thrift is expected to cost taxpayers $2.5 billion, much of the loss due to Wall's delay in closing it down.

Don't Play It Again, Uncle Sam

If, as seems entirely likely, there is no wholesale imprisonment of S&L scoundrels and no massive ouster of the politicians who betrayed us, who is going to feel most of the pain? You know the answer. You will, sucker. You, O citizen of this wretched Rome, are going to get *raptus regaliter*. Royally screwed.

Painful as the bailout cost will be, it is not nearly so painful and dangerous to the economic health of America as the shift in and concentration of the control of credit, which we are already beginning to see. Ten years ago there were about 4,500 S&Ls in the country. Now there are fewer than 3,000. By the time the bailout storm troops get through selling them off, the number is expected to be down around 1,500, with a corresponding drop in mortgage money. Most will have disappeared, via mergers, into super-S&Ls and superbanks whose social usefulness will be equivalent to supertankers like the Exxon Valdez.

The moneylenders, who were willing to take any risk for big borrowers in the 1980s, are now reluctant to take any risk for small borrowers. This, by the way, makes them lawbreakers, but they don't seem worried about that. The Community Reinvestment Act of 1977 declares that banks and S&Ls are chartered to serve the public and that they must help and give credit to low- and moderate-income citizens and small businesses.

Only once in its history has the Federal Reserve Board enforced that law. Today it is violated more than ever. Banks and S&Ls bailed out with your money are the stingiest of the lot. They have revived and pumped adrenaline into the ancient practice of redlining. In Texas, for example, where 40 billion bailout dollars have been lavished on banks and S&Ls in the past two years, virtually none have been reinvested as loans to minority neighborhoods. The Southern Finance Project found, for example, that although no banking establishment has grown fatter and wealthier from gobbling up failing banks and S&Ls in Texas than NCNB, in 1989 it loaned only one-half of 1 percent of its total mortgages in Houston, Dallas, San Antonio and Austin to minority borrowers.

Ordinary people are, obviously, being screwed—in the name of "reform." Whenever the money-masters of government carry out something "reformist," we are in deep trouble. The disastrous S&L rule changes of the early 1980s were called "reforms." Now the bailouts that concentrate wealth and credit are also called "reforms." And the George H. W. Bush administration has other even more noxious "reforms" planned for the immediate future.

Monopoly Capital

The plan adds up to the complete deregulation of commercial banks. Since 1985, when Vice President Bush was head of a task force studying financial market restructuring, he has been a patsy for the banks, which have been lobbying and finagling with considerable success to (1) reduce the S&L industry to an insignificant source for government-backed home mortgages (that goal is in sight), (2) allow banks to enter the securities business (the Federal Reserve recently made the first ruling in that direction) and (3) let banks do just about any damn thing they want to do.

The tainted S&Ls have provided the banks and the administration with a wonderful rationale: The S&Ls are booed as the bad guys—ruffians, vandals, thieves—and the banks are patted and praised as the gentlemen—decorous, well-regulated (by comparison), sound, safe. In fact, commercial banks are anything but. Since the mid-1980s they have been lending with as much abandon and stupidity as the S&Ls, and with as little supervision from the Feds. The industry has been falling apart for at least five years (Seidman's vaunted chairmanship of the F.D.I.C. notwithstanding).

Only ten banks, with assets totaling $232 million, failed in 1980. Eight years later, 220 banks, with assets of $54 billion, either closed or were given emergency cash injections by the Federal Reserve. Bad management, bad luck, fraud and lousy supervision by Seidman's cops all contributed. In 1986, with 1,400 of the nation's 14,500 banks in serious trouble, Seidman admitted that half the problem banks hadn't been examined in more than a year. "We're spread very thin," he said. "We don't have enough people to catch the problems."

Things didn't improve. Nor did thrifts have a corner on crooks. In 1987 the F.D.I.C. admitted that one-third of the banks that failed were brought down, at least in part, by insider dishonesty. The same year, with banks collapsing right and left, Stephen Aug reported on *ABC Business World* that "huge segments" of the commercial banking industry were "restructuring in what some say is a giant controlled bankruptcy organization." And much of the emergency oxygen was being fed to the giants—Citicorp, Chase Manhattan, Bankers Trust, Manufacturers Hanover and Bank America.

But most of the popular press, to the extent that it was writing about moneylenders' problems at all, was concentrating on the S&Ls. Don Dixon's prostitutes were much more entertaining than Chase Manhattan's disappearing Third World loans. And they were indeed disappearing. By last year all the big banks mentioned above were writing off huge portions—some by as much as two-thirds—of their Third World loans, thus admitting they would never be repaid.

In the past two years particularly, there was an orgy of bank gambling with leveraged buyouts and takeovers financed by junk bonds, and now the earth is beginning to shake. Indeed, the General Accounting Office has warned that seven of the nation's ten largest banks plunged so deep into those risky loans that if even one of the highly leveraged companies should go bankrupt, an extremely dangerous chain reaction could result. Oceans of speculative commercial real estate loans made during the 1980s are also turning rancid.

Back to the 1920s
Although it is obvious that the tottering commercial banking world needs tighter regulations than ever, the industry and the administration push on pell-mell for deregulation. In fact, the dismal condition of the industry is being used by the deregulating claque as their strongest, and weirdest, argument. Just as St. Germain, Garn, Pratt and Wall argued that the best way to help zombie thrifts recover was to remove all regulations so that they could "grow out" of their problems, now Bush, Fed chair Greenspan, Treasury Secretary Nicholas Brady, Seidman and

others demand that the government dismantle what Seidman calls the "archaic laws" that for many years have controlled commercial banking. They, too, want to "grow out" of their perilous condition. What these laws do is protect the banking industry from its worst instincts by insisting that banks remain banks, and not become gamblers, hucksters and hustlers in other lines as well.

The deregulators will probably make their big power-play next spring, when, under mandate from Congress, the Treasury Department must come up with its "reform" plans for the banks. You can expect the other side to try to sell some blind horses to us, like offering to swap a lower ceiling on deposit insurance for wholesale abandonment of regulations—as if the rotters wouldn't be just as happy engaging in risky activity under a lower ceiling as they have been gambling under the present one. If there is a double agent to be on guard against, it will be Donald Riegle, chair of the Senate Banking Committee. He and the moneylenders are—could any old saw be more apt?—thick as thieves. Riegle is recorded as receiving $200,000 from S&L officials and PACs between January 1981 and May 1990—second only to California's Senator Pete Wilson ($243,334). Now that S&L money is seen to be tainted, Riegle has scrambled to redeem his reputation by returning $120,000 of it. But the commercial banks have stuffed his pockets too, and there is no record of his having returned any of *that* money.

Recently Greenspan—that trustworthy fellow who guaranteed the morality of Keating and was one of the chief boosters of junk-bond purchases by S&Ls—guided his Fed colleagues into a disastrous decision. They ruled that J.P. Morgan (Morgan Guaranty Trust) could trade and sell corporate stocks. With this cloven hoof in the door, other banks will follow, and that will be the death of the Glass-Steagall Act, which Congress passed in 1933 to separate commercial banks from investment banks and thereby control some of the outlawry that had caused thousands of banks to fail. Next they will probably be targeting the Bank Holding Act of 1956, which was intended to keep banking out of commerce, and the McFadden Act, which limits interstate banking.

What Greenspan, Seidman and their gang say to critics is, Oh, we want banks to be banks, too, but we want them to be *universal* banks. Which can be translated to mean uncontrolled banks, banks completely unfettered by regulations that restrict their operations—in short, pretty much a return to the reckless and lawless 1920s and early 1930s, which, if measured by the drama and excitement of collapsing financial structures, had it all over the 1980s.

R. Dan Brumbaugh, Jr., for one, is dumbfounded by what he's seeing. "The administration and Congress just don't want to acknowledge the problem," he says with a sigh. "This is *déjà vu* all over again. You can't believe it's happening, but there it is."

Democratize the Fed?
For Starters

DOUG HENWOOD
June 27, 1994

For the fourth time in less than four months, the Federal Reserve has pushed up short-term interest rates. To lay observers, this is a pretty shabby way to treat an economy that's only in the early stages of recovery from a long swoon. To central bankers and their Wall Street constituency, it's appropriate medicine, with a few more doses probably on the way. And now we learn from Bob Woodward's new book, excerpted recently in the *Washington Post,* that Fed chair Alan Greenspan persuaded Bill Clinton to drop the modest public investment agenda he campaigned on in favor of hair-shirt deficit-cutting Who is this Fed, and can anything be done about it?

To financiers' eyes, the economy has just got too strong for comfort. Though current inflation rates are about as low as any we've seen in the past thirty years, there's profound worry among bankers and Fedsters that this relative price stability is about to end. Such price hawks are convinced that the U.S. economy cannot grow at a rate faster than 2.5 to 3.0 percent a year—quite slow by historical standards—without lapsing into a sickly inflation. If unemployment gets too low, meaning much below current levels, then workers might develop an attitude problem, and the twenty-year decline in real hourly wages might be reversed, however briefly. Wall Street wants the slow-growth, high-unemployment days of the early 1990s back again, and the Fed seems intent on fulfilling those wishes.

But wish fulfillment may not come so easily. History shows that once an economic expansion is under way, it often takes far more sustained and sharp increases in interest rates to slow it down than anyone guesses at first. A review of the past forty years by James Stack, who publishes the market newsletter *InvesTech* and who is one of the most astute observers of Fed policy around, shows that once central bank tightening begins, short-term interest rates usually rise by four points or more over roughly two years, meaning that there's lots more to come. By the way, if this tightening ripens into a full-blown recession, as it usually does, it would be very bad news for Bill Clinton, who would be running for re-election just as the economy heads downward.

Clinton's fate aside, Fed tightening just as prosperity is threatening to break out has revived calls for "democratization of the Fed." After all, an institution that views rapid growth as a threat rather than the goal of economic life seems almost un-American. Led by House Banking Committee chairman and Texas populist Henry Gonzalez, a number of Congressional Democrats have been calling for major changes at the Fed—more openness, a more democratic procedure for appointing the policy-making staff and a top-to-bottom audit of the institution's finances. More radical suggestions include bringing the Fed under the direct supervision of the Treasury Department and choosing Fed governors by election rather than by appointment. But how much real difference would it make to reform the central bank?

There's no question that the Federal Reserve is an affront to democracy in both form and content. From its founding in 1913, the Fed has consisted of twelve district banks scattered around the country—a concession to the decentralized traditions of American finance and politics—and a central governing board in Washington. The district Federal Reserve banks are technically owned by the private banks in their regions, which choose six of each district bank's nine directors. Of the New York district's nine, three are bankers, two are CEOs of Fortune 500 companies (A.T.&T. and Pfizer), another is the CEO of a large insurance company, one owns a small business, one runs an elite foundation (the Carnegie Corporation) and one is a union president (of the conservative United Federation of Teachers). Only two of the nine are outside the Big Business/Big Finance orbit—three if you want to count the foundation executive, since foundations usually have major financial holdings. So while the Federal Reserve System is technically part of the government, an important part of the system is owned and controlled by private interests.

Despite the original decentralizing intent of the district structure, power quickly gravitated toward two centers—Washington, where the Fed is headquartered, and New York, the site of the most important of the regional banks because of its location only blocks from Wall Street. The system's executive body is a Board of Governors, consisting of seven members nominated by the president and confirmed by the Senate, who serve for a term of fourteen years. That long term is supposed to insulate the governors from political pressures; in reality, it insulates them almost completely from anything like democratic accountability. From the seven board members, the president nominates, subject to Senate confirmation, a chair (currently Alan Greenspan) and a vice chair (Alan Blinder, current nominee), who serve four-year terms. From the chair down to the vice presidents and directors of the district banks, the Fed's senior staff is overwhelmingly male, white and privileged.

Unlike ordinary government agencies, the Fed is entirely self-financing; it need never go to Congress, hat in hand. Almost all its income comes from its portfolio of $350 billion in U.S. Treasury securities. It's not a difficult trick to build up a huge piggy bank when you can print money out of thin air, as the Fed does.

Monetary policy is set by a Federal Open Market Committee (F.O.M.C.), which consists of the seven governors plus five of the district bank presidents, who serve in rotation—five of the twelve votes are cast by the heads of institutions owned by commercial banks, a very strange feature in a nominally democratic government. Imagine the outcry if almost half the seats on the Labor Relations Board were given over to representatives with strong union ties.

The F.O.M.C. meets in secret every five to eight weeks to set the tone of monetary policy—restrictive, accommodative or neutral, in Fed jargon. Until very recently, the committee didn't announce policy decisions until six to eight weeks after they'd been made. (In a departure from almost eighty years of history, the four tightenings since February 4 have been announced immediately, a frank attempt to steal some of the reformers' thunder.) Also until very recently, the Fed has maintained that it didn't even take detailed minutes of these meetings; actually, it has been taping them for years and hid that fact from Congress for seventeen years. It repeated the denials to Representative Gonzalez last fall, when he pointedly asked about the existence of tapes or transcripts. Facing intensified Congressional scrutiny, Fedsters enjoyed a sudden onrush of recovered memory and acknowledged the existence of the tapes and transcripts.

Such secrecy has spawned the Fed-watching industry, a racket reminiscent of Kremlinology, in which every institutional twitch is scrutinized for clues to policy changes. Fed watchers, many of them recent alumni of the central bank, "earn" salaries well into the six figures for their work; greater openness at the Fed would reduce their importance, if not put them out of business, a rare form of unemployment that would be entirely welcome. Even though F.O.M.C. members would no doubt invent all sorts of clever euphemisms to express the dangers of excessively low unemployment, televising the F.O.M.C.'s proceedings on C-SPAN would still be an enlightening glimpse into the mentality of power.

The example of Congress on C-SPAN, however, should be sobering to those who think a round of *glasnost* might do the Fed some good. The proceedings of Congress, an elected body, are televised at narcotic length, but Congress still produces innumerable insults to democracy. The moneyed and powerful enjoy an access to Congress that mere citizens lack, a disparity that is well known; why should applying similar standards to the Fed produce any better results?

Procedure aside, the nature of the central bank may be less important than the broader institutions in which it is embedded. A comparison with other countries demonstrates the point. The most independent of the major central banks is the German Bundesbank (known as "Buba" to its friends); it does what it damn well pleases with an insouciance that even Alan Greenspan must envy. The least independent of the European central banks is the Bank of England; though it began its life in the seventeenth century as a private institution that served as banker to the state, it was nationalized in 1946 by the Labour government and still takes policy direction from the Chancellor of the Exchequer, the equivalent of our Treasury Secretary. Now it must be admitted that Buba has kept interest rates very high over the past several years, out of fear of the inflationary consequences of Bonn's hostile takeover of the former East Germany. Yet over the long term, by any standard—whether by hardheaded ones like growth rates and investment levels, or squishy-humanist ones like poverty rates and income distribution—the German economy has performed far better than the British one for decades.

It would be tempting to conclude from that comparison that maybe an independent central bank is a pretty good thing after all. But the Bank of Japan is largely subordinate to the Japanese Finance Ministry and by the same standards, tough or soft, Japan's economy has done far better than even Germany's over the past few decades. So maybe an independent central bank isn't such a good thing after all.

Or maybe the importance of the central bank is exaggerated. Unlike Britain and the United States, which suffer from loosely regulated financial systems and a shoot-from-the-hip stock market mentality, Japan and Germany have rather tightly regulated systems in which stock markets play a relatively unimportant role in both investment finance and corporate governance. Compared with these broader financial structures, the central bank's (in)dependence isn't quite so important.

Populist critiques of the Fed tend to concentrate excessively on its autonomous powers while overlooking the influence of the financial markets on the central bankers; the Fed follows interest rate trends as well as leading them. For example, creditors began selling their bonds, driving up long-term interest rates, several months before the Fed jacked up the short-term rates last February. They reinforced the message with repeated cries urging the Fed to tighten. Even after the Fed began tightening, Wall Street bayed for more. Similarly, Greenspan's urging of deficit-cutting on Clinton was done in the name of pleasing the bond market, a task the new president took to with great public fervor, despite the private reservations reported by Woodward. Were some reconstructed Fed to shift policy into a permanently stimulative mode, it would have to face the prospect of a capital strike on the part of the creditor class; it might be able to force short-term rates down, but long-term rates would quickly rise toward 20 percent. Any democratization of the Fed that didn't simultaneously take on the financial elite would quickly face such a disaster. Sure, the Fed should be opened up—its secrecy ended; its own finances brought into the general federal budget; its personnel made more broadly representative in terms of gender, race and class; and its narrow, austere criterion of economic management put on permanent furlough. But that kind of transformation could succeed only as part of a broader transformation of financial relations that would include, as a start: the establishment of nonprofit banks that would provide low-cost checking and savings accounts as well as low-interest loans for community and regional development; tight regulation of the existing for-profit banks; taxes on securities trading to cool speculative fevers; tight controls on international capital flows; reform of corporate boards to include worker, community and public sector representatives; a radically new approach to the management of pension funds; and a wealth tax that would simultaneously reduce the influence of the moneyed and provide funds for a vast rebuilding of our social and physical environment.

Short of these reforms—which, it must be emphasized, would be taken by Wall Street as revolutionary—reform of the Fed alone would turn out to be little more than cosmetic.

Breaking Glass-Steagall

EDITORS OF *THE NATION*
November 15, 1999

ALTHOUGH WALL STREET has pushed for financial deregulation for two decades, it was last year's merger of Citicorp and Travelers that set the stage for Congress's effective revocation of the Glass-Steagall Act in late October. The merger was a violation of the longstanding laws separating banking and insurance companies, but Citicorp and Travelers, because they well knew their power to ram deregulation through Congress, exploited loopholes that gave them a temporary exemption. Indeed, further proving that Wall Street and Washington are two branches of the same firm, the newly formed Citigroup announced only days after the deal that it had hired recently departed Treasury secretary Robert Rubin as a member of its three-person office of the chairman. With Citigroup's co-CEO Sanford Weill and lobbyist Roger Levy leading the charge, industry executives and lobbyists badgered the administration and swarmed the halls of Congress—vetting all drafts before they were introduced—as the final details of the deal were hammered out. Even more than usual, campaign contributions and lobby money greased the deal. The finance, insurance and real estate industries together are regularly the largest campaign contributors and biggest spenders on lobbying of all business sectors. They laid out more than $290 million for lobbying in 1998, according to the Center for Responsive Politics, and donated more than $150 million in the 1997–98 election cycle—a figure sure to be topped in 1999–2000. For their money, the finance industry bought not only the end of the Glass-Steagall Act but also the partial repeal of the Bank Holding Company Act. These landmark pieces of legislation, recognizing the inherent dangers of too great a concentration of financial power, barred common ownership of banks, insurance companies and securities firms and erected a wall of separation between banks and nonfinancial companies. Now the ban on common ownership has been lifted—and the wall separating banking and commerce is likely soon to be breached.

The misnamed Financial Services Modernization Act will usher in another round of record-breaking mergers, as companies rush to combine into "one stop shopping" operations, concentrating financial power in trillion-dollar global giants and paving the way for future taxpayer bailouts of too-big-to-fail financial corporations. Regulation of this new universe will be minimal, with powers scattered among a half-dozen federal agencies and fifty state insurance departments—none with sufficient clout to do the job. The final two major debates over the bill's provisions focused not on the core-questions of concentrated financial power and regulatory controls but on issues of privacy and lending practices. A coalition ranging from Representative Edward Markey to Senator Richard Shelby denounced the bill for permitting financial conglomerates to share customer information among affiliates, but their attempt to give consumers a right to block such privacy invasions failed. As a result, holding companies will be able to build individual marketing profiles that will include detailed personal data. Gaining this prerogative was a major consideration, as witnessed by the industry's threats to walk away from the bill if privacy protections were included. The final hurdle to passage of the bill was the Community Reinvestment Act (CRA), which obligates banks to provide credit to citizens in minority and low-aid moderate-income areas and which is the *bête noire* of Phil Gramm, chairman of the Senate Banking Committee. Gramm did not succeed in obliterating the CRA, but with the Clinton administration's acquiescence, he went a long way toward eviscerating it. Under the conference bill there will be no ongoing sanctions against holding company banks that fail to meet CRA standards. And it will lessen the number of CRA examinations, making it harder for regulators to insure that banks are complying with their obligations to the poor.

There is much more that is wrong with the bill: It does not include adequate protections against redlining; it does not require banks to provide basic services to the poor, leaving them at the mercy of check-cashing shops and similar ripoff outfits; and it opens the way for the new conglomerates to gouge consumers.

History will record this bill as a landmark in the march toward the consolidation of financial power in America.

The Rise of Market Populism: America's New Secular Religion

THOMAS FRANK

October 30, 2000

W HEN RICHARD HOFSTADTER wrote thirty years ago that "conflict and consensus require each other and are bound up in a kind of dialectic of their own," he was offering advice to historians examining the American past, but he might as well have been describing the culture of the 1990s. If there was anything that defined us as a people, we came to believe in that decade, it was our diversity, our nonconformity, our radicalism, our differentness. It was an era of many and spectacular avant-gardes, of loud and highly visible youth cultures, of emphatic multiculturalism, of extreme sports, extreme diets and extreme investing.

But even as Americans marveled at the infinite variety of the Internet and celebrated our ethnic diversity, we were at the same time in the grip of an intellectual consensus every bit as ironclad as that of the 1950s. Across the spectrum, American opinion leaders in the nineties were coming to an unprecedented agreement on the role of business in American life. The leaders of the left parties, both here and in Britain, accommodated themselves to the free-market faith and made spectacular public renunciations of their historic principles. Organized labor, pounded by years of unionbusting and deindustrialization, slipped below 10 percent of the U.S. private-sector workforce and seemed to disappear altogether from the popular consciousness. The opposition was ceasing to oppose, but the market was now safe, its supposedly endless array of choice substituting for the lack of choice on the ballot. Various names were applied to this state of affairs. In international circles the grand agreement was called the "Washington Consensus"; economics writer Daniel Yergin called it the "market consensus"; *New York Times* columnist Thomas Friedman coined the phrase "golden straitjacket" to describe the absence of political options. While once "people thought" there were ways to order human affairs other than through the free market, Friedman insisted, those choices now no longer existed. "I don't think there will be an alternative ideology this time around," he wrote in August 1998. "There are none."

It is this intellectual unanimity about the nature and the purpose of economies, as much as the technological advances of recent years, that we refer to when we talk so triumphantly about the "New Economy." It is this nearly airtight consensus—this assurance that no matter what happens or who wins in November, a strong labor movement and an interventionist government will not be returning—that has made possible the unprecedented upward transfer of wealth that we saw in the Clinton years, that has permitted the bull market without end, and that has made the world so safe for billionaires.

This is not to say that in the nineties Americans simply decided they wanted nothing so much as to toil for peanuts on an assembly line somewhere, that they loved plutocracy and that robber barons rocked after all. On the contrary: At the center of the "New Economy" consensus was a vision of economic democracy as extreme and as militant-sounding as anything to emanate from the CIO in the thirties. From Deadheads to Nobel-laureate economists, from paleoconservatives to New Democrats, American leaders in the nineties came to believe that markets were a popular system, a far more democratic form of organization than (democratically elected) governments. This is the central premise of what I call "market populism": that in addition to being mediums of exchange, markets are mediums of consent. With their mechanisms of supply and demand, poll and focus group, superstore and Internet, markets manage to express the popular will more articulately and meaningfully than do mere elections. By their very nature markets confer democratic legitimacy, markets bring down the pompous and the snooty, markets look out for the interests of the little guy, markets give us what we want.

Many of the individual components of the market-populist consensus have been part of the cultural-economic wallpaper for years. Hollywood and Madison Avenue have always insisted that their job is simply to mirror the public's wishes, and that movies and ad campaigns succeed or fail depending on how accurately they conform to public tastes. Similarly, spokesmen for the New York Stock Exchange have long argued that stock prices reflect popular enthusiasm, that public trading of stocks is a basic component of democracy. And ever since William Randolph Hearst, newspaper tycoons have imagined themselves defenders of the common man.

But in the nineties these ideas came together into a new orthodoxy that anathematized all alternative ways of understanding democracy, history and the rest of the world. An example of the market-populist consensus at its most cocksure can be found in "Fanfare for the Common Man," the cover story that *Newsweek* used to mark the end of the twentieth century. The story's title comes from a Depression standby (a 1942 work by Aaron Copland), and its writing recalls the militant populism of that era. Looking back on the events of the "people's century," it occurred to Kenneth Auchincloss, the story's author, that for once in the human experience "ordinary folks changed history." To nail it down he singled out a succession of popular heroes who changed things: Suffragettes, feminists, the antiwar and civil rights movement and, finally, "the entrepreneurs"—this last group illustrated with a drawing of Bill Gates. Even while hailing the richest man in the world as a champion of the common people, Auchincloss took pains to point out that the New Deal wasn't nearly as wonderful as everyone thought it was.

The other hero of the thirties, the labor movement, was not mentioned in the story at all.

This may seem egregious, but it was hardly atypical. Wherever one looked in the nineties entrepreneurs were occupying the ideological space once filled by the noble sons of toil. It was businessmen who were sounding off against the arrogance of elites, railing against the privilege of old money, protesting false expertise and waging relentless, idealistic war on the principle of hierarchy wherever it could be found. Their fundamental faith was a simple one: The market and the people—both of them understood as grand principles of social life rather than particulars—were essentially one and the same. As journalist Robert Samuelson wrote in 1998, "the Market 'R' Us." This is how a "Fanfare for the Common Man" could turn into yet another salute to Bill Gates and his fellow billionaires; how the New York Stock Exchange, long a nest of privilege, could be understood in the nineties as a house of the people; how any kind of niche marketing could be passed off as a revolutionary expression—an empowerment, even—of the demographic at which it was aimed.

And as business leaders melded themselves theoretically with the people, they found that market populism provided them with powerful weapons to use against their traditional enemies in government and labor. Since markets express the will of the people, virtually any criticism of business could be described as an act of "elitism" arising out of despicable contempt for the common man. According to market populism, elites are not those who, say, watch sporting events from a skybox, or spend their weekends tooling about on a computer-driven yacht, or fire half their workforce and ship the factory south. No, elitists are the people on the other side of the equation: the labor unionists and Keynesians who believe that society can be organized in any way other than the market way. Since what the market does—no matter how whimsical, irrational or harmful— is the Will of the People, any scheme to operate outside its auspices or control its ravages is by definition a dangerous artifice, the hubris of false expertise.

This fantasy of the market as an anti-elitist machine made the most sense when it was couched in the language of social class. Businessmen and pro-business politicians have always protested the use of "class war" by their critics on the left; during the nineties, though, they happily used the tactic themselves, depicting the workings of the market as a kind of permanent social revolution in which daring entrepreneurs are endlessly toppling fat cats and picking off millions of lazy rich kids. Wherever the earthshaking logic of the "New Economy" touched down, old money was believed to quake and falter. The scions of ancient banking families were said to be finding their smug selves wiped out by the streetwise know-how of some kid with a goatee; the arrogant stockbrokers of old were being humiliated by the e-trade masses; the WASPs with their regimental ties were getting their asses kicked by the women, the Asians, the Africans, the Hispanics; the buttoned-down whip-cracking bosses were being fired by the corporate "change agents"; the self-assured network figures were being reduced to tears by the Vox Populi of the web. A thousand populist revolts shook the office blocks of the world, and the great forums of market ideology overflowed with praise for in-your-face traders from gritty urban backgrounds, for the CEO who still retained the crude manners of the longshoreman.

How did populism ever become the native tongue of the wealthy? Historically, of course, populism was a rebellion against the corporate order, a political tongue reserved by definition for the nonrich and the nonpowerful. It was a term associated with the labor movement and angry agrarians. But in 1968, at the height of the antiwar movement, this primal set piece of American democracy seemed to change its stripes. The war between classes somehow reversed its polarity: Now it was a conflict in which the patriotic, blue-collar "silent majority" (along with their employers) faced off against a new elite, a "liberal establishment" with its spoiled, flag-burning children. This new ruling class—a motley assembly of liberal journalists, liberal academics, liberal foundation employees, liberal politicians and the shadowy powers of Hollywood—earned the people's wrath not by exploiting workers or ripping off the family farmers but by contemptuous disregard for the wisdom and values of average Americans.

Counterintuitive though it may have been, the backlash vision of class conflict was powerful stuff. Until recently American politics remained mired in the cultural controversies passed down from the late sixties, with right-wing populists forever reminding "normal Americans" of the hideous world that the "establishment" had built, a place where blasphemous intellectuals violated the principles of Americanism at every opportunity, a place of crime in the streets, of unimaginable cultural depravity, of epidemic disrespect for the men in uniform, of secular humanists scheming to undermine family values and give away the

Panama Canal, of judges gone soft on crime and politicians gone soft on communism. The thirty-year backlash brought us Ronald Reagan's rollback of government power as well as Newt Gingrich's outright shutdown of 1995. But for all its accomplishments, it never constituted a thorough endorsement of the free market or of laissez-faire politics. Barbara Ehrenreich, one of its most astute chroniclers, points out that the backlash always hinged on a particular appeal to working-class voters, some of whom were roped into the Republican coalition with talk of patriotism, culture war and family values. Class war worked for Republicans as long as it was restricted to cultural issues; when economic matters came up the compound grew unstable very quickly. Lee Atwater, an adviser to presidents Reagan and Bush, is said to have warned his colleagues in 1984 that their new blue-collar constituents were "liberal on economics" and that without culture wars to distract them "populists were left with no compelling reason to vote Republican."

Fortunately for the right, as the culture wars finally began to subside in the aftermath of the impeachment fiasco, a new variation on the populist theme was reaching its triumphant zenith. Market populism was promulgated less by a political party than by business itself—through management theory, investment literature and advertising—and it served the needs of the owning community far more directly than had the tortured populism of the backlash. While the right-wing populism of the seventies and eighties had envisioned a scheming "liberal elite" bent on "social engineering"—a clique of experts who thought they knew what was best for us, like busing, integration and historical revisionism—market populism simply shifted the inflection.

Now the crime of the elite was not so much an arrogance in matters of values but in matters economic. Still those dirty elitists thought they were better than the people, but now their arrogance was revealed by their passion to raise the minimum wage; to regulate, oversee, redistribute and tax.

There are critical differences between market populism and the earlier right-wing dispensation, of course. While the backlash was proudly square, market populism is cool. Far from despising the sixties, it broadcasts its fantasies to the tune of a hundred psychedelic hits. Its leading think tanks are rumored to pay princely sums to young people promising to bring some smattering of rock-and-roll street cred to the market's cause. And believing in markets rather than God, it has little tolerance for the bizarre ideas of the Christian right or the Moral Majority. Market populism has also abandoned the overt race-baiting of the backlash: Its "Southern strategy" involves shipping plants to Mexico or Guatemala and then describing this as a victory for the downtrodden Others of the planet. Market populists generally fail to get worked up about the persecution of Vietnam vets (they sometimes even equate new-style management theories with the strategy of the Vietcong); they have abandoned the "family values" of Reagan; they give not a damn for the traditional role of women or even of children. The more who enter the workforce the merrier.

By the middle of the nineties, this was a populism in the ascendancy. Leftoid rock critics, Wall Street arbitrageurs and just about everyone in between seemed to find what they wanted in the magic of markets. Markets were serving all tastes, markets were humiliating the pretentious, markets were permitting good art to triumph over bad, markets were overthrowing the man, markets were extinguishing discrimination, markets were making everyone rich.

In the right hands, market populism could explain nearly any social phenomenon. The "tiger economies" of Asia had collapsed, market populists told us, because they had relied on the expertise of elites rather than the infinite wisdom of the people. Similarly, the economies of Western Europe were stagnant because the arrogant aristocrats every red-blooded American knows run those lands were clinging to old welfare-state theories. Meanwhile, the NASDAQ was soaring because the buy-and-hold common man had finally been allowed to participate. And when the House of Morgan was swallowed up by Chase Manhattan, we were told this was because it was a snooty outfit that had foolishly tried to resist the democracy of markets.

More important, market populism proved astonishingly versatile as a defense of any industry in distress. It was the line that could answer any critic, put over any deregulatory initiative, roll back any tax. Thus economist Stanley Lebergott used it to blast a 1998 warning by Hillary Clinton against the values of consumerism. The consumer culture, he informed the First Lady from the *New York Times* Op-Ed page, and by extension the free market generally, was the righteous collective product of the people themselves. "Who creates this 'consumer-driven culture' but 270 million Americans?" he asked. Taking an indignant swipe at the carping snobbery of the "best and the brightest," Lebergott then asserted that criticism of business was in fact criticism of "other consumers," and that simply by participating in American life—by driving "a 1-ton car to the theater" or by "accumulat[ing] books and newspapers printed on million-dollar presses"—we authorize whatever it is that the market chooses to do.

On the *Wall Street Journal* editorial page, where the behavior of markets is consistently understood as a transparent expression of the will of the people, one saw market populism wheeled out to defend the advertising industry, to defend the auto industry, to bolster demands that the software industry be permitted to import more workers, to hail stock options as the people's true currency and, most remarkably, to defend Microsoft from its antitrust pursuers. Since a company's size (like the value of a billionaire's pile) was simply a reflection of the people's love, antitrust itself was fundamentally illegitimate, a device used by elitist politicians, the *Journal* once proclaimed, "to promote the interests of the few at the expense of the many." Even after the Microsoft verdict had been announced, the *Journal* continued to assert that the company "should have argued that we have a monopoly because our customers want us to have one." And when Al Gore began annoying the men of privilege with his recent attacks on big business, the paper responded in the most direct manner imaginable. "Mr. Bush should tell Americans," online *Journal* executive James Taranto opined in an Op-Ed late last summer, "when my opponent attacks 'big corporations,' he's attacking you and me."

Market populism can seem quite absurd at times. We are, after all, living through one of the least populist economic eras in the past hundred years. The "New Economy" has exalted the rich and forgotten about the rest with a decisiveness that we haven't seen since the twenties. Its greatest achievement—the booming stock market of recent years—has been based in no small part on companies' enhanced abilities to keep wages low even while CEO compensation soars to record levels. Market populism is, in many ways, the most blatant apologia for economic inequality since social Darwinism. But there can be no doubting the intensity of the true believers' faith. Only a few paragraphs after identifying "you and me" with "big corporations," for example, the *Journal*'s Taranto went on to declare that "thanks to the democracy of the market" and the widespread ownership of stock, "the U.S. is now closer to [the] Marxian ideal than any society in history." And unless you have a spare billion to tell the world otherwise with a thirty-second spot during the Super Bowl, you can count on listening to proclamations like that for years to come.

Hunting the Predators

BOBBI MURRAY
July 15, 2002

MARIO AND IVONNE LUNA got into trouble with their credit when a friend for whom they had cosigned on a loan ran up bills and left them for the Lunas to pay. As they contemplated borrowing money to pay off the debts, they got a call from Household Financial Services. "They said they had good news for me," says Mario, who cleans office buildings for a living. In June 2001 the Lunas borrowed against the equity on their home in Inglewood, just outside Los Angeles, purchased in 1996 for $107,000. Household added in $3,500 in credit insurance to the loan, with $11,000 in up-front fees known as "points," and when they balked at the latter, Luna says, the Household representative told them no one else would finance them and implied that the payments on the 10.8 percent loan would eventually drop. That hasn't happened.

"With interest and everything, I'll have to pay a half-million dollars on this house over thirty years," Luna sighs. He is trying to refinance with another bank and lower his $1,400 monthly payment.

Opponents call the practices that the Lunas endured "predatory lending," where unsuspecting borrowers are set upon by highly sophisticated hunters who prey on their desperation. The lending industry has other terms to describe their methods—flipping, stripping, packing, steering—just some of perhaps a dozen ways to get borrowers so mired in debt that they become permanent income streams for the lender.

But over the past five years, a movement has been building to take on predatory lending—and the financial institutions that profit from it. Advocates pursue a range of tactics, from local ordinances that ban municipalities from doing business with abusive companies, to state legislation outlawing the most egregious practices, to pressure on regulatory agencies. The Association of Community Organizations for Reform Now (ACORN) has targeted Household Financial Services, the nation's largest mortgage lender, with a national direct-action campaign, and has encouraged local divestment as well.

The fight is particularly tough because activists must not only be able to wield political clout but also rewrite complicated lending rules designed by financial institutions largely for their own benefit.

Predatory lending concentrates on what's called the subprime market, which refers not to the interest rate but to the credit rating of the borrower. Lenders say they're just giving people with blemished credit records access to credit, and that sky-high interest rates—24 percent is not unheard of—are necessary to offset the risk. Most advocates concede that the risk of lending to borrowers with poor credit justifies a higher rate, but not that high. "They use it as an excuse to exploit," says William Brennan Jr., program director for the Home Defense Program of the Atlanta Legal Aid Society. "Even 10 percent is outrageous, and some of these people are being charged 13, 14, 15 percent."

A recent study by ACORN reveals both the class and racial dimensions of the problem: Nationally, subprime loans made up 57.5 percent of refinance loans to low-income African-Americans, 31.1 percent for low-income Latinos and 25.5 percent for low-income whites; and 54.3 percent for blacks of moderate income, 33.5 percent for moderate-income Latinos and 24 percent for whites of comparable means.

A typical loan can average 10–13 percent in the subprime market, but predatory practices will pack them with extra fees and unnecessary insurance, all financed at high interest by the lender, with high-percentage prepayment penalties that tether a borrower to the loan, or balloon payments that will force them to borrow still again, charged a few thousand dollars in "points" each time. Such repeat refinancing, with no benefit to the borrower, is called "flipping" the loan. Default can mean the loss of a home.

Predatory lending pumps wealth out of communities that can least afford it and into the coffers of some of the wealthiest companies in the country. The transfer amounts to $9.1 billion annually, according to a study by the Durham, North Carolina-based Self-Help Credit Union. Subprime lending has boomed by 1,000 percent since 1992—a surge fueled in part by relatively new practices that transfer mortgage money straight to Wall Street in the form of mortgage-backed securities.

Ideally, Congress would pass legislation to outlaw predatory lending practices, and activists praise Maryland Democratic Senator Paul Sarbanes for drawing attention to the issue as head of the Senate Banking Committee with a series of hearings in 2001. He introduced strong pro-consumer legislation in January of this year, while Democratic Congressman John LaFalce introduced a comparable bill on the House side.

But Margot Saunders, an attorney with the Washington, D.C. based Consumer Law Center, notes, "We won't get a bill through Congress unless the industry wants one to pre-empt all these state laws." This past April, the Georgia state legislature passed the strongest state-level predatory-lending bill ever. "Georgia is now setting the stage," explains Atlanta Legal Aid's Brennan, who spent hundreds of hours reviewing the legislation to make sure it was strong enough to vanquish the worst abuses. "The industry is talking about going to Congress—they call it balkanization, all the different state laws."

The struggle around pre-emptive legislation is central to the predatory lending fight. The past three years have seen activists gain ground locally, putting in place ordinances at the city or county level that attack predators and their practices. Banking interests have responded with attempts to pre-empt them at a state level—which they have done most recently in Colorado, with a weak law that putatively addresses predatory lending practices but would override stronger local legislation. The tactic has also been used in Florida, Pennsylvania and Ohio. Hence the possibility that the industry backlash against the Georgia legislation could move the pre-emption fight to Washington.

Ohio Republican Bob Ney is expected to announce a legislative proposal at the annual meeting of the National Association of Mortgage Brokers in Cleveland in late June, and insiders say that the industry is likely to be pleased. But the short time left on this session's clock makes it unlikely that a measure will move forward in Congress this year, and Sarbanes is expected to stand staunchly against any legislation that would counter his.

Meanwhile, the battle continues to rage in the states, with activists racking up some impressive victories. North Carolina first broke ground in 1999 with a law that consumer advocates then called the most comprehensive in the country, and California followed, albeit with less muscular legislation. But Georgia's bill is modeled on North Carolina's and outmatches it. Like the North Carolina bill, it essentially tightens a federal law passed in 1993, the Home Ownership and Equity Protection Act (HOEPA), which defines abusive loans as those with interest rates 10 percent or more above comparable Treasury rates the day the loan is issued. That now hovers at 5 percent; so a loan could have an interest rate as high as 15 percent before being considered a bad one. In addition, points and fees can be as much as 8 percent. Certain abusive practices are prohibited in loans over those thresholds—a good idea, activists say, but a high bar. The pre-emptive state legislation promoted by the industry is usually similar to HOEPA, while also including a poison pill that automatically overrides stronger local measures.

The new Georgia law defines a first mortgage as high-cost—the range in which predatory practices are most common—when its interest rate is 8 percent or more than the current prime for Treasury bonds; 10 percent above for second mortgages. Loans with points and fees that exceed 5 percent are also defined as high-cost. Either the interest rate or the fees can "trigger" the outright prohibition of many abusive practices, such as balloon payments.

Essential to the victory was the coalition pulled together by State Senator Vincent Fort, whose 2001 anti-predatory lending legislation was sandbagged by colleagues in cahoots with the Georgia Mortgage Bankers Association. The alliance, which included AARP, the NAACP, the Georgia AFL-CIO and the Atlanta Labor Council, convinced Governor Roy Barnes that it was worth his while to support a strong anti-predatory measure. Barnes was a wild card—as an attorney, he had won a $115 million judgment against Fleet Finance in 1993, but his ownership of a community bank worried advocates about where his loyalties might lie. Yet Barnes brought his clout to bear on behalf of the legislation Fort had promoted last year, and this time it weathered a blistering assault from industry.

The tactics in the battle between anti-predator activists and their industry opponents are escalating: The fight in Georgia was far more contentious than the one around North Carolina's 1999 law. Because it was a first, the industry was not up in arms, and North Carolina's unconventional coalition even included lenders. By 1998, Self-Help Credit Union, founded in 1980 to bring credit to capital-starved communities—mostly African-American—had seen many of their clients refinance with a notorious lender, Associates First Capital (the Associates). With eighty-eight branches throughout North Carolina, "just one predatory lender like the Associates was doing more harm than all the good we had done over all that time," recounts Eric Stein, Self-Help's research director.

So Self-Help founder and CEO Martin Eakes took the lead in founding the North Carolina Coalition for Responsible Lending, which included the NAACP, AARP and other lenders, banks and credit unions with sound lending practices who didn't want their names sullied by the predators. The North Carolina Credit Union League and the North Carolina Bankers Association endorsed the bill. Self-Help's Stein says that there's been a drastic drop in the number of victimized clients coming to their credit union, and a marked reduction in flipping, since the law passed.

The industry was on its toes by the time a state-level proposal started moving forward in California in 2000. ACORN had already campaigned in Oakland to pass an ordinance that outlawed major abuses. The American Financial Services Association filed suit against the city, and the industry was on high alert when a coalition that included ACORN, AARP, the Consumers Union, the Congress of California Seniors and the California Reinvestment Committee moved forward on a bill. The state bill is weaker than the Oakland legislation, with higher percentage rates allowed, so the industry pushed—unsuccessfully—for language that would pre empt the local ordinance. AFSA also tried this tack in court, but in November the judge denied a preliminary injunction, ruling that the ordinance will stay in effect until all appeals are exhausted.

The California law has received lukewarm praise from some advocates, who are critical of a section that assigns liability only to the broker who sold the loan, leaving no remedy for borrowers whose loans are sold to other companies. "We've been very clear all along that this bill does a lot of things very well, but it is modest and a first step," responds ACORN organizer Brian Kettenring. It prohibits one of the industry's biggest abuses, credit life insurance, a product advocates call worthless and which the lender rolls into a loan and finances at a high fee. Most lenders have stopped promoting it, but the legislation puts the prohibition into law.

Legislative counterattacks by the industry have drawn blood in several states—like in Pennsylvania. After a yearlong fight, in 2000 the City of Philadelphia passed the "limousine of ordinances," in the words of ACORN organizer Jeff Ordower, with both regulatory and divestment features. Banking interests went to the state legislature, which outlawed the Philadelphia measure and added an exemption for mortgage lending from the state fair-practices law. ACORN has now drafted model legislation for the state and hopes to inject the issue into the November governor's race.

But in Illinois antipredators leveraged a legislative failure into a double victory. The National Training and Information Center

(NTIC) and the Illinois Coalition Against Predatory Home Loans provided the pressure and political cover for State Representative Dan Burke to introduce a bill in January 1999 to stop predatory practices. The coalition even elicited a promise of neutrality from the Illinois Bankers' Association, but the industry went on to crush the legislation, which would have banned prepayment penalties and excessive fees and points. At the same time in Chicago, however, both grassroots pressure and his own abhorrence of abandoned housing led Mayor Richard Daley to introduce an antipredatory ordinance. Daley is the kind of mayor who tends to get what he wants; the ordinance passed unanimously. Militant action by the NTIC affiliate network, National People's Action, kept the heat on. Meanwhile, coalition members had been meeting with Governor George Ryan about state regulations against predatory lending. Ryan, who had been looking to Chicago for cues, introduced regulations in December 2000 after the local ordinance passed; they were approved by the legislature in April 2001.

Fights are ongoing in New York State, where a coalition led by AARP is promoting antipredator legislation and trying to beat back industry attempts to assign liability only to the broker who sold the initial loan. In New York City, an ACORN-backed initiative that would stop the city from doing business with banks that securitize the loans is moving through the City Council—a potentially staggering blow on Wall Street's home turf. And activists scored a mid-June victory against an attempt to weaken a measure making its way through the New Jersey legislature.

Ohio is faced with an interesting fight: The industry interests have passed a law that in effect reiterates the weak HOEPA standards while it pre-empts local legislation, but the City of Cleveland went ahead and passed a stronger anti-abuse law anyway. Toledo is gearing up to do the same. These are city governments that have seen predatory lending-linked foreclosures devastate whole areas of their cities, says Kathy Keller of AARP, one of 200 member organizations in the Ohio Coalition for Responsible Lending, which has mobilized members at the state and local levels. Any new ordinances will undoubtedly be taken to court by the industry, leaving it up to a judge to determine whether they will take effect.

The National Association of Consumer Advocates' Ira Rheingold says that the antipredatory movement has passed at least one milestone—it has defined the debate. "With predatory lending, we were able to define it before the banks could respond," he says. Atlanta attorney Brennan concurs that activists have ratcheted up the political pressure, citing Bank of America's cessation of predatory practices last year. "All the advocates can take credit for getting the Bank of America out of that business," he says.

But the industry is not about to quit. Citing "the specter of predatory lending," leaders at the National Home Equity Mortgage Association's annual meeting in March asked members to pony up $365 a person to the NHEMA's political action committee to "keep our legislators focused on what their job is— and that's promoting free enterprise," according to NHEMA's president.

In the meantime, Mario Luna is working with ACORN to re-finance his home, and has testified before the Los Angeles City Council—which is considering an anti-predatory lending law—about abusive lending practices. "I don't know what's going to happen," he says. "At least now I have someone who can advise me about my situation ... I've begun to feel much better."

The One-Eyed Chairman

WILLIAM GREIDER

September 19, 2005

WHEN ALAN GREENSPAN retires as Federal Reserve chairman early next year, we can expect waves of adulation for his extraordinary eighteen-year reign over the American economy. The financial press is already offering nostalgic retrospectives on the highlights: the crash of '87 and rapid rebound, the chairman's total victory over price inflation, his swift interventions to avoid financial panics and to reverse the stock market's massive meltdown of 2000–2001. In tempestuous times, this Fed chairman acquired a godlike aura—the inscrutable wizard with a nerdish charisma, his wisdom cloaked in financial doubletalk. How will the nation get along without him?

A different assessment was expressed last winter by the Senate minority leader, Harry Reid. "I'm not a big Greenspan fan," the Nevada Democrat allowed. "I think he's one of the biggest political hacks we have in Washington." His harsh comment was politely overlooked in governing circles, like an off-color joke told at a Washington dinner party.

When the adulation fades and people begin to understand the full weight of Greenspan's legacy, however, they should be able to see that Reid had it right. Indeed, the Senator's critique did not go far enough. The central banker is a hack, yes, but also a man of conviction.

Alan Greenspan is the most ideological Fed chairman since the 1930s. Without ever acknowledging his intentions, he enlisted himself and the awesome governing powers of the central bank in advancing the "reform" agenda of the Republican right. The chairman thus became an important actor in achieving the profound transformations that occurred during the last generation: the retreat of government, the rise of market ideology and the financialization of American economic life. The "money guys" gained hegemony over the "real economy" of production and work—the people and businesses who make things. The consequences imposed on society are often described as "the tyranny of the bottom line." In numerous ways, the Greenspan Fed helped make it happen. However, the chairman did not produce what conservative doctrine promises—stable and secure prosperity.

Greenspan crossed a line previous Fed chairmen had always gingerly honored: the appearance of political neutrality. That's what angered Reid—this chairman made himself a player on highly partisan matters, using his status as the influential arbiter of "sound economics" to prod Congress and the public to accept the right's larger goals. After years of hectoring Democrats to cut spending and eliminate federal budget deficits, the chairman turned around and endorsed George W. Bush's massive, regressive tax cuts. Democrats fumed, since they had been snookered by Bill Clinton and his Treasury Secretary Robert Rubin into accepting the Fed's agenda, with never a complaining word. But Wall Street loved the wizard, who had gratuitously embraced the GOP plan to deform Social Security by turning over its trillions to the private investment houses.

Trespassing in party politics is not a trivial offense. The so-called "independent" Federal Reserve, from its origins in 1913, has in theory been a cloistered, technocratic institution that has stayed above the fray, making "scientific" decisions on money and credit, acting like a "governor" that regulates the engine of economic growth for long-term stability. The notion of a de-politicized central bank is illusory, of course, since banking interests have always hovered intimately around the Fed's policy decisions. But the myth is useful cover and necessary to sustain the Fed's privileged status as a government agency exempted from normal scrutiny and criticism, deliberately shielded from accountability to the voters—that is, shielded from democracy.

But if the Fed chairman is acting as an errand boy for special interests—in this case for concentrated financial power and wealth—why should the central bank continue to be granted its protected status? Why not bring the institution out into full sunlight, scrub away the pseudo-scientific mystique, make it accountable to elected officials and let Americans learn how to engage with the political–economic issues that govern their lives?

Like other good questions prompted by Greenspan's distinctive performance, this debate is unlikely to be heard, not yet anyway. The bipartisan deference to the central bank remains too strong. Reform-minded politicians have dwindled to a handful. Someday, however, the partisan question might come back to haunt the Federal Reserve and the right-wing Republicans, too.

From Active Government to Laissez-Faire

The ideological shift executed by the Greenspan Fed is more extreme than generally recognized. There has been nothing like it since the New Deal years, when Marriner Eccles was Fed chairman and collaborated closely with FDR to reform the central bank and convert it to the economic understandings grounded in Keynesian liberalism. Eccles and Greenspan are like historic bookends on the long, gradual transition in economic thinking from left to right, from active government intervention to the current faith in laissez-faire markets.

Eccles was a Republican Mormon banker from Utah who became a leading architect of New Deal reforms (including issues beyond monetary policy). In the crisis of the Great Depression such odd political convergences occurred. The self-taught Eccles (he never went to college) personally intuited what John Maynard Keynes developed as a formal theory: The national government, including the Fed, must become the intervening balance wheel in a modern industrial economy—the stabilizing force that, when necessary, stimulates the economy to encourage faster growth and full employment, while at other times it puts the brakes on economic activity to avoid inflation. Eccles essentially invented the modern Federal Reserve, liberating the central bank from the 1920s hard-money orthodoxy of banking and finance, an inflexible doctrine that gravely worsened the Depression.

Greenspan, one might say, devoted his tenure to eliminating vestiges of Eccles and FDR. He resurrected the financier's lost religion, now dignified by conservative economists as the new theory of "efficient markets." Keynesian demand-side stimulus, they contended, produces no lasting effects for the economy, so nothing will be gained by worrying about wage incomes and the consuming power of workers. Wages should be determined by the marketplace and are none of the government's business, except when it wants to squelch price inflation.

The best government can do for the economy, conservatives argued, is to boost the "supply side"—that is, favor wealth holders so they will have more capital to invest in new factories and production. This logic led to huge tax cuts for high-end citizens and for business. It meant liberating and protecting financial markets to do their thing: distributing capital for productive uses in the most efficient (and often ruthless) manner. It convinced Greenspan's Federal Reserve, though a principal regulator of banking and finance, to no longer believe in regulation.

In that sense, Greenspan was the perfect chairman for this era. His monetary policy directly supported all of the various doctrinal strands of the right's ascendant ideology. He deliberately restrained economic growth for many years, effectively suppressing employment and wages. The economy, he argued, cannot grow faster than 2–2.5 percent without igniting price inflation, so the Fed was duty bound to prevent it. (That's not exactly laissez-faire policy, but never mind the contradictions.)

Capital gained in value as a result. Labor took it in the neck. Economic ideologies are often elaborate rationales to justify taking care of some folks and neglecting others.

Meanwhile, protecting the supply side of the economy, the chairman came to the rescue of the financial system and financial firms again and again, whenever they encountered serious peril or the stock market seriously wilted. The 1998 collapse of Long Term Capital Management was interpreted as threatening the safety of the financial system, so the Fed stepped in (what happened to the therapeutic effects of market discipline?). Likewise, the Fed reacted aggressively to the Russian debt crisis that year and the jitters over the "Y2K crisis" of 2000, and Greenspan provided quick liquidity or interest-rate cuts to calm other financial-market upsets.

Greenspan did not formally try to deregulate the banking system, but simply declined to use the Fed's regulatory powers to enforce regular order or discipline fraudulent behavior. In the name of greater efficiency he engineered legal approval for new megabanks like Citigroup even before Congress changed the law. These "too big to fail" financial conglomerates promptly rewarded the chairman's faith by engineering their own massive scandals—the Enron-style corporate frauds and dishonest balance-sheet maneuvers that bilked investors.

Bubbles and Meltdowns

Greenspan's finance-friendly passivity was demonstrated most fatefully when the stock market developed its infamous "price bubble." The chairman refused to take preventive action. Some

$6 trillion was lost by investors in the meltdown, but Greenspan treated it like an unfortunate act of nature. Government does not know enough, he insisted, to intervene in such situations. All it can do is clean up the mess afterward. Greenspan was frequently compelled to do so.

The governing culture at the Fed was also changed dramatically under Greenspan's tutelage. Libertarian clones were appointed to various top positions—officials who take principled pride in their refusal to act as vigilant regulators. The president of the Richmond Federal Reserve Bank warns of the danger of policing the banking industry's "predatory lending" practices too stringently. The Chicago Fed president attacks public schools as a government monopoly. A Federal Reserve governor (and former bank lobbyist) testifies on the need for the Fed to provide larger subsidies for the major banks.

The contrast with Greenspan's predecessor, Paul Volcker, is instructive. Volcker was a savvy and imperious career regulator, adept at befogging politicians and willing to impose harsh discipline on the economy (his long, brutal recession in 1980–82 launched the process of disinflation that Greenspan completed). But Volcker also distrusted the lemming-like behavior of bankers and the faddish enthusiasms of financial markets. He managed his monetary policy close to the vest, hoping to keep the "money guys" off balance and a little intimidated by the Fed's power. Greenspan wanted markets to trust him, even like him. If he provided ample "information" and sprung no surprises, he thought financial-market participants would behave in reasoned, responsible ways. Never happened. But they did like him. They knew he was on their side.

While many contradictions accumulate around Greenspan's governance, none are more obvious than this: The chairman ruled like a one-eyed king, who chose to see only half of the reality before him. He applied rigorous discipline to the real economy, always ready to slow things down to block any price inflation in goods and services, especially in wages. Often he erred deliberately on the side of pre-emptive toughness—tamping down economic growth even when there was no price inflation at all.

Yet the king simultaneously ignored the truly ferocious price inflation under way in financial markets during his long tenure. If working-class wages rose smartly, that was a sign of inflation threatening prosperity. If stock prices rose explosively, that was evidence of good times ahead. For true believers in the conservative orthodoxy, there was no contradiction—capital was growing, unions were being decimated. If you embraced "efficient markets" theory, you would naturally be reluctant to go against the stock market's soaring valuations. If you thought markets were self-regulating, you could count on them to correct themselves. In a way, they did—eventually and violently—by succumbing to a massive "correction"—much to the sorrow of millions of hapless investors, pension funds and others who had gotten no timely warnings from their government about what was ahead.

Greenspan could not claim ignorance. In private meetings with Federal Reserve Board colleagues as far back as 1996, he was repeatedly warned of the dangers posed by the growing stock-price bubble. He declined to take any action or even warn the public. Yale economist Robert Shiller, whose book *Irra-*

tional Exuberance impressively predicted the coming blood-bath, was a rare critic. A public official who fails to alert investors to such risks "is no better than a doctor who, having diagnosed high blood pressure in a patient, says nothing because he thinks the patient might be lucky and show no ill effects," Shiller wrote.

The Price of "Sound Money"

The lopsided focus of Greenspan's Fed—exalting financial markets over the real economy—is perhaps his greatest ideology-driven error, and it caused the deepest damage to society. Congress by law instructs the Federal Reserve to pursue twin goals—stable money and full employment—and there is always a natural tension between those two objectives. Maintaining low price inflation gets much more difficult when the economy expands more vigorously, so the central bank traditionally tried to sustain a rough balance. Greenspan resolved the tension easily (as most conservatives probably would) by tipping the scales in favor of sound money.

The strategy produced very low price inflation, as close to zero as possible, which boosted prices for financial assets, stocks and bonds but also pumped up the financial bubble even further. Soaring stocks encouraged "New Economy" fantasies that the good times would last forever. His fans call Greenspan's era "the great moderation" because there were fewer and shorter recessions, but that leaves out the deeper-running consequences of his reign. In reality the Fed was acting as a principal source of the growing inequalities in American society.

Greenspan's ultimate dilemma—his essential governing failure—was that he didn't know how to handle "success." He had pushed too far in one direction, hardening money's value year after year, but he couldn't push price levels any lower without igniting a destructive deflationary spiral. How to turn around? Conservative orthodoxy provided no good answers to this dilemma, since it claims that zero inflation is a state of perfection. In fact, it is the most dangerous terrain in capitalism. Preventing deflationary calamities was one of the main reasons the Federal Reserve was created.

After years of doing the opposite, the chairman belatedly took his foot off the brake pedal and decided to let the economy grow faster. His shift generated full employment and rising wages—the chairman was celebrated as an economic genius—but booming relief for the real economy came too late to last, given the other imbalances Greenspan had fostered. Faster growth perversely expanded the stock market's delusions, and the price mania spiraled to new heights. Remember the predictions of Dow 35,000? Instead of confronting the real problem, the financial excesses, Greenspan once again turned on the real economy and hammered it with increased interest rates, deceitfully claiming he was attacking wage-price inflation. He lost his gamble on both fronts. The financial bubble did not moderate; it collapsed. And so did the short-lived boom. The national economy was deeply wounded by these events and it is still struggling to recover.

Beware of economic policy-makers who go to extremes in defense of ideological convictions. Essentially, that is the nature of Greenspan's grave failure. The real world did not cooperate with his right-wing beliefs, but he persisted anyway. In the hydraulics of monetary policy, his posture set in motion deep waves of economic extremes: fabulous personal wealth alongside a deeply indebted populace; extraordinary corporate profits alongside stagnant wages and surplus labor; too much capital and not enough consumer demand. These exaggerated waves, and some others, are still sloshing back and forth in the U.S. economy. They will for years ahead, with more crises to come. Greenspan collected much praise for his swift and daring rescue missions—the nimble fireman rushing from blaze to blaze, putting out fires before they destroyed the economy. What many people did not understand is that it was Greenspan who lit the match.

The great irony of the Greenspan era is that conservative ideology turned out to be not conservative at all. It was instead recklessly experimental, testing out its new theories in the human laboratory and ignoring any negative results. Who can still believe in "efficient markets"? Not the folks who lost $6 trillion in the stock market. Who can seriously argue that capital investors need still more "supply side" favors from government, when even Bush's economic adviser complains of a "global savings glut"? Who still wants to liberate the fraud-happy bankers and financiers from the dead hand of government regulation?

My point is, the market ideology is in deep trouble—intellectually, if not politically. If you go behind the mystique and examine Greenspan's performance, there is abundant evidence that demonstrates in real terms the right's economic fallacies, never mind its moral failings. It is premature to talk of an ideological crackup—the right still holds power—but it is not too soon to develop the case for counter-reformation. Most academic economists wouldn't touch it, but maybe some young grad students will decide their right-wing professors are full of crap and undertake the search for alternative thinking. That is how reigning economic ideologies often crumble—when the next generation sees that the old orthodoxy can no longer cope with the facts.

The prospects for political reform are gloomier. Democrats tossed away their populist credentials years ago, and with few exceptions are utterly subservient to the Fed mystique. But there's strong, critical material for the reform minded citizens and public officials who are not intimidated. What might they say? That the Federal Reserve has violated its basic obligations to democracy and it's time to revise its peculiar charter. It is wrong for a government institution to sit by silently and watch a slow-motion disaster unfold for citizens, as Greenspan did. It is also wrong—both politically and economically—to ignore the legal mandate and simply serve one realm of the economy over everyone and everything else. In a democracy, government at least owes citizens fair notice—a timely warning of what it's doing to them. The Fed never, never honors this obligation, for obvious reasons; but then neither do many politicians. That's the basic reason democratic discourse and accountability are so necessary—the hope that somebody somewhere in the government will have the decency to tell the people.

What He Leaves Behind

Which brings us to current circumstances. The Greenspan era, unfortunately, will not end when he departs. The instabilities and ruptures he sowed will still be with us, and he would be wise to get out of town before people recognize the full depth of his destructive legacy. The U.S. economy is not strong and self-confident or even especially efficient. It is stumbling along under subnormal conditions, losing ground and taking on enormous debt from abroad. Nor is the United States free of the follies and risks generated during Greenspan's reign, including financial delusions and the threat of deflation. His successor will presumably be a right-winger too, but one hopes for a more supple, flexible intellect.

The weak-willed economy is an apt illustration of where Greenspan's lopsided policies have led. Four years after the 2001 recession ended, the economy is still struggling to overcome its "jobless" recovery (or "job-loss" recovery, as manufacturing unions call it). Corporate profits have rebounded to extraordinary levels, but companies are reluctant to invest the capital. Wages, meanwhile, remain flat or falling, especially for working-class occupations. Forty-six months into this expansion cycle, the total hours worked in nonsupervisory jobs have risen only 2 percent since the recession ended—compared with rebounds of 9–16 percent after the four previous recessions. Manufacturing, once the vital core of U.S. prosperity, is still losing jobs every month. Its total working hours are down 9 percent since 2001.

This is the most sluggish recovery on record, which seems to puzzle the Fed chairman. But it reflects the Greenspan style of running things; he presided over a similarly tepid recovery in the early 1990s. Tom Schlesinger, director of the Financial Markets Center, a monetary-policy watchdog, thinks the lopsided economy is the most disturbing hallmark of Greenspan's governance. "The Fed has said almost nothing about this, except [vice chairman] Roger Ferguson says there's nothing the Fed can do particularly," Schlesinger complains. "The jobless recovery appears to be a new feature of the U.S. business cycle. Yet the principal agent of economic management says nothing."

In fact, Americans seem to be confronted with the very conditions Keynes warned against: an economy performing, more or less permanently, far below its potential. That situation proves satisfactory for the affluent and for business enterprise, since wage pressures are muted, but it makes life insecure or miserable for most everyone else. The logical response is a fundamental policy shift in favor of work and wages—boosting incomes and demand—but that approach would require taboo measures from the Keynesian past that even most Democrats don't understand or support.

Meanwhile, the financial froth of speculative bubbles—and their dangers—are another enduring legacy of the Greenspan era. "Irrational exuberance really is still with us," Robert Shiller wrote in the new, revised edition of his book. Notwithstanding the earlier meltdown, the stock market remains dangerously overvalued by historical measures, Shiller warns, and is now accompanied by dramatic price inflation in real estate. These two bubbles are false valuations by markets and will burst sooner or later. Shiller urges investors to recognize the "risk that in 2010 or even 2015, the stock market will be lower still in real, inflation-corrected terms, than it was in 2005."

Why do these financial delusions keep arising among investors? Shiller describes many causes, and they include Alan

Greenspan's Fed. The chairman's earnest solicitude for financial markets, Shiller explains, contributed to the "gold rush" psychology, convincing financial players that the central bank would always come to their rescue and never turn against them. Their sloppy exuberance is the opposite of the manly competitive ethos and market discipline preached by Greenspan and the right. Worse, it is bound to injure innocent people. "Things happen during a speculative bubble that can ruin people's lives," Shiller noted. "Little will be done to stop these things if public figures consider themselves beholden to some overarching efficient markets principle and do not even recognize overspeculation as a real phenomenon."

The specter of deflation is, meanwhile, still hanging over the United States. Greenspan initially took dramatic action to avoid the same fate Japan suffered after its financial bubble collapsed in 1990—a low-grade depression and a decade of sputtering stagnation. Cutting interest rates to near zero, the Fed succeeded, at least for the short run. But unless the economy gains more normal balance and energies in the next year or so, the United States may yet be facing the same ditch. The problem, explains William Gross, managing director of PIMCO, a major bond investment house, is that long-term rates have already fallen about as far as they can in real terms. "The Fed may soon be running out of fuel," Gross warns. "If the asset pumps run dry and the kerosene cans empty, the inevitable path of the U.S. economy will reflect slow growth at best and recession as a realistic alternative."

Greenspan, meanwhile, is once again targeting the real economy, raising interest rates to gain some leverage but also flirting with a recession of his own making. He appears to be slyly hoping that higher rates will moderate the speculative bubbles without crashing the economy. Let's hope he wins the gamble this time.

The one-eyed king is in a corner and running out of moves, yet sticking with his failed convictions. Like it or not, we are still living in the lopsided world he made. And this half-blind king is still scary.

Part Two

Alarm Bells

▼ ▼ ▼

Why the Bubble Popped

ROBERT SHERRILL

May 3, 2004

THIS CLUTCH OF BOOKS* offers an excellent retrospective on the recent stock-market crash, which wiped out $8.5 trillion in market value. The value of individual retirement accounts dropped by one-third, and in just twelve months, 2 million Americans lost their jobs.

But the lessons from the crash will probably soon be shrugged off. Memory will be softened by a market that is beginning to recover at an impressive pace. The NASDAQ index, a swamp where tech alligators lurk, is double its value of eighteen months ago. That's a pity. Politicians never work up the nerve to really reform Wall Street until, as after the 1929 collapse, half the population in some cities is unemployed and ex-millionaires start jumping out of windows.

Many of the exploiters and attitudes and wobbly rules that launched the crash are still with us. A sign of the unchanging times could be found in the February 25 *Wall Street Journal*,

---

The Great Unraveling: Losing Our Way in the New Century by Paul Krugman (Norton); *Origins of the Crash: The Great Bubble and Its Undoing* by Roger Lowenstein (Penguin Press); *After the New Economy* by Doug Henwood (New Press); *Contours of Descent: U.S. Economic Fractures and the Landscape of Global Austerity* by Robert Pollin (Verso); *The Roaring Nineties: A New History of the World's Most Prosperous Decade* by Joseph E. Stiglitz (Norton); *American Sucker* by David Denby (Little, Brown).

which reported that Goldman Sachs is once again suspected of violating securities rules, this time by charging excessive bond-trading price markups. The accompanying report also sounds normal: Goldman's chief executive took home $21 million last year, a 75 percent increase over 2002.

Still, we can try to read the future in these analyses of the past. Paul Krugman's essays have the snappy smartness his followers have come to expect, but for me the best interpretations of the marketplace and the so-called New Economy come from Robert Pollin, a University of Massachusetts professor of economics, who for one thing helps strip the populist mask from Bill Clinton; Doug Henwood, whose tart humor keeps one awake even when he discusses Wagnerian topics, as in the chapter on globalization, where he calls Ralph Nader "a special case, a man who seems proud of his (locally produced) hair shirt"; Joseph Stiglitz, a Nobel Prize–winning economist who writes with admirable candor about the sellouts of some of his colleagues in the Clinton years; and Roger Lowenstein, a master (as I first learned from his book *When Genius Failed*) at making our financial pirates as interesting as those who sailed with Long John Silver. David Denby's *American Sucker* is not so much a critique of the era as it is a tragicomic, introspective tale of how much it can cost an ignorant investor to learn the true character of Wall Street. Denby, a film critic for the *New Yorker,* lost nearly a million.

Most of these writers properly feel that the crash was caused by a combination of all or most of these influences: deregulation to the point of anarchy; a towering secrecy that conceals the financial world from ordinary investors; greed that distorts capitalism and the character of those who administer it; a justice system that Wall Street malefactors know they need not fear; and, to personalize the problem, we are offered Alan Greenspan and his fellow conspirators, chief of whom were Clinton and his Treasury Secretary, Robert Rubin, who was a top exec at Goldman Sachs before joining Clinton's Cabinet and a top exec at Citigroup after leaving it. In Lowenstein's opinion, Clinton was, except for Ronald Reagan, "the most market-oriented president since the Roaring Twenties."

If the crash proved anything, it was that crime pays. Sufficient tax credits were claimed to offset the measly $1.4 billion fine that J. P. Morgan, Morgan Stanley, Merrill Lynch, Credit Suisse First Boston, Citigroup, Goldman Sachs and four others agreed to fork over for misdeeds that, as Stiglitz says, "put most acts of political crookedness to shame. ... The scale of theft achieved by the ransacking of Enron, WorldCom and other corporations in the nineties was in the billions of dollars—greater than the GDP of some nations."

Punishment of Wall Street's brigands has been neither swift nor sure. As of late February, seven of Enron's top executives had confessed to robbing the public, and eleven others were under indictment for that crime—but not one was behind bars. As for the top dog, Kenneth Lay, he seems to have been forgotten.

Lowenstein reminds us that at the start of the 1980s, 90 percent of the money managed by pension funds was invested in bonds, bills and cash. Stocks had had such a middling performance for half a century that they were considered to be just a little better than mattress stuffing. But "by the late 1990s, America had become more sensitive to markets, more ruled by markets, than any country on earth. This is the culture that led to prosperity and also to Enron. Markets became virtually sovereign—unchecked by corporate watchdogs or by government."

Unchecked, indeed. Out of control is more like it. The root cause of the lawless boom and the crash that followed was the deregulating mania that started with Reagan and Bush I. For a dozen years their administrations, in the words of Stiglitz, "glorified free markets and demonized government regulations," and this attitude was carried over into the Clinton administration. Robert Pollin agrees that Clinton's administration was defined by "virtually unqualified enthusiasm for ... the deregulation of financial markets—with Alan Greenspan providing crucial leadership in granting to financial traders the leeway they had long sought to freely speculate with other people's money."

The deregulation tide that began in the 1970s became a huge wave. Electricity was deregulated. Telecommunications was deregulated. And Wall Street, of course. The most disastrous deregulation resulted from the killing of the venerable Glass-Steagall Act, which had been around since 1933. The purpose of Glass-Steagall was to maintain a wall between commercial banks and investment banks. The former take our deposits and lend money to people and corporations that can prove they have a good credit rating. The much more profitable investment banks dote on risks and get huge fees for helping corporations issue new bonds and stocks. The reason for the wall between the banks was obvious: If it were removed, the commercial side of the bank would be pressured to join the dangerous fund, lending money to companies that didn't deserve more credit—even companies teetering on the brink of bankruptcy—so that the investment-banking side could continue getting their lush kickback fees.

That's exactly what was done by many of the banks, including the banking sections of the giant brokerage firms, after Glass-Steagall was "reorganized" out of existence by the Clinton administration. The lure of more mega-fees kept them propping up behemoth clients they knew were dying of their own excesses.

Another reason banks kept propping them up was that they feared that if the corporations did go bankrupt, the banks' own nefarious participation would be exposed. As indeed it usually was.

Consider WorldCom's support by Citigroup (an octopus including Citibank, Travelers Insurance and Salomon Smith Barney brokerage). That octopus, which lent many millions to WorldCom and was lead underwriter of a $5 billion debt, kept touting WorldCom stock as a "strong buy" almost to the day the company went under.

The investment banks' advance troops in the assault on the gullible public were the analysts. Some of these extremely effective pitchmen, Doug Henwood reminds us, were "publicly recommending stocks that they privately disdained ... stocks that no sane, fully informed persons would ever have bought." Henry Blodget, an analyst at Merrill Lynch whom David Denby had the misfortune to befriend, gained notoriety for promoting a stock that he privately described as a "piece of shit." Merrill Lynch, which must have known that sort of thing was going on, was fined a trifling $100 million for failing to stop the conflict of interest within its walls. As for Blodget, his punishment was to be banned for life from the securities industry, but that hardly reduced him to poverty or refilled the pockets of those, like Denby, he helped fleece.

And the same can be said for the closing-the-barn-door banning of Jack Grubman, whose allegedly fraudulent research brought tens of millions of dollars to Salomon and sometimes as much as $20 million a year to his own pockets. In his role as cheerleader for telecommunications, he foresaw a glorious future for WorldCom, Qwest and Global Crossing, now all wreckage.

Henwood's quote from former investment banker Nomi Prins, describing what happened to the telecom industry in the second half of the 1990s, is the abbreviated morality tale of the decade:

Wall Street raised $1.3 trillion of telecom debt and sparked a $1.7 trillion merger spree, bagging $15 billion in fees for the effort. Then, the accumulation party ended. The industry collapsed amidst a $230 billion pile of bankruptcies and fraud, wiping out $2 trillion in market value and defaulting on $110 billion of debt (half of all defaults). Telecom execs pocketed $18 billion before they cut 560,000 jobs. And in 2003, over 96 percent of the capacity built lies dormant.

The Accounting Game

Much of the genius behind the bubble's inflation must be credited to crooked accounting practices. To sucker the public into buying their stock, corporate accountants juggled the books so that profits seemed much higher than they were and losses could be hidden.

Enron, for example, entered into contracts that would have produced profits many years ahead, if ever, and claimed them as current profits. And many millions of dollars in stock options that corporate executives gave themselves should have been counted as expenses, but usually weren't. Paul Krugman gives an example: "In 1998 Cisco reported a profit of $1.35 billion; if it had counted the market value of the stock options it issued as an expense, it would have reported a loss of $4.9 billion."

This kind of crookedness had gone on for years, but in 1993 the Financial Accounting Standards Board (FASB) recommended a rule that would have ended it. The rule was immediately and fiercely opposed in Congress by members who had received bountiful gifts from both Wall Street and the accounting industry. None were more grateful for their largesse than that odd Democrat from Connecticut, Senator Joseph Lieberman.

He sponsored a resolution condemning the FASB's proposal on humanitarian grounds, even though, throughout the corporate world, "75 percent of options went to people who ranked in the top five in their companies. More than half of the remainder went to the next fifty managers ... an unprecedented accumulation of private wealth," writes Lowenstein. But Senator Lieberman made it sound like "millions of ordinary workers would now be cast into a cold, optionless world ... back to breadlines and hawking apples."

The FASB Surrendered

Why, sometimes it almost seemed that those seeking deregulation were selfishly motivated. Even as his wife sat on Enron's board, Senator Phil Gramm pushed through legislation exempting the corporation's practices from regulation. And when

Gramm left the Senate, says Krugman, he joined UBS Warburg, the company that bought Enron's trading operations.

Speaking of corruption, what happened to Arthur Andersen, one of the most venerable of the Big Five accounting firms (established in 1913), really shook Wall Street. If the Big Five couldn't be trusted to give reliable accounting, the stock market had truly become a gambling den. There had been whispers of Arthur Andersen's unreliability ever since its part in the savings and loan scandal. Actually, these whispers made it more attractive to some clients. Pollin points out that in 1990 George W. Bush had successfully called on Arthur Andersen to OK his questionable books at the Harken Energy Corporation; and in a promotional video in 1996, Dick Cheney, then chairman of Halliburton, had come straight to the point, praising Arthur Andersen for giving him "good advice ... over and above the just sort of normal by-the-book auditing arrangement."

Enron, WorldCom, Global Crossing and Tyco International also got more than "normal by-the-book" auditing on their way into oblivion, and Arthur Andersen soon felt the flames as well.

The Good Old Reliable SEC

Having killed Glass-Steagall, the deregulators would have liked to kill the Securities and Exchange Commission (SEC), too. But they knew they couldn't dare even suggest that. The SEC had been an almost sacred regulator of the securities market since its founding in 1934, when it became the cop on the corner empowered with regulations that were meant to build a sense of ethics among market professionals and give the public confidence that somebody was trying to protect them from the hustlers.

But if they couldn't kill it, they could sure weaken it. The SEC has always been "ludicrously underfinanced," Krugman says quite accurately. "Staff lawyers and accountants are paid half what they could get in the private sector, usually find themselves heavily outnumbered by the legal departments of the companies they investigate, and often must do their own typing and copying." George W. Bush would see that this continued.

The public's outrage over the stock-market collapse and the accounting scandals forced Congress in the summer of 2002 to pass the Sarbanes-Oxley Act, which was aimed at increasing regulation of public corporations' accounting practices. The SEC would implement the act. Bush grudgingly signed the act into law, but (according to Pollin's view of the episode) the president got to strike his customary low blow by slashing the SEC's budget 27 percent below what the legislation had proposed.

More accurately, that was the first low blow of the day. His second was to appoint William Webster to head the auditing oversight board set up by Sarbanes-Oxley. Obviously, if Bush wanted the board to fail, he chose the right man. Webster had previously directed two failed agencies, the FBI and the CIA, and was currently, writes Pollin, "a board member of a company under investigation for securities fraud." Press contempt for that appointment forced a mediocre replacement, and all things point to the SEC's withering away.

And Then There Was the Fed

There has been no bureaucrat more exalted by the business world, by Congress, by Clinton and his predecessors, and by the press than Alan Greenspan, chairman of the Federal Reserve Board. And there is no stranger phenomenon in recent history than that exaltation, for Greenspan has proved himself to be a very anti-everything that keeps us going.

He is an anti-inflation, antitax, antispending, antiregulation, antigovernment nut. Admittedly, his mistakes have sometimes been fortuitous. In 1974, as chairman of the Council of Economic Advisers, he was so eager to fight inflation (which wasn't really high) that he persuaded President Ford to cut government spending right in the middle of a sharp recession, which just made the recession worse. Angry voters dumped Ford in 1976.

The Federal Reserve System, which was set up in 1913, is the most undemocratic part of our government. Although its actions affect every legal or illegal resident of the country, it has no input from the general public. The Fed is literally owned by the largest national banks, and the Fed's board, which meets in secret, has never had a member who came from the labor movement or at least momentarily entertained a populist thought. The Fed has two mandates from Congress: Adjust the interest rates in such a way as to maintain a healthy economy, and promote employment. A moderate amount of inflation—meaning more money in circulation—is good for employment. But banks hate it because it lowers the value of the dollar. So the Fed has always ignored the second half of its mandate. Consequently, says Stiglitz, "there is little doubt that many of the postwar recessions have been caused by the Fed, as it has stepped on the brakes too hard in its fixation that unless it does so, inflation will break out."

Chairman Greenspan has religiously followed that absolutely-no-inflation dogma as it affected money (creating the recession that doomed the elder Bush at the polls). But he has not minded the inflation of asset values on Wall Street, and by ignoring them he helped create the boom-bust.

In 1996, when the Standard & Poor's Index (S&P) stood at 740, Greenspan asked, "How do we know when irrational exuberance has unduly inflated asset values?" But three years later, when the S&P had doubled and signs of the bubble were everywhere, he still took no action. In a 2002 speech to his chums at Jackson Hole, he tried to defend his inaction, claiming "it was very difficult to definitively identify a bubble until after the fact—that is, when its bursting confirmed its existence." And there was nothing he could have done about it anyway, he said. "Is there some policy that can at least limit the size of a bubble and, hence, its destructive fallout? ... The answer appears to be no."

Actually, the answer appears to be yes, and he knew all along what it was. He could have raised the market's margin requirements, thereby reducing how much stock people could buy with borrowed money. Krugman reminds us that at the September 1996 meeting of the Federal Open Market Committee (F.O.M.C.), Greenspan told his colleagues, "I recognize that there is a stock market bubble problem at this point" and that it could be solved by "increasing margin requirements. I guarantee that if you want to get rid of the bubble, whatever it is, that will do it."

But he didn't do it. Nor did he lobby behind the scenes against the huge capital gains tax cut of 1997, which fed the market with another torrent of investor money. Not only did he do nothing to tame the market, writes Stiglitz, "he switched to becoming a cheerleader for the market's boom, almost egging it on, as he repeatedly argued that the New Economy was bringing with it a new era of productivity increases."

Readers who pay attention to these books will have to conclude that the system is broken. Or maybe they won't. If, despite what happened to their 401(k) last time, they still want to try the market, then they will probably agree with what Henry Blodget told David Denby at their last tête-à-tête in 2001:

> People have now lost a lot of money. They can say, "I made a mistake, I lost a lot," or they can say, "Somebody fucked me." It's so much easier to say the latter. In two years, the revisionist view will be that nothing bad would have happened if the system weren't broken. But nothing would be further from the case. It was a bubble. This is just the way the markets behave and the way that people behave.

Bush's House of Cards

DEAN BAKER

August 9, 2004

THE LATEST DATA ON GROWTH suggest that the economy may again be faltering, just when President Bush desperately needs good numbers to make the case for his re-election. As bad as the Bush economic record is, it would be far worse if not for the growth of an unsustainable housing bubble through the three and a half years of the Bush administration.

The housing market has supported the economy both directly—through construction of new homes and purchases of existing homes—and indirectly, by allowing families to borrow against the increased value of their homes. Housing construction is up more than 17 percent from its level at the end of the recession. Purchases of existing homes hit a record of 6.1 million in 2003, more than 500,000 above the previous record set in 2002. Each home purchase is accompanied by thousands of dollars of closing costs, plus thousands more spent on furniture and remodeling.

The indirect impact of the housing bubble is at least as important. Mortgage debt rose by an incredible $2.3 trillion between 2000 and 2003. This borrowing has sustained consumption growth in an environment in which firms have been shedding jobs and cutting back hours, and real wage growth has fallen to zero, although the gains from this elixir are starting to fade with a recent rise in mortgage rates and many families are running out of equity to tap.

The red-hot housing market has forced up home prices nationwide by 35 percent after adjusting for inflation. There is no precedent for this sort of increase in home prices. Historically, home prices have moved at roughly the same pace as the overall rate of inflation. While the bubble has not affected every housing market—in large parts of the country home prices have remained pretty much even with inflation—in the bubble areas, primarily on the two coasts, home prices have exceeded the overall rate of inflation by 60 percentage points or more.

The housing enthusiasts, led by Alan Greenspan, insist that the run-up is not a bubble, but rather reflects fundamental factors in the demand for housing. They cite several factors that could explain the price surge: a limited supply of urban land, immigration increasing the demand for housing, environmental restrictions on building and rising family income leading to increased demand for housing.

A quick examination shows that none of these explanations holds water. Land is always in limited supply; that fact never led to such a widespread run-up in home prices in the past. Immigration didn't just begin in the late nineties. Also, most recent immigrants are low-wage workers. They are not in the market for the $500,000 homes that middle-class families now occupy in bubble-inflated markets. Furthermore, the demographic impact of recent immigration rates pales compared to the impact of baby boomers first forming their first households in the late seventies and eighties. And that did not lead to a comparable boom in home prices.

Environmental restrictions on building, moreover, didn't begin in the late nineties. In fact, in light of the election of the Gingrich Congress in 1994 and subsequent Republican dominance of many state houses, it's unlikely that these restrictions suddenly became more severe at the end of the decade. And the income growth at the end of the nineties, while healthy, was only mediocre compared to the growth seen over the period from 1951 to 1973. In any event, this income growth has petered out in the last two years.

The final blow to the argument of the housing enthusiasts is the recent trend in rents. Rental prices did originally follow sale prices upward, although not nearly as fast. However, in the last two years, the pace of rental price increases has slowed under the pressure of record high vacancy rates. In some bubble areas, like Seattle and San Francisco, rents are actually falling. No one can produce an explanation as to how fundamental factors can lead to a run-up in home sale prices, but not rents.

At the end of the day, housing can be viewed like Internet stocks on the NASDAQ. A run-up in prices eventually attracts more supply. This takes the form of IPOs on the NASDAQ, and new homes in the housing market. Eventually, there are not enough people to sustain demand, and prices plunge.

The crash of the housing market will not be pretty. It is virtually certain to lead to a second dip to the recession. Even worse, millions of families will see the bulk of their savings disappear as homes in some of the bubble areas lose 30 percent, or more, of their value. Foreclosures, which are already at near record highs, will almost certainly soar to new peaks. This has happened before in regional markets that had severe housing bubbles, most notably in Colorado and Texas after the collapse of oil prices in the early eighties. However, this time the bubble markets are more the rule than the exception, infecting most real estate markets on both coasts, as well as many local markets in the center of the country.

In this context, it's especially disturbing that the Bush administration has announced that it is cutting back Section 8 housing vouchers, which provide rental assistance to low income families, while easing restrictions on mortgage loans. Low-income families will now be able to get subsidized mortgage loans through the Federal Housing Administration that are equal to 103 percent of the purchase price of a home. Home ownership can sometimes be a ticket to the middle class, but buying homes at bubble-inflated prices may saddle hundreds of thousands of poor families with an unmanageable debt burden.

As with the stock bubble, the big question about the housing bubble is when it will burst. No one can give a definitive answer to that one, but Alan Greenspan seems determined to ensure that it will be after November. Instead of warning prospective homebuyers of the risk of buying housing in a bubble-inflated market, Greenspan gave Congressional testimony in the summer of 2002 arguing that there is no such bubble. This is comparable to his issuing a "buy" recommendation for the NASDAQ at the beginning of 1999. More recently, Greenspan has done everything in his power to keep mortgage rates as low as possible, at one point even offering markets the hope that the Fed would take the extraordinary measure of directly buying long-term Treasury bonds. The man who testified that the Bush tax cuts were a good idea apparently has one last job to perform for the president.

Leaking Bubble

DOUG HENWOOD
March 27, 2006

Housing inflation is the American national religion," as the late market pundit Ed Hart of the late Financial News Network used to say. And as everyone knows, we've been going through a particularly pious phase for the past few years. But it's looking like the housing religion is on the verge of a crisis of faith.

By just about any metric, the past several years have seen the most extraordinary boom in the U.S. housing market in history, rivaling the dot-com stock market madness of the late 1990s. In the third quarter of 2005, the average new house sold in the United States cost 4.9 times the average household's yearly income, up from 3.9 in the late 1990s and eclipsing the previous record of 4.3 set in 1989. But it's not just price that set records last year—it's also the rate of turnover. Turnover of new and existing houses in the third quarter of last year was more than 16 percent of GDP, way above its long-term average of 9 to 10 percent, and easily beating the levels reached in the housing frenzies of the 1970s and 1980s.

But that's not all, as they say on TV. People haven't merely been buying houses, they've been conducting scary experiments in financial innovation. Time was, you had to come up with a hefty down payment to buy a house. No longer: In 2005 the median first-time buyer put down only 2 percent of the sales price, and 43 percent made no down payment at all. And almost a third of new mortgages in 2004 and 2005 were at adjustable rates (because the initial payments are lower than on fixed-rate loans). At earlier peaks interest rates were near cyclical highs, but the past few years have seen the lowest interest rates in a generation. So adjustable mortgages are likely to adjust only one way: up.

But there's more! People haven't been borrowing aggressively merely to buy houses—they've been borrowing against the appreciated value to buy all kinds of other stuff. Americans have been using their houses as MasterCards, turning about $726 billion of their home equity into (borrowed) cash between 2001 and 2005. That's a big number, even by the standards of the U.S. economy; it's equal to almost 40 percent of the growth in personal spending, and a nice compensation for the failure of the economy to generate new jobs at a vigorous pace. But since we're saving nothing these days—the personal savings rate went negative in 2005 for the first time since the Great Depression—the cash had to come from abroad. Since 2001 U.S. foreign debt has increased by a stunning $2 trillion.

One thing can be said for the housing mania: It's kept the economy afloat since the bursting of the stock market bubble in 2000. (Wall Street economists estimate that 40 to 50 percent of the growth in GDP and employment over the last several years has been driven by the housing boom.) When the dot-coms went up in smoke, Alan Greenspan's Federal Reserve drove interest rates down to 1 percent to contain the economic fallout. But that "cure" is what got the housing mania going; low interest rates made borrowing irresistible, and the nation's speculative spirits were diverted away from Wall Street and toward home sweet home.

But now that all looks like it's coming to an end, thanks in part to the Fed's round of interest-rate increases. Sales volumes are slowing, prices are flattening or even declining, mortgage demand is easing and the inventory of unsold houses is rising.

So what's next? Deflating the housing bubble is likely to take some time. The housing market isn't like the stock market; it's a lot slower, and its harder to dump one's house in a panic than 1,000 shares of Pets.com. But removing the stimulus responsible for about half the economy's recent growth has to have an effect. That effect could be anything from a mild drag on an already limp economy to a real financial crisis. What it is depends on whether other sectors pick up some of the slack—say, if businesses were to start hiring and investing rather than hoarding their plentiful cash or distributing it to their stockholders.

If they don't, things could get quite unpleasant. So many households have taken on so much mortgage debt that if prices merely stop rising, they're going to find themselves under water. And the broad economy has become so dependent on home-equity credit that its withdrawal could come as a terrible shock. Maybe the economy will finally have to face the consequences of the collapse of the 1990s stock-driven boom that it managed to avoid by speculating on housing instead. In fact, the main thing arguing against that possibility is the economy's stunning ability to evade its dates with destiny time after time.

Show Me the Money

WALTER MOSLEY
December 18, 2006

THE RICH GET RICHER ..." This truism is irrefutable. "... and the poor get poorer." We look away from ourselves, and our loved ones, when the latter phrase is used to complete the saying.

Often only the first part of this age-old axiom is quoted. It's as if we are silently saying, "There's no reason to talk about the poor, about poverty. Let's just accept the notion that money migrates toward money and leave it at that."

But where does this money, which moves so unerringly into rich folks' pockets, come from? This is one of the most important questions in everyday working people's lives. Because the money that makes the rich richer comes out of the sweat, the sacrifice and ultimately the blood of working men and women.

Many people deny that they are the victims in the proverb because even though the rich make money off them, too, they are also making money, being middle class, off the working and lower classes.

It's an imagined pyramid scheme, and like all its brethren, a scam.

So-called middle-class people look at working people and say to themselves, "I'm not doing so bad. Look at that poor slob. He's the one getting poorer. I'm traveling along in the wake of the rich. I don't have a mansion, but I own a mortgage on a house."

This is what the poor Irish and Italians and Jews told themselves about black people in late nineteenth- and early twentieth-century New York.

Today people say it about the Mexican and Central and South American migrant laborers who toil in our fields and factories. "They are the ones who live in squalor and poverty."

What is the difference between the working class and the middle class? Is it a clearly demarcated line dividing those who pass on wealth and those who accrue it?

Most people I know consider themselves middle-class workers. They're making good money, they say, and have good credit at the bank. Their children will go to good colleges and get better jobs. They will retire in comfort and travel to Europe (or Africa) to see the genesis of their culture.

These self-proclaimed middle-class citizens feel a certain private smugness about their proven ability to make it in this world while those in the working and lower classes—because of upbringing, lack of intelligence or will, or bad luck—are merely the fuel for the wealth of the nation.

But how do you know where you fit in the class system? Is it a level of income? Is it defined by education or the kind of job you possess? Is class a function of your relationship to your labor? For instance, are you in the middle class because you own your own business? Or are we defined by our rung on the ladder? As long as we are not at the bottom (or the top), then we can say we are in the middle.

It's a difficult question because the economic state of everyone's life in this world is in perpetual flux. Depression, inflation, recession—all these and many other economic events continually change our finances and redefine our position in society. Our money grows in the bank, but at the same time it loses value. Our property increases in value, but taxes and expenses also rise. We say that we own the mortgage on our home, but more often than not the mortgage controls us. To buy a $10,000 home we pay $40,000 over thirty years. Where did that extra $30,000 go?

It seems to me that we need a rule-of-thumb definition of class. We can't use the pristine forms of geometry to prove where we are and what we're worth. Mathematical sums don't define wealth; the ability to control your time and quality of life does.

I'd like to put forward a system of class definition that is grounded in what I believe to be a common-sense approach to the issue.

Poverty is defined, in my system, by people not being able to cover the basic necessities in their lives. Indispensable medical care, nutrition, a place to live; all these essentials, for poor people, are often and chronically beyond reach. If a poor person needs $10 a day to make ends meet, often he or she only makes eight and a half.

Wealth, in my definition, is when money is no longer an issue or a question. Wealthy people don't know how much money they have or how much they make. Their worth is gauged in property, natural resources and power, in doors they can go through and the way that law works. Wealth moves like a shark over the rockbound crustaceans of the poor and working classes.

The middle classes, which logic would tell us occupy the space between poverty and wealth, are made up of two very different subspecies. One is the working class; the other is the class of limited privilege.

It is my proposition that the great majority of us fall into the former group. The privileged middle class are people who have to work for a living but who can buy almost anything they desire: a summer cottage, a prestige car, berths at the finer schools for their children. These people are lawyers, real estate developers, the owners of small and successful businesses. If someone in the class of privilege were to lose their job or experience reversals in their business, they would have time (between nine and twelve months) to consider their options before any part of their lifestyle would necessitate change. Their children could stay in private schools, they could still go to fine restaurants and the opera on Friday nights, and even donate to the same charities.

But if a person from the working class loses her job, she would have to find an equivalent one within the month or it'll be fast food and junior college for everyone in the family.

Working-class people are (excuse the Marxism) wage-slaves. Those in the working class live on the edge of poverty, saying to themselves that they are doing all right. They drink and watch far too much TV. They buy Lotto tickets and live moderate lives that are far beyond their means. The profit they generate flows to the rich, and they borrow to fill out the coffers.

Most Americans are working-class wage-slaves, arguing that they're better off. This fantasy, more than any other confusion, hobbles us. Because we fear to see how delicate our economic state is, we cannot motivate ourselves to demand change.

Capitalism, the accrual of wealth from labor, is the religion of America; poverty our cardinal sin. To recognize our position in relation to wealth would be perceived as a confession of wrong-doing, and so we stoically bear up, pretending we are doing all right. And because we don't see ourselves clearly, we have poor healthcare, no adequate insurance for old age, poisons in our water and our food and the continual nagging fear that things may at any moment fall apart.

Where is the money? It's not in our bank accounts or serving our people. It's not in affordable housing, quality education or the development of sciences that would better the species and the planet. It's not being used for the purpose of global peace.

America is the wealthiest nation in the world, by far, but we the American people are not wealthy. We, most of us, live on the border of poverty. In the distance are towering silvery skyscrapers housing our corporations and our billionaires. But do not be fooled. This skyline does not belong to us. We are not partners in the corporation of America.

The money we make, the wealth we have created, is paradoxically beyond our reach. We live in a separate America. An America that is heated by oil that we may or may not be able to afford; an America that makes profit off of cigarettes, alcohol and imperialist incursions into underprivileged nations; an America that cares more for corporations than it does for its living, breathing citizens.

Where is the money? It has been turned into gold and laid upon our willing backs. We struggle under the weight of the wealth of America, and there we are ground down until, in the end, it shall be soaked in our blood.

This knowledge, as depressing and oppressing as it is, is also a harbinger of hope. Poverty is not our fault or our destiny. We, the poor and working class, have built this nation and it, along with all its fabulous wealth, belongs to us. From the Atlantic to the Pacific we, the workers, are the ones who hold sway. And every vault, every clinic, every drop of sweat fallen upon American soil is our democratic birthright.

The rich don't own anything that we haven't built. The government means nothing that we don't endorse. These are the secrets that need to be made public. There may be charities to help with income and profession, there may be those who lend a helping hand. But the helpers and the help are equals in this country, in this nation. There are no hierarchies of class in a democracy. There is only freedom and debt owed to the millions upon millions who have labored to make us great.

The greatest service that could be given to the poor and working classes is the knowledge that they, that we, all deserve the best that America has to offer, and if there are those who try to diminish us because of our bankbooks or our education this is a crime against our Constitution. We carry this nation on our backs, and everything it has done is our property and our responsibility.

A man can be rich, but only a nation can be wealthy. And if any person of any age suffers from poverty, then our whole country bears the shame.

Monetary Zombies

NICHOLAS VON HOFFMAN

January 17, 2006

NEXT TO PUBLISHING LISTS like the top ten, ten best or ten worst of any damn thing you can think of, what journalism loves most is a first. So here is a first to thrill any editor's heart: Two thousand and five was the first year since the Great Depression that Americans spent more money than they earned.

Ordinarily a statistic like that is grounds for giving the public a good scolding for its spendthrift ways, followed by a prediction of chaos and mass bankruptcy to come. But that may not be how this story plays out. Jesse Eisinger of the *Wall Street Journal* writes that the outcome may be a society of millions of consumer "zombies," individuals and families who are financially half alive and half dead, shackled by debts that keep growing and that they cannot pay off but prevented by their credit card companies from taking the final plunge and declaring bankruptcy.

Something like that happened in Japan fifteen years ago, after the banks there had lent trillions to companies unable to repay their loans or even keep up on the interest. The size of these bad loans would have put Japan's banks into bankruptcy except for an arrangement worked out with all interested parties to freeze everything. The banks agreed not to demand the money they were owed by the companies, and the Japanese government pretended that the banks were still solvent. As a result the Japanese economy, prevented from regaining strength through the cathartic benefits of bankruptcy, floated in a chilly world of zombie companies and financial institutions on life support. Companies had just enough cash to keep going but not enough capital to expand and develop.

If individuals and families continue to spend more than they make, millions of us may also end up in the land of the living dead. After inflation is taken into account, the wages of 80 percent of working people have been trending slightly downward for the past four years. At the same time the clamor to get people to buy and spend does not abate and will not, since the masters of the universe have determined that the prosperity of the entire globe depends on Americans continuing to visit the mall.

We are seeing early signs of the zombie syndrome. It first appeared in the American automobile industry and latterly at Wal-Mart and the other big, lower-price retail chains. When faced with a choice of selling fewer cars at a profit or more cars at a loss, the automobile companies made the zombie choice to sell more, lose money and sink closer to bankruptcy. This past holiday shopping season retailers, faced with the possibility of lower sales than last year, elected to cut their already thin profit margins to keep their increasingly strapped customers at the checkout lines with their shopping carts full and their bank accounts empty.

Obviously, after a certain point price-cutting and discounting is going to land retailers in the soup. Presumably stores are also pushing their suppliers to cut prices and, if they oblige as they are wont to do, they will slip into the red themselves. We may wind up in a comic book universe with everyone losing money and thrashing for air in the pool.

Home equity loans or refinancing one's ever-appreciating home have compensated for flat or declining earnings, but that particular ATM machine has closed with the leveling off of the housing market. For many people, the only readily available credit left this side of bankruptcy is their credit cards.

Delinquencies among credit card holders have been running around 4 percent. The credit card business is so lucrative the banks that own the card companies have no problem with that. If that number were to gradually climb to 12 percent or even 15 percent, they would have a problem. Since they have to pay the merchants whose customers used the card regardless, delinquency rates at those levels would take a noticeable bite out of profits.

If the companies use the new laws to force their customers into bankruptcy, zombie status is practically automatic. Under the new law the bankrupt does not have his debts washed away, only reduced. If the credit card companies do not drive their card holders into bankruptcy, the payment arrangements they make will zombify their debtors anyway.

There is another way. The bankruptcy law in the early Roman Republic tolerated no zombie-ism:

"A person who admits to owing money or has been adjudged to owe money must be given thirty days to pay.

"After then, the creditor can lay hands on him and haul him to court. If he does not satisfy the judgment and no one is surety for him, the creditor may take the defendant with him in stocks or chains. He may bind him with weights of at least fifteen pounds.

"On the third market day, the creditors may cut the debtor to pieces. If they take more than they are due, they do so with impunity."

Henry Paulson's Treasury

NOMI PRINS

June 26, 2006

I N THE COVERAGE OF President Bush's nomination of Henry J. "Hank" Paulson to replace John Snow as Treasury Secretary, I've lost count of the number of mainstream media discussing the "well-worn path" between Goldman Sachs and official Washington. But just because a road is well traveled doesn't mean it leads in the right direction.

Tapping officials from the venerable investment bank for policy-making positions in government is a practice that dates back to the Eisenhower administration, when John Foster Dulles, whose law firm represented Goldman Sachs, was appointed Secretary of State.

In more recent history, Goldman Sachs co-CEO Robert Rubin instigated massive banking deregulation in the five years he served as Treasury Secretary in the Clinton administration. Rubin quit in 1999 for a multimillion-dollar position at Citigroup. Around the same time, Jon Corzine lost an internal political battle as Paulson's co-CEO, rebounding first as the Democratic senator of New Jersey and now as governor.

In March 1999, Joshua Bolten left Goldman Sachs to become policy director of the Bush-Cheney campaign, later serving as policy adviser, director of the Office of Management and Budget and ultimately White House Chief of Staff. Stephen Friedman, former Goldman co-CEO with Rubin, was appointed National Economic Council director by Bush from 2002 to 2005.

Enter Hank Paulson, who has spent the past eight years as Goldman Sachs chairman and CEO. He joined the firm in 1974 after serving as a member of the White House Domestic Council in the Nixon administration.

Under Paulson's leadership, Goldman Sachs has become one of Washington's most generous patrons. Paulson is a top donor—mostly to the G.O.P. (To the chagrin of critics on the right, Paulson is also an ardent environmentalist and is chairman of The Nature Conservancy.) As Treasury Secretary, Paulson may have to dump some stock (he is the single largest shareholder in Goldman Sachs according to its 2006 proxy statement, with 4.6 million shares) to decrease his overwhelming conflict of interest, but even if he sells his unrestricted stock, he'll still have several hundred million bucks in RSU (restricted stock unit) awards, which are not immediately sellable. This could place him in a position where maintaining his financial well-being could necessitate supporting policies positive to Goldman's short-term stock price over long-term needs of the general economy, like dividend tax cuts.

What first struck me upon news of Paulson's possible appointment was that he's too smart to take on this task, with Bush's approval ratings for his economic policies hovering around 40 percent. Then, I got it. Paulson is Bush's last hurrah—and his last chance. Known as a pragmatic and decisive leader, Paulson will likely be more proactive than Snow, whose sole job essentially was traipsing up to Congress once a year and urging lawmakers to raise the U.S. debt cap by another trillion dollars so we wouldn't default on our interest payments to China.

Bush's economic legacy is a weak dollar (who wants to invest in a country teetering on the brink of default?) and tax cuts for the super-wealthy that have created an outrageous deficit and debt. And that legacy benefits men like Paulson at the expense of middle-class Americans and the working poor. It will be a stretch for him to argue for prudent budgeting, while facing the country's highest national debt ever, without cutting social programs to get there.

This shaky economic legacy also makes Paulson's possible appointment more challenging and hence more potentially dangerous than Rubin's. He must rally citizens into believing their individual economic condition is better than it is. Plus, he needs to convince international investors that the dollar isn't in free fall, despite the abundance of American debt. That's a lot harder than convincing a board of peers as chairman to compensate your fellow senior executives hundreds of millions of dollars.

When Robert Rubin hit Washington, mega-consolidation in the banking industry that led to "Enronian" corporate scandals had yet to be given the 1999 legislative go-ahead that smashed Glass-Steagall, FDR's New Deal Act separating commercial banking from investment banking. Today, things are more complicated and less regulated.

Separately, the fact that Paulson presided over Goldman Sachs during a period when the firm increasingly transformed itself from a classic investment bank relying heavily on profit from stable fees into something resembling a hedge fund, in which record profits were based on trading bets made with borrowed funds, doesn't make him the most credible proponent of debt or deficit reduction.

So for Paulson to nab the top Treasury spot is multiples worse. Still, he is strong and confident. That's the scary part. Bush gets a cheerleader to help cement his ideas of individualism, from more tax cuts for the rich to privatization of anything politically viable at the moment.

In a highly touted post-Enron-implosion speech at the National Press Club in mid-2002, Paulson urged reform in the financial system in three areas: accounting policy, standards of corporate governance and conflict of interest. "Conflicts are a fact of life in many, if not most, institutions, ranging from the political arena and government to media and industry," he said. "The key is how we manage them."

Or how we ignore them. The question isn't how it's a conflict of interest for Paulson to preside over our country's economy but how it's not. According to the first general statement laid out in the "Standards of Ethical Conduct for Employees of the Executive Branch": "Public service is a public trust requiring employees to place loyalty in the constitution, the laws and ethical principles above private gain." Even if Paulson ultimately sells all his stock and finds a way to offload his restricted stock, he will wield in the meantime enormous influence over the Treasury bond and foreign currency trading positions of Goldman, with every policy decision on debt issuance or the dollar that he makes. What's good for Goldman isn't necessarily good for Middle America. Therein lies the conflict of a man whose entire career has been predicated on successfully promoting corporate welfare over public interest.

Born-Again Rubinomics

WILLIAM GREIDER

July 31, 2006

WHEN ROBERT RUBIN speaks his mind, his thoughts on economic policy are the gold standard for the Democratic Party. The former Treasury Secretary, now executive co-chair of Citigroup, captured the party's allegiance in the 1990s as principal architect of Bill Clinton's governing strategy, the conservative approach known as "Rubinomics" (or less often "Clintonomics"). Balancing the budget and aggressively pushing trade liberalization went hard against liberal intentions and the party's working-class base. But when Clinton's second term ended in booming prosperity, full employment and rising wages, most Democrats told themselves, Listen to Bob Rubin and good things happen.

So it's a big deal when Robert Rubin changes the subject and begins to talk about income inequality as "a deeply troubling fact of American economic life" that threatens the trading system, even the stability of "capitalist, democratic society." More startling, Rubin now freely acknowledges what the American establishment for many years denied or dismissed as inconsequential—globalization's role in generating the thirty-year stagnation of U.S. wages, squeezing middle-class families and below, while directing income growth mainly to the upper brackets. A lot of Americans already knew this. Critics of "free trade" have been saying as much for years. But when Bob Rubin says it, his words can move politicians, if not financial markets.

Rubin has launched the Hamilton Project, a policy group of like-minded economists and financiers who are developing ameliorative measures to aid the threatened workforce and, he hopes, to create a broader political constituency that will defend the trading system against popular backlash. A strategy paper Rubin co-wrote defines the core problem: "Prosperity has neither trickled down nor rippled outward. Between 1973 and 2003, real GDP per capita in the United States increased 73 percent, while real median hourly compensation rose only 13 percent."

A storm is coming, Rubin fears. He wants a new national debate around these facts. In an interview, he explains the danger he foresees for global trade: "Where there's a great deal of insecurity, where median real wages are, roughly speaking, stagnant ... where a recent Pew poll showed 55 percent of the American people think their kids will be worse off than they are, I think there is a real danger of heightened difficulty around issues that are already difficult, like trade. ... Look at the difficulty around immigration."

Princeton economist Alan Blinder, a Hamilton participant and Federal Reserve vice chair in the Clinton years, describes the "difficulty" in more ominous terms: "I think the prospects for the liberal trade order are not great," he says. "There's a whole class of people who are smart, well educated and articulate, and politically involved who will not just sit there and take it" when their jobs are moved offshore. He thinks CNN commentator Lou Dobbs, who has built a populist following by attacking globalization and immigration, "is just the beginning—nothing compared to what's going to happen in the future."

What should we make of Rubin's heightened concern for the "losers" who, he now recognizes, include a vast portion of the populace? Many view the Hamilton Project as just more talk-talk. I regard it as an important event—a "course correction" in elite thinking that, given Rubin's influence, may reshape the familiar trade debate, at least among Democrats. Rubin's central objective, however, is to control the terms of debate: to address the economic disparities globalization has generated but without disturbing anything fundamental in the global system itself.

His program consists mostly of familiar ideas that might soften the pain for displaced workers. But I doubt the Hamilton proposals will do much, if anything, to reduce the global forces that are depressing incomes for half or more of the American workforce. Even Rubin is uncertain. When I ask if his agenda will have any effect at all on the global convergence of wages—the top falling gradually toward the rising bottom—he says: "Well, I think that's a question to which nobody knows the answer. I think the proposals and approach we are proposing are the way to get the best possible outcome for the United States in a complicated world. ... But whether that's going to stop the global convergence of wages, I don't know the answer to that. I would guess the answer is no."

Despite my skepticism about his policy ideas, I think Rubin is providing a significant opening for the opposition—a new chance for labor-liberal reformers to make themselves heard with a more fundamental critique of globalization. Up to now, the standard trade debate has been utterly simpleminded—"free trade good, no trade bad"—and anyone who opposes trade agreements or WTO rules is dismissed as a backward "protectionist." The enlightened position, as major media always explain, is to support the "win-win" promise of globalization.

Only Rubin is departing a bit from that script, effectively accepting the opposition's central complaint that "win-win" is a cruel distortion of what's happening. If so many Americans are actually losing ground, Rubin asks, shouldn't government do something about that? Yes, certainly, but that admission invites a different question: Are his establishment proposals actually likely to improve the American condition, or does the wage deterioration require more aggressive reforms?

Ideas do matter. My hope for more complex and honest debate may sound too wishful, but I was struck in our lengthy interview by Rubin's willingness to discuss contrary propositions, and by his disarmingly self-effacing and reflective manner (the transcript is posted at www.thenation.com). Several times, I was taken aback when his comments made tentative concessions to the opposition's argument. He even endorsed, though only in broad principle, some objectives for reforming global trade that his critics have long advocated.

I suggest that reformers test his sincerity. In the same spirit, they might try to initiate a conversation about what Rubin calls the "conceptual framework" for reform. He says he would welcome the discussion.

The Hamilton Project's early policy output, I concede, doesn't encourage a belief that reasoned dialogue with dissenters is what Rubin has in mind. Advisory board members see themselves as progressive-minded, but they do not stray from the mainstream's conventional wisdom—lots of Harvard, Princeton and Berkeley, no one from the ranks of "free trade" skeptics. The twenty-five-member board includes thirteen investment bankers, venture capitalists and hedge-fund managers from Wall Street and the West Coast—guys who, like Rubin, do the investment deals at home and abroad.

There's already a warm political glow. At the Hamilton launch in April, Senator Barack Obama hailed the group as "some of the most innovative, thoughtful policy-makers ... the sort of breath of fresh air that I think this town needs." Senator Hillary Clinton's recent economic speeches are, not surprisingly, a good fit with Rubin's thinking, since the pair's political closeness is well-known. Washington's Clintonistas-in-waiting embrace and amplify Rubin's ideas. He helps them arrange financing for new projects, like John Podesta's Center for American Progress. Democratic candidates seeking Wall Street campaign money hope for Rubin's blessing, a seal of approval that can open checkbooks.

The "soft" ideas in the Hamilton Project playbook are mostly old ideas—improve education and retraining, provide "wage insurance" payments to dislocated workers, increase public investment in industrial development and infrastructure. All are worthy things to do, but they seem like tinkering around the edges. Ron Blackwell, chief economist of the AFL-CIO, observes, "What they've got going are these little ideas that sound like they are forward-looking and respond to the problem of living standards, but they don't speak to power."

The right-of-center tilt of Rubin's group is reflected in some secondary proposals that are sure to rattle Democratic constituencies: Reform education by weakening teacher tenure, linking it to student performance; reform the system for tort litigation to eliminate what Rubin describes as "vast excess today" (his own firm suffered from tort litigation when it had to pay billions to settle investor lawsuits for Citigroup's role in the financial fraud at Enron and other corporate scandals).

The "hard" economic propositions in Rubin's agenda are essentially the same ones he pushed successfully in the Clinton administration: Balance the budget to boost national savings and thereby (Rubin assumes) reduce the country's horrendous trade deficits and enormous capital borrowing from abroad, where the creditors are led by China and Japan; advance more trade agreements if possible, but don't tamper with the trading rules or international institutions that currently govern the system.

In other words, born-again Rubinomics. Peter Orszag, the young economist who is Hamilton's director, doesn't quarrel with the label, saying, "This is almost like Clintonomics 2.0." Rubin says, "The basic principles of sound economic policy I don't think change." The script sounds a lot like the "putting people first" platform Bill Clinton ran on back in 1992, though in office he abandoned most public investment in favor of deficit reduction. Orszag calls it a "warm-hearted but cool-headed" agenda. But will it work? That's the question I would like to hear debated among Dems before they sign up for more Rubin magic. Clinton's second-term boom did temporarily reverse the downward wage trends, though economists still argue over the cause and effect. But balancing the budget again is unlikely to produce the same results, for lots of reasons. While increasing national savings is a very important goal, the world is now awash in surplus capital. And the United States is in a much deeper hole, borrowing $700 billion a year from abroad to sustain the domestic economy.

More to the point, Rubinomics in the 1990s did not reverse the long-term trend of rising trade deficits in goods and services or the deepening current-account deficits in capital borrowing from abroad, which could bring on a crisis if foreign lenders decide to pull the plug. In fact, both capital and trade deficits exploded at the very moment Clinton's budget was coming into balance. As the budget moved from deficit to surplus, the U.S. current-account deficit nearly tripled, from 1.6 to 4.2 percent of GDP (it is now around 7 percent).

Rubin is sticking to his convictions, though respected conservative economists no longer believe in the "twin deficit" relationship. Studies by the Federal Reserve and the I.M.F. found the relationship too weak to matter much. The I.M.F. estimates that balancing the budget now would reduce the current-account deficit only slightly, while the required fiscal austerity would produce a five-year loss of more than $300 billion in economic output.

Rubin defends his thesis by blaming the rising trade deficit on inflexible currency exchange with China and other Asian nations. Correct that and everything will be fine, he says. Further, he explains that the capital deficits in the Clinton years were actually a good thing because the high-tech investment boom was drawing in more foreign investors. He neglects to mention that the boom included the high-tech stock-market "bubble" that collapsed a year later on George W. Bush's watch, with $6 trillion in losses for investors.

In any case, Rubin sees nothing in the trading system itself that needs fixing. "Maybe I'm missing something," he says, "but I don't think there's anything in the design of the system we would have done differently."

Another debatable tenet in Rubin's thinking is the familiar mantra that more education will save us in the long run—that is, improving Americans' skills and knowledge will offset the low-wage competition. Rubin's tone is sympathetic to workers, but some acolytes pushing this logic sound like they are "blaming the victim." U.S. educational attainment levels, after all, rose robustly during the last generation with no effect on job losses or wage stagnation. "I actually think education is key," Rubin insists. "I'm granting I think your point is right—the cost gap," the cheaper labor abroad, which may pull down U.S. wages for another generation. But to some extent, he says, "the cost gap will, over time actually, probably get partially solved by their increasing wages (in China and India), hopefully with as little as possible our wages coming down. ... The more productive we are, the better we can compete with them."

There's one large and looming problem with that logic: The number of "losers" whose jobs are outsourced to foreign labor markets is getting much larger than the establishment had envisioned, and the job losses are creeping up the income ladder to undermine people in well-educated, highly paid occupations. In a startling *Foreign Affairs* essay, Alan Blinder warned that "tens of millions" of job losses are ahead from outsourcing, not for the already decimated blue-collar workers in manufacturing but for accountants, software designers and other high-status professions. These are people who presumably did the "right thing" by getting advanced educations. How, I ask Blinder, does educational improvement help them, since they are already well educated? "I wish I knew the answer to that," Blinder replies. "On balance, more education is better than less education, but it's not a panacea." He talks vaguely of changing the style of American schooling.

Blinder's ominous forecast for high-skilled jobs is another belated recognition by establishment authorities that they were wrong, since the process of moving engineering work to Asia, where they could hire cheaper engineers, started two decades ago. Free-trade advocates like Blinder are complacent about the loss of manufacturing jobs, comparing it to the technological changes that wiped out agricultural employment a century ago. "It's pretty inevitable," he says. They seem more worried now that white-collar jobs are being wiped out. But they think it would be a big mistake to interfere. "It's like global warming," he explains. "If there is severe global warming, you may have to change the preparations for bad weather." But Blinder's "global warming" metaphor actually expresses the viewpoint of the other side. Like global warming, the trading system is not an act of nature. It is a set of man-made rules—protecting capital and ignoring labor. Finance and industry persuaded government to adopt these terms. But they can be altered, just as government can order industry to reform itself to curb the dangers of global warming. That difference—deference to the status quo versus a vision for reform—is the nut of the argument between the two sides.

When I asked Rubin to consider labor's critique and its argument for global labor standards, I was pleasantly surprised that he did not brush off the question. Instead, we had an engaging back-and-forth.

Without global rights for workers to organize and some version of a minimum wage pegged to each country's economic conditions, the "race to the bottom" is sure to continue, I suggest. When workers start mobilizing for higher wages, multinationals counter by moving production to the next available cheap labor market. Middle-class wages fall at the top, but the bottom does not rise as rapidly as it should. "But it's a complicated question," Rubin responds. Improving the distribution of incomes in poorer countries "is in everybody's interest," he agrees. "On the other hand, I've had exposure to people who make that argument, and I think they make it as a way to prevent trade liberalization. ... The one hope some of these countries have to take people out of abject poverty is that their labor-cost advantage will result in a shift of production to their countries. ... Would you say the people of Sri Lanka have to stay in abject poverty to keep that from happening?"

Labor rights, I counter, do not prevent the very poorest countries from developing on the advantage of their cheap labor, but reform would require all developing countries to operate so that wage levels can rise proportionate to the economy's rising productivity and profit, however that is measured. "Something like that ought to be an objective of the global system," Rubin agrees. But he says he has never seen a convincing model of how this might work. He remains skeptical. He admits it is disturbing that economic advances in some countries "still have had very little effect on the poverty rate, and middle-income people haven't done all that well either. So the political economic elites had all this economic benefit, and they were in-different to poverty, to the poor."

The global system, I point out, protects capital by imposing dense rules on how a developing nation must treat investment capital, banking, patents and intellectual property rights. If a poor country doesn't accept the rules for capital, it doesn't get to play in the global system. Yet when organized labor seeks basic rights for working people around the world to organize unions and bargain collectively, they are denounced as "protectionist" and denied any recognition. Is that fair? "Well, I guess it's true," Rubin says hesitantly. "You can say, Why distinguish between those (rules for capital) and labor conditions?" Perhaps it is justified, he says, because labor and especially environmental rights are "a bit further removed" from trade. "I think it's the right objective," Rubin says. "But I still think it's a very complicated question whether you put labor conditions in an agreement. I would not hold back from going ahead on a trade agreement because another country refused to accept labor standards."

To my surprise, Rubin next recalls the work of John Kenneth Galbraith and his famous concept of "countervailing powers." Market-based capitalism, Rubin explains, is kept stable, broadly prosperous and equitable because its excesses are checked by labor unions, government and other institutions with countervailing power. "If you have a big company negotiate with its workers and the workers aren't organized, it isn't real negotiations," he says, adding, "If one side has no negotiating power, that isn't really a market-based system. It's an imposition of one on the other." This is a startling statement: The man from Citigroup has articulated the essential reasoning that makes the case for including labor rights in the global trading system.

That conversation has convinced me that outgunned reformers ought to make use of Rubin's musings. Knock on his door and try to initiate a dialogue. If the critics come forward and offer their ideas on a "conceptual framework" for reform, I ask, would the Hamilton Project be willing to discuss them? Rubin reiterates his doubts and reservations. "But the answer is yes," he says. "The answer is absolutely yes." Skeptical friends and kindred spirits will probably say to me, You have been conned. I would say back to them, What have you got to lose by talking to the man?

The Hamilton Project is a sophisticated example of what I call "deep lobbying"—developing well in advance of the 2008 presidential election an agenda that safely avoids critical challenges to the global system and defines the terms of debate in very limiting ways. Democratic hopefuls who sign on can gain the cover of Rubin's respectability. Long before voters even know who the candidates are, the party's debate might be over before it begins. Given this prospect for premature consensus, it might be a good idea to start the debate right now.

In some ways, Robert Rubin reminds me of the original Progressives of the early twentieth century, reformers drawn from the emerging middle class of managerial and professional people. They tried in various ways to reconcile the tumultuous conflicts between capital and labor but without getting blood on their hands. They were horrified by the greed and inhumanity of industrial capitalism but also wished to keep their distance from Socialists and the struggling labor movement.

Rubin is a "nice guy"—even adversaries say so—and I suspect he feels similar tensions. He sincerely would like to work things out—find some kind of reasonable balance—but without interrupting the creative destruction under way in the global system. The big difference separating him from the Progressives is that Rubin and his investment-banking colleagues are men of capital. At Goldman Sachs, Rubin was doing major deals in Mexico before he came to Washington to push NAFTA and balanced budgets. At Citigroup he travels to Beijing and Shanghai, promoting client interests. I don't question his sincerity. But as a reformer, he has competing demands on his loyalty.

My hunch is that Rubin won't succeed any more than the original Progressives in reconciling the competing forces (the New Deal eventually did). The tumult most likely will grow louder and possibly violent before reformers gain the political power to accomplish their serious goals. Meanwhile, if popular anger does erupt here and around the world, there won't be much space left for "nice guys" seeking a reasonable discussion.

The Loan Shark Lobby

GARRETT ORDOWER

April 9, 2007

THE MID-MARCH COLLAPSE of the nation's second-largest subprime mortgage lender caused a panic in the financial

markets and sparked calls for regulating the high-interest predatory loans given to those with bad credit. But much of the damage has already been done, with millions of homeowners facing
foreclosure at the hands of an industry allowed to run wild.

As its business has exploded—last year subprime loans grew
into a $600 billion industry, more than triple the 2002 volume
and accounting for one-fifth of all mortgages—the predatory
mortgage industry has done its best to make sure Congress
wouldn't rein it in, spreading its largesse to Democrats and Republicans: Nearly half of House Financial Services Committee
members, including chairman Barney Frank, have received
money from New Century Financial Corp., the subprime
lender that recently collapsed. Democratic presidential candidates Hillary Clinton and Chris Dodd, head of the Senate
Banking Committee, have been some of the largest beneficiaries
of the mortgage banking industry, whose dollars have provided
a strong incentive for Congress to sit tight and hope the subprime bubble wouldn't burst.

But it has. According to the Center for Responsible Lending, one out of five subprime mortgages inked in the past two
years will end in foreclosure. The losses are staggering: It is estimated that homeowners will collectively be out $164 billion,
with millions of families stripped of their most valuable asset.

This was not an unavoidable tragedy. Subprime mortgages
prey on the poor, the uninformed and minorities. They offer
high-credit-risk clients homeownership at interest rates well
above the going rate—above what many can pay. Common sense
suggests mortgages shouldn't be sold to those who can't afford
them, certainly not in such massive numbers. On March 13 Rep-

resentative Frank acknowledged as much, saying that "we plan to legislate to restrict those kinds of mortgages going forward."

Such legislation, however, has existed from nearly the beginning of the subprime-lending boom. While millions of homeowners were being mortgaged into ruin, the bills have sat dormant. Part of the reason for that—not surprisingly—might be the money. New Century, for example, which is nearing bankruptcy and under criminal investigation, has profited immensely from the subprime boom; insiders there made $103 million from selling stock. The company has given nearly $700,000 in campaign contributions to legislators since 2004.

And all any of New Century's Congressional patrons had to do was insure that legislation helping consumers didn't gain traction. While it would not necessarily have been a cure-all, it would have gone a long way toward providing safeguards for those targeted by subprime lenders. The most popular legislation, the Prohibit Predatory Lending Act, with nearly seventy co-sponsors, would have required that a borrower receive counseling, would have set limits on fees and would have prohibited balloon payments, "teaser" rates and lending without taking into account whether the loan could be repaid. It would also have prohibited mandatory arbitration, which most subprime lenders require and which leaves little room for borrowers to seek redress. Representatives Brad Miller and Mel Watt, both North Carolina Democrats, introduced this legislation in 2005 along with Barney Frank, who as ranking committee member failed to gain widespread support for the bill, a version of which is expected to be introduced this year.

Representative Stephanie Tubbs Jones, whose home state of

Ohio has among the highest foreclosure rates in the nation, introduced the Predatory Mortgage Lending Practices Reduction Act in 2005, which contained many of the same safeguards. It would also have provided grants for predatory lending education and given the Department of Housing and Urban Development, the Federal Reserve and the Federal Trade Commission the ability to define and take action against "unfair or deceptive" lending practices. Tubbs Jones is a member of the Congressional Black Caucus, which has strongly supported these measures, since blacks are nearly three times as likely to take out subprime loans. (Representative Dennis Kucinich, also a supporter of Tubbs Jones's bill, opened subprime hearings after the New Century collapse.)

Both bills died after being referred to financial services subcommittees, whose current and former heads have received money from New Century: Representative Paul Kanjorski has seen $42,095; Spencer Bachus, $31,743; and Richard Baker, $7,000.

New Century did take the lead in pushing for some legislation—the Responsible Lending Act, which would have hurt consumers by narrowing the definition of subprime mortgages and pre-empting stricter state laws. The bill's patron saint was Bob Ney, the Ohio Representative now serving a thirty-month federal prison sentence for corruption. New Century has spent more than $1.6 million lobbying in the past three years, and over time has contributed to the campaigns of nearly 60 percent of those who co-sponsored Ney's bill, including $49,300 to Ney himself.

With Democrats in control of Congress, the prospects for meaningful subprime legislation may have improved, but don't hold your breath. When the collapse became front-page news, prominent Democrats, including Hillary Clinton, jumped on the bandwagon calling for Congressional action, but it may be difficult for them to withstand the blandishments of the lobbyists. Mortgage bankers gave 40 percent of their $6.6 million in contributions to Democrats in 2006, before the party gained power, and eleven of the top twenty recipients were Democrats, including the top recipient, Clinton, who took in $108,100. Senator Dodd joined Barney Frank in a vague call for legislation but added that he is "a strong advocate of subprime lending." New Century has given Dodd $15,000 since 2003, and Frank ranked ninth on the list of mortgage banking contributions, with $54,550 in 2006.

Congress now has a decision to make: Should those thousands of dollars be in their pockets, or in those of the millions losing their homes?

Hedging Bets

JORDAN STANCIL

June 14, 2007

HEDGE FUNDS seem to have been designed as the ideal plutocratic villain for some novel of financial intrigue. These highly secretive investment groups control more than $1 trillion in assets but are so heavily leveraged that their total positions are thought to equal more than $3 trillion. The essence of their business is speculation, which they engage in on the basis of proprietary mathematical models that are guarded more closely than state secrets. The managers rake in obscene sums of money—the highest-paid made $1.7 billion in 2006. And yet they are virtually unregulated by any government.

The Bush administration sees nothing wrong with this situation. For two years it has stalled efforts by Germany to push the G-8 to monitor hedge funds. The funds, and their private-equity cousins, are controversial in Germany because they've been "restructuring" many old-line German companies. Germany's vice chancellor has referred to the funds as "locusts," and the Schröder government started investigating ways to make the industry more transparent. Current Chancellor Angela Merkel has continued that effort, and the German finance ministry drew up plans for a code of conduct for G-8 leaders to approve at the June G-8 summit. But even a voluntary code of conduct was too much for the Bush administration. In the end, the G-8 leaders did little more than agree to remain "vigilant" regarding the systemic risks posed by hedge funds.

The problem is that regulators don't even collect information about the industry they're supposed to be vigilant about. Since hedge funds are open only to limited numbers of big investors, they escape all the usual reporting requirements. Even the timid attempt by the Securities and Exchange Commission to impose a registration requirement was struck down by a federal court last summer.

The upshot is that this increasingly significant portion of the capital market—investment volumes have tripled in the past five years—is totally opaque, which recently led former SEC chair William Donaldson to call the hedge fund industry "a ticking time bomb that is going to blow up at some point." Since major banks and pension funds increasingly invest in hedge funds, the direct effects of this time bomb would extend well beyond the wealthy individuals who are typically thought to be the funds' main customers.

The hedge funds tell us not to worry. Instead, we should thank them for providing needed liquidity to the financial system. Of course, they do this by being so heavily leveraged, but they claim this is safe because their secret strategies are so flexible and ingenious. Regulation would hamper their ability to engage in these brilliant financial acrobatics, they say.

In fact, it seems that no discussion of hedge funds is ever complete without mentioning how complicated and sophisticated their strategies are, as if complicated things somehow deserve to be free of regulation. It is true that some hedge funds consult with Nobel Prize–winning economists and financial theorists. But the essence of their strategy would have been immediately recognizable to the provincial nail manufacturer in Stendhal's *The Red and the Black,* Monsieur de Rênal, whose financial acumen consists of "getting himself paid exactly what he's owed, while paying what he owes as late as possible." Rarely has the concept of leverage been more clearly explained. Nobel prizes aside, that's basically what many of the hedge funds are doing.

It's a strategy that works great right up to the point when it doesn't, which is what happened to Long-Term Capital Management (LTCM) in September 1998, when the Russian government defaulted and the hedge fund suddenly had to pay what it owed before it got paid. That led to an almost $4 billion bailout orchestrated by the Federal Reserve amid concerns by U.S. financial officials that world credit markets would, as New York Fed president William McDonough quaintly put it at the time, "possibly cease to function for a period of one or more days and maybe longer."

The point here is not to engage in populist mockery of people who are in fact extraordinarily brilliant but simply to question the idea that they are morally and intellectually infallible. That's essentially what you need to believe if you want to categorically oppose hedge fund regulation, as the Bush administration does.

Former Treasury Secretary Robert Rubin, hardly known for his hostility to capital flows, hints at this point in his memoirs, where he writes that his first reaction to the news of LTCM's collapse was to say, "I don't understand how someone like [head of LTCM] John Meriwether ... could get into this kind of trouble." After all, Rubin notes, Meriwether was one of the country's leading financial minds, and he had two Nobel laureates working with him. But they were "betting the ranch on the basis of mathematical models."

As with any bet, the only way to be sure you'll win is to see into the future. Since hedge fund managers, like other human beings, lack this ability, and since it is widely accepted that their business poses a significant risk to the world economy, it is unclear how there can be a good argument against some form of regulation. The issue is not whether hedge funds are inherently good or bad. The issue is that the hedge funds' best argument boils down to nothing more than two words: Trust us.

Smashing Capitalism

BARBARA EHRENREICH

August 20, 2007

SOMEWHERE IN THE HAMPTONS a high-roller is cursing his cleaning lady and shaking his fists at the lawn guys. The American poor, who are usually tactful enough to remain invisible to the multi-millionaire class, suddenly leaped onto the scene and started smashing the global financial system. Incredibly enough, this may be the first case in history in which the downtrodden manage to bring down an unfair economic system without going to the trouble of a revolution.

First they stopped paying their mortgages, a move in which they were joined by many financially stretched middle class folks, though the poor definitely led the way. All right, these were trick mortgages, many of them designed to be unaffordable within two years of signing the contract. There were "NINJA" loans, for example, awarded to people with "no income, no job or assets." Conservative columnist Niall Fergusen laments the low levels of "economic literacy" that allowed people to be exploited by subprime loans. Why didn't these low-income folks get lawyers to go over the fine print? And don't they have personal financial advisers anyway?

Then, in a diabolically clever move, the poor—a category which now roughly coincides with the working class—stopped shopping. Both Wal-Mart and Home Depot announced disappointing second quarter performances, plunging the market into another Arctic-style meltdown. H. Lee Scott, CEO of the low-wage Wal-Mart empire, admitted with admirable sensitivity that "it's no secret that many customers are running out of money at the end of the month."

I wish I could report that the current attack on capitalism represents a deliberate strategy on the part of the poor, that there have been secret meetings in break rooms and parking lots around the country, where cell leaders issued instructions like, "You, Vinny—don't make any mortgage payment this month. And Caroline, forget that back-to-school shopping, OK?" But all the evidence suggests that the current crisis is something the high-rollers brought down on themselves.

When, for example, the largest private employer in America, which is Wal-Mart, starts experiencing a shortage of customers, it needs to take a long, hard look in the mirror. About a century ago, Henry Ford realized that his company would only prosper if his own workers earned enough to buy Fords. Wal-Mart, on the other hand, never seemed to figure out that its cruelly low wages would eventually curtail its own growth, even at the company's famously discounted prices.

The sad truth is that people earning Wal-Mart-level wages tend to favor the fashions available at the Salvation Army. Nor do they have much use for Wal-Mart's other departments, such as Electronics, Lawn and Garden, and Pharmacy.

It gets worse though. While with one hand the high-rollers, H. Lee Scott among them, squeezed the American worker's wages, the other hand was reaching out with the tempting offer of credit. In fact, easy credit became the American substitute for decent wages. Once you worked for your money, but now you were supposed to pay for it. Once you could count on earning enough to save for a home. Now you'll never earn that much, but, as the lenders were saying—heh, heh—do we have a mortgage for you!

Payday loans, rent-to-buy furniture and exorbitant credit card interest rates for the poor were just the beginning. In its May 21 cover story on "The Poverty Business," *BusinessWeek* documented the stampede, in just the last few years, to lend money to the people who could least afford to pay the interest: Buy your dream home! Refinance your house! Take on a car loan even if your credit rating sucks! Financiamos a Todos! Somehow, no one bothered to figure out where the poor were going to get the money to pay for all the money they were being offered.

Personally, I prefer my revolutions to be a little more proactive. There should be marches and rallies, banners and sit-ins, possibly a nice color theme like red or orange. Certainly, there should be a vision of what you intend to replace the bad old system with—European-style social democracy, Latin American–style socialism, or how about just American capitalism with some regulation thrown in?

Global capitalism will survive the current credit crisis; already, the government has rushed in to soothe the feverish markets. But in the long term, a system that depends on extracting every last cent from the poor cannot hope for a healthy prognosis. Who would have thought that foreclosures in Stockton and Cleveland would roil the markets of London and Shanghai? The poor have risen up and spoken; only it sounds less like a shout of protest than a low, strangled, cry of pain.

The Housing Bubble Pops

DEAN BAKER

October 1, 2007

THE HOUSING MARKET is in its worst downturn since the Great Depression—and it's taking the rest of the economy down with it. Most forecasters insist there won't be a recession, although the August job losses forced even optimists to acknowledge that the meltdown is causing serious economic problems. (When it comes to recessions, the professionals seem to be the last to find out: On the eve of the last downturn, in the fall of 2000, all the Blue Chip 50 forecasters predicted solid growth for the following year.)

The downturn should not have been a surprise. House prices rose at an unprecedented rate over the past dozen years. For a hundred years, from 1895 to 1995, house prices nationwide increased at the same pace as the overall inflation rate. Since 1995 inflation-adjusted house prices have risen by more than 70 percent. It should have been clear to economists that this run-up was being driven by a speculative bubble. There was no change in the fundamentals of supply or demand that could have explained the rise.

Like Japan's in the 1980s, the U.S. housing bubble coincided with its stock bubble. While the two bubbles burst simultaneously in Japan, in the United States the stock collapse actually fueled the growth of the housing bubble. Investors, after losing much of their wealth in the stock crash, viewed housing as safe.

The housing bubble in turn fueled the recovery of the U.S. economy from the stock crash recession of 2001.

Soaring home prices pushed construction and home sales to record levels. Even more important, the run-up in home prices created more than $8 trillion in housing bubble wealth. This wealth fueled a consumption boom, as homeowners withdrew equity from their homes almost as it was created. The savings rate plummeted to near zero in 2005 and 2006. People used their homes as ATMs, borrowing to take trips, buy cars or just to meet expenses.

This pattern of growth could not be sustained. Record house prices were supported by a tidal wave of speculation, as millions of people suddenly became interested in investment properties. As prices soared, financing arrangements became ever more questionable. Down payments went out of style. Adjustable-rate mortgages and interest-only loans, even negative amortization loans (in which mortgage debt grows month by month), became common.

The worst of the speculative financing was in the subprime market, where moderate-income home buyers were persuaded to take out adjustable-rate mortgages, which generally feature very low "teaser rates," typically reset after three years, often to levels that are five or six percentage points higher. Millions of families who could afford the teaser rates cannot possibly afford the higher rates. This is leading to a huge wave of defaults and foreclosures—which is just beginning, as homeowners who took out mortgages in 2004 are now hitting their three-year mark.

The subprime scandal would not have happened if the mortgage market had not been transformed over the past quarter-century. Banks used to hold the mortgages they issued, which gave them a strong incentive to be careful (often too careful) not to issue a mortgage the borrower could not pay. In the current market, the mortgage issuer typically sells it off in the secondary market, where it becomes the basis for mortgage-backed securities that are then sold throughout the world. This is why the subprime crisis is leading to failures of banks and funds in France, Germany, Australia and elsewhere.

Mortgage credit has frozen up for all but the safest loans. This showed up starkly in a 12.2 percent drop in the July pending sales index, which measures the number of sales contracts signed each month. While this is an extraordinary decline, the reality is almost certainly much worse than the data show, since many of these contracts will fall through because buyers can't get mortgages.

The price data also scream trouble. Formerly supercharged markets like Las Vegas, Miami and San Diego are experiencing double-digit price declines, while the slightly less bubbly markets of New York, Boston and Washington are seeing declines in the single digits. With record numbers of unsold and vacant homes, it is difficult to see how prices will stop falling anytime soon.

The basic story is a downward spiral as the housing sector interacts with the rest of the economy: lower house prices, more foreclosures, fewer jobs in housing and less consumption, a weaker economy and less demand for housing. Throw into the mix declining state and local tax revenues due to the loss of construction fees and property taxes, and you have a further source of bad economic news.

There will be no quick fixes. As former Federal Reserve chairman Alan Greenspan discovered in 2002, it is not easy to boost the economy out of a recession caused by a burst financial bubble. Since housing wealth is far more evenly distributed among households than stock, it will be even harder to recover from the housing crash than the stock crash. But we can implement policies to get the economy on the right track.

First, it is important to protect the subprime home buyers who were tricked into taking out mortgages they could not afford. President Bush has proposed measures that would encourage lenders to renegotiate mortgage terms to allow people to stay in their homes and would provide additional support from the Federal Housing Authority. These are steps in the right direction, but they will not help the vast majority of the subprime homeowners at risk of losing their homes. The simplest and quickest way to help them is to adopt the "own to rent" policy, by which subprime homeowners facing foreclosure are allowed to remain in their homes indefinitely as renters paying the fair market rent. This assures them a roof over their head, with no new bureaucracy and no tax dollars.

Tax cuts directed at low- and moderate-income families are a good way to jump-start the economy, as would be government investment aimed at neglected infrastructure needs, such as rebuilding New Orleans and preventing the collapse of more bridges. Pushing down the value of the dollar should also be a top priority. There is no way to correct our trade imbalance with an overvalued dollar providing a massive subsidy for imports and imposing a tariff on U.S. exports. A lower dollar will make U.S. manufactured goods far more competitive in the world economy, and will thus create a large number of relatively high-paying jobs. One benefit of the housing meltdown is that it should be much easier to get our trading partners to go along with a lower dollar now that we can show them how much money they lost by investing in U.S. financial assets that have gone bad.

Finally, we must get people on the Federal Reserve Board who take financial bubbles seriously. Greenspan recently asserted that "the human race has never found a way to confront bubbles." But it is possible for the Fed to do so, most obviously by repeatedly and publicly warning against stock, housing or other market bubbles as they arise. This would educate even the stupidest hedge fund managers, or at the very least make them fear personal liability for mismanaging billions of dollars. Clearly, Greenspan was not up to the job. We will need more qualified people running the Fed in the future.

The Coming Foreclosure Tsunami

CHRISTOPHER HAYES

November 13, 2007

UNLIKE MOST HEARINGS on the Hill, last week's meeting of the Joint Economic Committee actually got more interesting the longer it went on. While the first half-hour featured Federal Reserve chairman Ben Bernanke offering his modest, softly downbeat but not panicked predictions about how the unfolding subprime mess would affect the broader economy, the last hour provided an opportunity to hear committee members give their own often eccentric diagnoses and predictions.

Kansas Republican Senator Sam Brownback opined that tax cuts, shockingly, were probably the best way to deal with the current crisis. New Hampshire Republican Senator John Sununu spent much of his allotted time pointing out that he'd done a better job of predicting future trends of housing inventories in March than the chairman. "I was right," he told Bernanke with a smirk, "and you were wrong." ("Well, Senator, you were right and I was wrong," Bernanke intoned back into the mic with a deadpan expression that basically said, "Satisfied, dick?") And Senator Robert Bennett, a Republican from Utah, offered a refreshingly honest articulation of the conservative view of the unfolding debacle: "Markets make better decisions than governments do, and the market will punish, the market will reward and the market will ultimately stabilize. For the market is a just and wrathful God!" (OK, I made up that last sentence.)

But amid the grandstanding, Maryland Congressman Elijah Cummings injected some welcome perspective. "Many members of Congress now, Chairman, are holding forums in their districts, as I will be doing very shortly, to help people who are coming to our doors literally with tears in their eyes and trying to figure out how they're going to manage a foreclosure that's right around the corner. ... It seems like you have painted a very rosy picture, but if you came and walked through my district, I think people would be very ... surprised that you seem so calm."

Bernanke was defensive: "Congressman, first, I don't know how you got the impression that I was unconcerned about foreclosures."

"I didn't say you were unconcerned," Cummings shot back. "I just said you seem to be pretty calm about it." Foreclosures in Maryland were up more than 400 percent in the third quarter, compared with the first. Minority homeowners, like those in Cummings's inner-city Baltimore district, are getting hit particularly hard. "I know that so often what happens is that when we're making decisions in the suites, we forget about the people who actually have to go through this," Cummings said. But "we're becoming a bit alarmed."

In past financial implosions, of S&Ls in the eighties or Long Term Capital Management in the nineties, it was easy to name the villains but far trickier to find the victims. Not so here. They're everywhere, not just in inner-city Baltimore. There are subdivisions in the exurbs that are beginning to resemble ghost towns.

So what is to be done? The long-term challenge is to regulate an industry that, left to its own devices, seems to have eaten its young. Last week the Mortgage Reform and Anti Predatory Lending Act of 2007 passed out of Barney Frank's House Financial Services Committee with the support of nine Republicans. It's far from perfect, but it represents a small step in the right direction. The mortgage industry is fighting it tooth and nail.

The more immediate issue, though, is what to do about the millions of people who live in homes that are in danger of going under in the coming tidal wave of foreclosure. North Carolina Democratic Representative Brad Miller has proposed one common-sense solution. He has sponsored a bill that would allow bankruptcy judges to amend the terms of home mortgages. As the law currently stands, the terms of a mortgage on a yacht or a vacation home can be adjusted during bankruptcy, but the primary residence is off-limits. "This makes no sense," said Eric Stein of the Center for Responsible Lending in testimony before the House Judiciary Committee Subcommittee on Commercial and Administrative Law. "The current bankruptcy law deprives mostly low-wealth and middle-class families of protections available to all other debtors and grants lenders on home mortgages a special protection not available to any other type of lender."

Correcting this quirk of bankruptcy law seems like the kind of fairly straightforward modification you might want your Democratic Congress to make in the midst of a massively disruptive financial crisis. But if you've been following the Democratic Congress, you've probably already predicted that some in the caucus are circling the wagons to defend the mortgage industry. A few weeks ago, sixteen "Blue Dog" Democrats from conservative districts sent a letter to House Judiciary Committee chairman John Conyers, asking him to delay considering Miller's bill because it might undermine the provisions of the bankruptcy bill that President Bush signed into law in 2005. That bill, which made it harder for the broke and desperate to declare bankruptcy, stands as one of the most egregious examples of legislative malpractice of the last five years.

"Guns are one thing," wrote blogger Matt Stoller on OpenLeft in response to the letter, "but there is no strong grassroots movement in conservative districts on behalf of big banks.

These people are simply whores for credit card companies and banking interests building profitable de facto debtors prisons."

If the Blue Dogs think that standing with lenders against borrowers makes for good politics or good policy, perhaps they should go take a walk through Representative Cummings's district.

Or, you know, their own.

The Subprime Swindle

KAI WRIGHT

July 15, 2008

GEORGE MITCHELL'S WIFE, Lillian, took her last breath in the house she loved, on New Year's Day 2006. "Right there in that spot," says George, 77, nodding to the far end of his worn, floral-print couch. "I think the last words she spoke was my name."

"Yup," confirms his youngest daughter, Chandra Chavis. "I was trying to perform mouth-to-mouth resuscitation at the time." She points out the living room window to the small, sloping front yard and drive. "There was no address on the house, so I had to stop doing that to get the ambulance to come in."

_____

Research support was provided by the Investigative Fund of The Nation Institute.

But Lillian's heart had seized, and Chandra knows there's not much she could have done anyway. She figures if even the trauma team at Atlanta's century-old public hospital couldn't revive her mom, she must have been long gone. "Nobody can bring you back if the Lord calls you," concludes an older daughter, Gwen Russell.

It was Lillian's tenacity that led the Mitchell family to Atlanta's Westwood neighborhood, in 1968. "She was determined," Chandra explains, "not to have her children in an apartment—I know the story; I've heard it a million times—so she found somebody, a real estate agent, and they came out and they looked in this neighborhood. I don't know what brought them to this part of town, 'cause at the time they were living in Dixon Hills"—then an up-and-coming black neighborhood—"but she decided she wanted a house, and this is where she found it."

"All I did was sign the paper," says George with a shrug.

That made the Mitchells one of the first African-American families to move into Westwood. Atlanta has long been known as the "black Mecca," a place where African-Americans have been able to claw up the socioeconomic ladder and plunge into America's consumer culture. Nowhere is that striving more visible than in the massive subdivisions of large, new homes that Atlanta's black bourgeoisie have erected, reaching far into the suburbs. But the process began generations ago in a cluster of inside-the-beltway neighborhoods wedged into the city's southwestern corner, including Westwood. Today that area is reeling, having been one of the nation's communities hardest hit by the one-two punch of subprime lending and home foreclosures. The Mitchells have not been spared. Like hundreds of thousands of Americans, they are scrambling to keep the house Lillian found for them.

Nearly 18,000 homes faced foreclosure in the Atlanta area during the first quarter of 2008, an almost 40 percent jump from the first quarter of 2007. In Fulton County, which encompasses most of the city's core and is heavily African-American, one in 122 homes was in foreclosure in the first week of April. A digest of Atlanta's March 2008 "foreclosure starts" was as thick as the phone book, and the Mitchells's 30310 ZIP code topped the list.

The area boasts an old stock of quaint, mid-century houses painted in bright yellows and crisp blues, accented with quirky touches that now feel more haunting than homey. On block after block, as many homes sit vacant or bank-owned as not. Boarded-up windows lurk behind white-columned front porches, and the yards are slowly going to weeds and trash. On one block, eleven boarded-up houses line the street, making the area look like it's been hit by a natural disaster.

But the disaster is depressingly man-made. And this neighborhood reveals a deeply troubling dimension of it, one that will echo long past the recovery everyone hopes will soon come: for black America, the "mortgage meltdown" looks less like a market hiccup than a massive strip mining of hard-won wealth, a devastating loss that will betray the promise of class mobility for tens of thousands of black families.

As the mortgage crisis unfolded, observers of all political stripes repeated a boilerplate line: the "affordability products" that have flooded the lending market in recent years—from subprime to interest-only loans—have done more good than bad by fueling a surge in black and Latino homeownership. But while minority homeownership may have grown in the short term, the long-term outlook promises quite the opposite, as southwest Atlanta painfully illustrates.

First-time homebuyers have originated less than a tenth of all subprime loans since 1998, according to a 2007 Center for Responsible Lending analysis. As recently as 2006, just over half of all subprime loans were refinances of existing home loans. The expected foreclosure toll from these loans will outpace the ownership gains by nearly a million families, the center estimates.

That's particularly true in established black neighborhoods like Westwood, where banks and brokers targeted vulnerable longtime homeowners and lured them into needless and rapidly recurring mortgages they clearly couldn't afford and from which they never stood to gain. More than half of all refinance loans made to African-Americans in 2006 were subprime, according to an analysis by the advocacy group ACORN. That's nearly twice the rate among white borrowers. Among low-income black borrowers, 62 percent of refinance loans were subprime, more than twice the rate among low-income whites.

"It actually started in communities like Atlanta," says Nikitra Bailey, a Center for Responsible Lending researcher who has studied the Southeastern U.S. housing crisis. "A lot of our older African-Americans were house rich but cash poor. So lenders came up with these scams to siphon the wealth away."

It's a loss black America can scarcely afford, because black wealth has long been enormously dependent on home equity. In 1967, the year before the Mitchells bought their house, homes accounted for 67 percent of black wealth, compared with 40 percent of white wealth. The disparity has only grown, pushed by the turn-of-the-millennium stock market boom. Without counting home equity, black net worth in 2004 was just 1 percent of that for whites, according to research by New York University economics professor Edward Wolff.

This wealth gap makes the disaster unfolding in neighborhoods like Westwood all the more catastrophic. As the Mitchells sit in George's cluttered living room, wending their way through their past, they bump against memories of family after family who are in quandaries just like theirs—friends and neighbors struggling to hold onto homes they bought decades ago. "It's a crying shame," Gwen rails. "People been living around here forever! I think it's wrong," she complains, throwing up her hands in resignation. "But what can I say?"

The Mitchells mark time by the particulars of their history. They know, for instance, that George retired from thirty years of delivering mail to his neighbors in 1985, because that's when Chandra came back from Germany with her newborn son. And they know they moved into this house forty years ago, because that's when Gwen had her child. "Yup, Kipper would have been 40 this year," Gwen says, nodding for emphasis as she mentally links the house's life span with that of her son, who died in 2000 in a car accident. "Forty years in this house right here."

George doesn't remember his white neighbors giving the family any trouble when they moved in, but they didn't roll out the welcome mat either. He still laughs at one neighbor's reaction when he and the realtor stopped in front of the guy's house. "The dude, he broke out the house like somebody hit him with a hot poker! He was talking about how he built this house and he did it for his family and he didn't want nobody in it. And all I did was look at the house. But I tell you, the next time I went through there it was some black ones in it—'cause he was gone." Before long, so were all of the Mitchells's white neighbors.

George and Lillian took over a previous owner's $16,000 mortgage for their 1,600-square-foot home. With two incomes, they easily managed the monthly note. Then and now, the house offered the family security and stability.

"I was 6," Chandra proudly declares of the age at which she began living here. "My son grew up in this house, too," she adds. They've all lived here at some point over those decades. George's four kids and six grandchildren have spread out around the South—a son in Fayetteville, Georgia; a middle daughter in Birmingham, Alabama—but this has always been what Gwen calls the "home house."

Gwen stays here three days a week, when she's off from her job as a live-in nurse. Chandra and her husband own a home a few neighborhoods over. But her 20-year-old son, Marcus, lives here with his aunt and grandpa. Chandra frets that "the knucklehead" won't get his life together and go to college or take real steps toward his dream of opening an auto-body shop. But she knows he's got a roof over his head and, in time, will sort it out. "You can always come home to Momma and Daddy when times get tough," Gwen says affectionately.

George and Lillian were lucky to get the house, because African-Americans were largely locked out of the massive mid-twentieth-century, public-private effort to expand access to credit and homeownership.

America hasn't always been a majority "ownership society," as George W. Bush likes to call it. The nation's first homeownership boom came after World War II, when the government used the Federal Housing Administration's (FHA) mortgage insurance to lower the cost of buying. Banks extended credit lines to middle-class borrowers in ways that encouraged long-term ownership—thirty-year mortgages covering 80 percent to 90 percent of the buyer's costs with interest rates of about 6 percent. By 1960, the American homeownership rate had shot up from less than half before the war to nearly 65 percent, where it remained until the modern housing market took off.

Black communities were excluded from this rising tide. The FHA's underwriting manual guaranteed insurance for segregated white neighborhoods only, until a series of court cases between 1948 and 1953 struck down the rule. Even then, the policy changed in word alone: 98 percent of the 10 million homes federal money had backed by 1965 went to whites, and banks' redlining of black neighborhoods went on for years thereafter. As a result, the black-white disparity in homeownership hasn't dropped below 20 percentage points since 1940; it was at 25 percentage points in 2007.

The 1977 Community Reinvestment Act (CRA) aimed to end the lending bias in the housing market. The complex law boils down to a simple principle: anywhere a federally insured bank or thrift takes deposits, it must give out credit. The law also set up regular audits of the institutions' lending practices to police compliance.

Today, when industry backers aren't touting the good that subprime mortgages have done, they're arguing that the CRA set the stage for the market's current collapse by encouraging lending to "risky" borrowers. But subprime lending didn't start with the demand that banks serve the community; it grew out of the removal of usury laws that governed how much banks could charge for their lending services. Having fought the CRA tooth and nail in the late seventies, by 1980 the banks were pushing for regulatory changes that would allow them to profit from the requirement. Says the Center for Responsible Lending's Nikitra Bailey, "It's like once we got in the game, the rules changed."

So did the loan products offered by banks. Subprime loans emerged in the 1980s and slowly multiplied, driven in part by the new deregulation and in part by an explosion of brokers and other unregulated lending entities—many of them subsidiaries of traditional, otherwise regulated banks. These products were supposed to be tools to firm up poor credit and bridge low-income borrowers to prime loans. For years, they remained a tiny, if troubling, share of overall lending, accounting for just 5 percent of all mortgage originations in 1994. The problems started when the housing market took off at the turn of the millennium, driven by historically low interest rates, skyrocketing sales prices and the resulting global rush to invest in the U.S. mortgage market. Suddenly, subprime loans turned into trapdoors—increasingly exotic products through which lenders, desperate to feed the mortgage investment beast, lured people into needless debt. By 2004 subprime loans were 20 percent of home loans—and half of all home-purchase and refinance borrowers had one in 2006.

The Mitchells, for their part, started out OK. Guarded by Lillian's caution, they leveraged their new house to get opportunities otherwise beyond their grasp. The Mitchells paid for the final two years of Chandra's bachelor's degree at Clark—one of Atlanta's famed historically black colleges—with their first refinance, in 1981; her Clark sticker is still in the upstairs window. "I thought she needed an education," George explains. "She wanted one. So I saw to it she had it."

And for the next two decades, the Mitchells's lending history remained a relatively quiet, measured affair—a few more mortgages on the home, all for less than $40,000. Then, in 2003, the deed record for their house suddenly erupts into a line of increasingly large refinance loans, falling one after another in quick succession.

It starts with a $68,000 loan in May 2003—that's the one they made for the new siding. By that December, they'd already refinanced for $100,000. In December 2006, there's another loan, with now-defunct NovaStar Mortgage, for just over $116,000. Two months later there's a package of two more loans, totaling about $125,000 and owed to California-based IndyMac Bank. The IndyMac loan package is a classic subprime product—interest-only payments for five years, at a fixed rate of just over 6 percent, then adjusting upward to about 9 percent plus the principal.

"That is just not an appropriate loan product for someone who's 76 years old and who's on a fixed income," says Atlanta Legal Aid Society attorney Sarah Bolling, who's representing the Mitchells in their effort to keep their house. "The only calculation that would make this make sense is to say, 'Well, we'll give him a low rate and in five years he won't be alive.' But that's pretty cynical." Not that it mattered: George managed to pay the loan for only two months before falling behind. Within a year, he was in default.

It's a familiar story in 30310. Not far away from the Mitchells, the Hoods are desperately trying to hold onto a house they bought in 1975. A retired couple living largely on Social Security, they owe $176,000 on a house that may be worth just over $100,000. A broker from Maryland had cold-called them and talked them into a series of refinances. Another senior citizen, Jennie McCaslin, bought her house in 1970. In 2005 a broker sold her a $67,000 rehab loan, then flipped her through a series of refinances that left her owing $102,000, with an adjustable interest rate that can reset as high as 17 percent. One of the loans was co-signed by a 21-year-old niece, another by a son who was in jail at the time. McCaslin is functionally illiterate.

The Mitchells, Hoods and McCaslins are the "risky" and "irresponsible" borrowers cited in press coverage and policy debates about the foreclosure crisis. For months, the Bush administration's mantra has been that whatever remedy Washington comes up with, it mustn't let borrowers off the hook for making bad choices. "I believe most Americans want to protect homeowners who played by the rules. They don't want to reward risky financial behavior," Assistant Secretary for Housing Brian Montgomery told the House Financial Services Committee in April.

The administration and industry lobbyists have buttressed this rhetoric with claims that large numbers of those facing foreclosure are merely "speculators." "The strength of our economy relies on the willingness of people to take risks," Mortgage Bankers Association chair-elect David Kittle told an April 16

House Financial Services subcommittee hearing, "but risk means one does not always win."

It's a stunning statement when considering just how much risky speculating lenders themselves have engaged in during the past decade. The vast majority of homes facing foreclosure are owner-occupied. Aggregate data on those homeowners is spotty at best, but consumer advocates insist they look a lot like George Mitchell—people shoved into large, needless loans so that lenders could profit from the fast-growing securities market.

Much has been written about the role of the byzantine derivatives trade in the housing market's balloon and bust. Investment banks have been bundling pools of mortgages and selling them as securities since the mid-1980s. But when the housing market exploded in the early 2000s, those pools became immensely profitable. Banks started gobbling up mortgages from lenders, who in turn frantically cranked up their lending volume to cash in on the new demand. Brokers raked in money as banks offered incentives for them to close larger and larger loans. Investors worldwide poured cash into the profitable mortgage pools that formed.

If the securities market was the bonfire, borrowers were the kindling. Had lenders not sought out and made loans to people without regard to their ability to pay, the fire would have burned itself out long ago. Instead, when the supply of reliable borrowers was depleted, the subprime lending products that Reagan-era deregulation helped usher in kept the flames lapping. Undocumented loan applications, interest-only payment plans and teaser interest rates are all just the tools lenders used to forage for new borrowers. "The purpose of those products was to convince these people that they could get in," says Legal Aid attorney Bill Brennan.

George Mitchell, who, his daughters believe, suffered at least two strokes between 2003 and shortly after his wife's 2006 death, barely remembers taking out the February 2007 IndyMac loan that he's now suffocating under. Asked to recount how and why he took out any of the refinances he's made since his original 2003 siding loan, George furrows his brow and stares out from his thick gray beard in silence.

"Papa don't remember," a frustrated Gwen explains. She suspects he got calls from banks and brokers offering him new loans. "I'm almost sure," she says, noting that the house phone rings incessantly with marketers asking for her father by first name, as if they're old friends. "He orders things off TV. He doesn't realize he orders it. The pimple stuff?" She shoots a disgusted look at her dad when recalling that absurd package's arrival. "He says he didn't order it, but it came."

Despite their close role in George's life, none of the Mitchell children knew about the recent loans until February 2007. That's when George called Chandra and asked her to come by the house to witness him signing for one of the two loans in the IndyMac package. "I came over here with the intention of not signing the papers," Chandra says, recounting the frenzied afternoon. But the IndyMac loan officer, who Chandra says was at the house for just fifteen minutes, convinced her otherwise. "She told me you could not cancel the loan."

George explained to Chandra that he'd had trouble keeping up with that loan and with his credit cards since Lillian's death, due to the loss of her $500 a month in Social Security. "I read through what I could understand," Chandra says of the few minutes she was given to browse the IndyMac package. "It was really thick, and I don't know legalese, especially when it comes to loans. The only question that I had for her was, Could he cancel it, honestly?" Having been persuaded he could not, Chandra signed as a witness and hoped for the best.

George's signature is scrawled on the bottom of each of the loan's densely packed pages, as well as those of his initial loan application. But when Legal Aid's Sarah Bolling reads the application details back to him, he nearly leaps out of his recliner with shock. It lists his income as $4,725 a month. He collects $300 a month from Social Security and $1,400 a month from his Postal Service pension. Nothing in the loan file documents the inflated income claim—a practice known as "no doc" and "low doc" lending that has displaced the once-standard step of proving income to an underwriter.

The application also says George had nearly $8,000 in the bank at the time. "No way!" he gasps. "Ain't never been that kind of money in there." Again, nothing in the file documents the claim, and nothing about it raised flags for IndyMac's underwriters. Nor did it matter to the underwriters that the application appraised the house at more than $135,000. "The tax assessor thinks it's worth $73,000, and that's on the public record," says Bolling. "I mean, it might only be worth $70,000 at this point."

Even without these whoppers, it should have been clear to the bank's underwriters that George never stood to gain a thing from the loan—other than a larger, more dangerous debt burden. All but $361.74 of the $125,000 that didn't go to pay off NovaStar went to IndyMac's fees and closing costs. He nominally lowered his interest rate for a few years, but the loan value had ballooned so high—to more than double the original 2003 loan—that the interest rate was irrelevant. Whatever choices George made, the most dubious decision was IndyMac's willingness to make such a plainly bad loan.

"He was in foreclosure the day he signed the papers," says Legal Aid's Bill Brennan. Brennan has been fighting predatory lending in Atlanta for three decades, and to his eye the current crisis has less to do with exploding interest rates than the fact that banks, eager to profit from the surging securities market, simply approved any loan that came in the door. "They ran out of legitimately eligible borrowers a long time ago," he says.

The rapidity with which borrowers have fallen into foreclosure is telling. Georgia law requires lenders to publish foreclosure filings once a month, so Brennan's research team culled through Fulton County's 1,600 listings for last November. Three-quarters of the foreclosures were for loans made since 2005, half were made in 2006 and one in ten had been made that same year. That sort of turnover used to be remarkable. "Even a few years ago, it was unusual to see a foreclosure that occurred in less than two or three years," Georgia Tech researcher Dan Immergluck told the Georgia business newsletter *Daily Report*. He added that he has not seen foreclosures turn over that fast in the fifteen years he's been following the local market.

It's also clear that banks and brokers targeted African-American neighborhoods when mining for these loans. The Dekalb County community development office likes to show two maps to illustrate the point. One map shows Atlanta neighborhoods with the densest populations of people of color who could benefit from CRA lending. They are clumped together in a butterfly, centered on the city's south side. A nearly identical butterfly appears on the second map, which shows neighborhoods that had a foreclosure rate over 20 percent between the first quarters of 2000 and 2005.

"It used to be that you couldn't get credit, but now I tell people to just stay away from it," Brennan says. "You don't want it. It's toxic."

After taking the IndyMac loan, George Mitchell kept the seriousness of his financial troubles to himself until last summer, when the kids were all home for the Fourth of July. He told them then that the gas company was about to shut off his service. "We found out when everything was behind and the hounds was at the door," Chandra says.

He'd been paying the mortgage intermittently, but by the time he told his children about the problems he was at least two months behind. He'd also fallen even further behind on his already substantial credit card debt. The gas card had racked up. The water and light bills were past due as well.

"Once I paid the mortgage, there wasn't enough to cover—" George starts to explain, but Chandra cuts him off. "Actually, there was." She shares her mother's discipline, and she chides George for not adapting to the situation his IndyMac loan put him in. "Holly Golightly here wanted to go out and do other things. But you don't have money to do extra things now."

Chandra's frustration is understandable, because the crisis has affected more than just George's finances. All of the kids are chipping in to cover the sprawling costs. Gwen pays the water bill. Chandra and her husband pick up the phone bill and keep everybody fed by cooking enough for both households—that way George can focus on his mortgage payments and credit card debt. "Sometimes it's hard," Chandra says, "but this is family. And you have to do what you have to do for family."

Economists say this dynamic of wealth and resources flowing backward—from kids to parents—rather than forward is typical in black families, and an important part of what separates blacks and whites who, by other measures, are nominally of the same class. Researchers are hotly debating the details of what is expected to be a historically large intergenerational transfer of wealth in America over the coming decades. But one fact is clear: blacks won't participate in it. In 2004, one in four whites reported having received an inheritance; fewer than one in ten blacks said the same, and the amount they got was, on average, half that of whites.

The foreclosure crisis makes the picture look bleaker still. Estimates vary on the amount of wealth lost, but they are all in the hundreds of billions of dollars. A United for a Fair Economy estimate in January put the wealth loss for people of color at between $164 billion and $213 billion, roughly half the nation's overall loss.

State Senator Vincent Fort pads around the Georgia Capitol with the wan look of a man who knows where the bodies are buried. Fort, who represents the tract of Atlanta that's been hardest hit by foreclosures, saw the crisis coming. He wrote and managed to pass a law that would have averted the whole mess—if financial industry lobbyists hadn't flooded Georgia and got it repealed a year later. Now he's relegated to the role of gadfly, resubmitting the prescient bill each session and getting nowhere. Sitting in his office after the close of this winter's session, he rocks back and laughs at it all: "It's like getting pickpocketed at eighty miles an hour."

Fort's bill passed in 2001, with the strong-arm help of Democratic Governor Roy Barnes. The law was meant to strengthen a 1994 Congressional measure, the Home Ownership and Equity Protection Act, which polices high-interest loans but has proven ineffective because its trigger is set too high. The Georgia law lowered the interest ceiling at which tougher rules kick in. And among other things, it forced lenders to demonstrate a "tangible net benefit" to the borrower for any refinancing of a home loan less than five years old.

The law was based on a 1999 North Carolina bill. Together, the two measures were the tip of what looked to be a building wave of state-level efforts to head off subprime lending—and the financial industry went all out to stop them. According to the *Wall Street Journal,* between 2002 and 2006 industry lobbyists poured tens of millions of dollars into state-level campaigns to prevent or undo subprime lending regulations.

Ameriquest, the now-defunct mortgage company that was one of the nation's largest subprime lenders, led the fight in Georgia. It handed out tens of thousands in political donations, according to the *Journal,* and threatened to stop doing business in the state unless Senator Fort's law was repealed. Standard & Poor's chimed in, announcing that it wouldn't offer ratings for any mortgage securities with Georgia subprime loans in them, citing liability concerns.

"What we had in 2002 and 2003 was the most powerful companies in the world focused on Georgia," Fort says with a sigh.

He relates how he was deluged from the moment he announced plans to write the bill, after hearing a presentation on subprime lending at a Department of Housing and Urban Development conference. He stood up and announced that he planned to address the problem in Georgia, and an industry lobbyist immediately approached him to offer "help." "I guess I learned a lesson: don't tell your enemy what you're going to do."

Within months of Standard & Poor's announcement, the Georgia legislature repealed Fort's law and replaced it with one that removed the requirement that lenders show a tangible net benefit for refinance loans. The same process unfolded in New Jersey, where the legislature passed a tough law in 2003. Lobbyists, led by Ameriquest, descended on the state. Standard & Poor repeated its refusal to rate securities with subprimes from New Jersey. And in 2004 the legislature unanimously replaced the tough law with one that deleted the tangible-net-benefit rule.

"It's useless," Brennan says of the new Georgia law. "They would not have come back to Georgia if the 2001 bill had stayed in place. That was the purpose of the bill, to drive the predatory lenders out of the state." Indeed, North Carolina, where the net-benefit law held up, is today one of the states least impacted by the foreclosure crisis.

As Washington gears up for its belated response, industry lobbyists are once again warning against regulating lenders' behavior. During his April 16 House testimony, Mortgage Bankers Association's David Kittle described at length his members' voluntary efforts to work with borrowers to prevent foreclosure. "The key is to find solutions that help borrowers but do not violate the agreements with investors who now own the securities containing these loans," he cautioned.

The Bush administration has joined the industry in opposing any measure that would force lenders to restructure loans or write-down their values. Bipartisan bills in the House and the Senate would do just that by empowering bankruptcy judges to force loan modifications for borrowers facing foreclosure on mortgages larger than the market value of their homes. Neither bill has gained traction.

Meanwhile, Congressional Democrats and the administration have agreed on using the Federal Housing Administration to spur voluntary loan restructuring. They disagree mightily on how far to go, however.

An administration plan announced in early April would let select subprime borrowers who are behind on their payments refinance into an FHA-insured loan; for loans larger than a house is worth, lenders would have to write the principal down. The administration predicts the plan will help 100,000 homeowners. In June the Senate reached a compromise for a competing Congressional plan—a version of which passed the House in May—that would offer the same deal but with larger write-downs and would be available to far more borrowers, an estimated 400,000. The White House threatened to veto it, citing its cost and added taxpayer liability.

The Senate deal had enough support to override a presidential veto. But more than 2 million loans were at least sixty days delinquent in April, according to data from the Hope Now program, set up by the banking industry to facilitate voluntary workouts of troubled loans. Which means Washington will ultimately have to revisit the question of how to save people's homes, not to mention how to prevent new predation once this crisis passes.

Notably, Barack Obama has backed housing advocates' primary demand: allow bankruptcy courts to modify loans. He's also supporting a key part of the Senate plan, which would create a fund for local governments to buy foreclosed properties and thereby reverse the building glut of vacant, unsold housing. John McCain, meanwhile, has shifted his stance, initially echoing industry rhetoric about not aiding "irresponsible" borrowers, then unveiling a plan he said would help about 200,000 borrowers.

The Senate's homebuying fund is key because, as the slow machinery of Washington grinds along, neighborhoods like Westwood are falling further and further into decay. The ugly reality is that banks can foreclose on properties, but they can't resell them. With thousands of already overvalued homes up for sale, the market is flooded, further driving down property values. Banks, however, are hostage to the securities on which they gambled and cannot price the foreclosed homes at their actual value.

So the houses sit there, many with overgrown lawns, busted windows and piling trash. Squatters and drug dealers break in; scavengers mine them for copper and other valuable metals. Municipal tax bases drop, even as the vacant properties spawn crime and fires, which demand greater public service costs. "It's a major drain on the community and its resources," says Senator Fort.

The Atlanta Legal Aid Society is trying to slow the decay one house at a time. For senior borrowers like George Mitchell,

Brennan's team is betting on a strategy using a reverse mortgage. Under these complex deals, a lender gives an older borrower a loan for an agreed-upon percentage of the house's appraised value—usually about 60 percent. The borrower never has to pay that loan, but it accrues interest until the borrower dies. At that point, whoever inherits the estate has twelve months to either pay the principal plus interest or turn the house over to the lender.

Legal Aid secures a reverse mortgage, then offers the money from it to the foreclosing bank as a settlement—along with a threatening letter outlining the ways they believe the borrower was preyed upon. The message is clear: take this much and call it even or deal with a messy lawsuit. It's no universal solution, but as of January Brennan and Bolling had used it to save a couple dozen homes.

The Mitchells are hoping to join the list, but it'll mean a seemingly endless struggle to stay ahead of foreclosure. The eldest daughter, Patricia Taylor, is approaching retirement, when she had planned to move back to Atlanta from Birmingham and take over the Westwood home. The family figures if it can get George a reverse mortgage and make a deal with IndyMac, Patricia can in turn get her own reverse mortgage to pay off George's. That'll be a victory, of course, but one born from a sobering reality: forty years after George and Lillian Mitchell achieved the hallmark of American socioeconomic stability, their children embark upon a decades-long hustle to rescue what should have been capital-building equity from the grasp of paralyzing debt.

Lawyers for the Poor Muzzled in Subprime Mess

LAURA K. ABEL

January 16, 2008

IN THE NEXT TWO YEARS, 2 million families who took out subprime loans will face losing those homes to foreclosure. Their families will suffer, neighborhoods will be devastated and local governments will lose significant tax revenue. Economists trace the problems back to careless and sometimes fraudulent mortgage lending practices. Some lenders coaxed first-time low-income home-buyers to take out mortgages, or long-time homeowners to take out second mortgages, without disclosing the high monthly rates they eventually would have to pay. Not surprisingly, the homeowners cannot afford the monthly payments, and when they fall too far behind foreclosure proceedings start.

Now policy-makers are asking how we could have allowed such a widespread financial disaster to occur. They point to lax federal and state regulators, irresponsible mortgage companies and a financial sector too reliant on the housing bubble to examine the mortgages in which it invests. There's another cause, though, which is largely ignored: restrictions that have prevented federally funded civil legal aid lawyers from fully addressing the problem from its inception.

Civil legal aid lawyers, who work for non-profit organizations around the country, represent low-income people in the sorts of civil cases most important to their daily lives: housing issues, child custody, wage and hour law violations and consumer fraud. They are an essential part of our nation's law enforcement apparatus, because they ensure that the businesses and government agencies that operate in low-income communities do so according to the rule of law. Civil legal aid attorneys also serve as a detection and warning system for problems plaguing low-income communities. As the people most familiar with the legal problems of the communities in which they work, often they are the first to learn of new legal abuses occurring in those communities. Over the years, civil legal aid lawyers have spoken out and prompted change when the police refuse to respond to domestic violence calls, when foster care agencies place children in unsafe foster homes and when local employers repeatedly fail to pay the minimum wage.

But since 1996, civil legal aid attorneys have been muzzled. Congress has barred them from using some of the legal tactics that are most effective at enforcing the law for entire communities. Civil legal aid lawyers who receive any Congressional funding through the federal Legal Services Corporation cannot call legislators to warn of new problems facing their communities and suggest legislative fixes. They cannot represent clients seeking to use the class action mechanism to compel repeat offenders to obey the law. They cannot use statutorily available fee awards to make it too expensive for repeat offenders to continue breaking the law. They cannot use private funds, donated by private foundations or individuals, to provide client communities with any of these services. And because their funding has eroded over the years, they cannot represent millions of people who seek help every year.

These restrictions and inadequate funding have allowed the mortgage crisis to fester since the mid-1990s. Since then, civil legal aid lawyers have watched as predatory lenders targeted the communities they serve. They have successfully represented homeowners seeking compensation from law-violating lenders. But because they are barred by Congress from bringing a class action to require a lender to compensate all affected community members, they have watched helplessly as the same lender continues to strip equity from the homes of hundreds or thousands of other community members. The Legal Assistance Foundation of Metropolitan Chicago, for example, helped a 75-year-old woman keep the home she had lived in for thirty years, after a contractor took out a fraudulent loan in her name. Now they watch as the same contractor sends out mailings seeking new victims.

They, and other civil legal aid lawyers, have represented countless homeowners fighting foreclosure. But their foreclosure cases have dragged on for years, taking up valuable attorney hours, because legal aid attorneys cannot use the attorneys' fee award mechanism Congress intended clients to use to persuade lenders to settle cases earlier rather than later. And they have turned away thousands of other homeowners seeking help, because they lack the funding to help. In September, with foreclosures in New York City at twice the level they were at in 2005, South Brooklyn Legal Services stopped taking any new foreclosure cases. In March, Jacksonville Area Legal Aid did the same.

The lawyers have hoped and prayed that legislators would finally understand the gravity of the situation and take action. But they haven't been able to call those legislators to warn them and suggest legislation to fix the problem, because they are congressionally barred from lobbying. Now that the markets are affected, and Congress is taking note, legislators are calling civil legal aid attorneys to testify at hearings examining the mess. What a shame the attorneys couldn't call the legislators to warn them, years ago.

While policy-makers hold hearings, draft legislation, and tighten regulations, they should consider a cost-free measure: lifting the restrictions on civil legal aid lawyers handling foreclosure cases. And while they consider bailing out financial institutions suffering from the subprime scandal, or homeowners fighting foreclosure, they should consider taking the preventive measure of funding civil legal aid programs to fight predatory lenders.

Youth Surviving Subprime

ALLISON KILKENNY
March 17, 2008

WHEN I HEARD ABOUT the subprime mortgage crisis, it sounded eerily similar to the shady credit card lending practices found on most college campuses. I imagined yet another financial bubble floating down from Wall Street, filled with the gelatinous slime of adjustable interest rates; one that would inevitably pop somewhere over Poor People, U.S.A., blanketing the unsuspecting citizens below.

I knew the country's economic situation was bad, and as usual, the poor would suffer the most. However, I did not foresee the trickle-down effect of the subprime fiasco where even my peers—recent college graduates and first time homeowners—would feel the sting from predatory lenders.

"They go after young adults because they know we have to start building our credit and that we need money," says 25-year-old Vanessa Valenzuela from Norwalk, California. She and her husband went bankrupt after dealing with predatory lenders.

College Loan Connection

But Vanessa and her husband aren't alone. Predatory subprime lenders prey on the ignorance of inexperienced homeowners, especially young couples, who know little about the dangers of adjustable interest rates.

Andrew Lockwood and Peter Ratzan are co-owners of College Planning Specialists in Florida and post debt-related advice on their website, College Planning Advice (www.college planningadvice.com). They instruct families on how they can send the kids to school without the family going broke, and are also deeply aware of the connection between the subprime crisis and student debt.

"Unfortunately, most parents and college-bound students do not realize that student borrowers are not-so-distant cousins to headline-making borrowers with subprime mortgages," Lockwood points out. "In fact, many experts believe that the student loan market is poised to experience the devastation currently affecting the subprime mortgage industry."

This consensus comes after bond-rating agencies noticed an increase in defaults on private educational loans, and the U.S. Department of Education reported that nearly 12 percent of all federal loans due in 2001 are already in default. Experts worry that millions of college grads have borrowed too much in loans, which creates parallels to the subprime crisis when students, like homeowners, inevitably default on overwhelming debt.

"The main culprit behind the subprime crisis are adjustable-rate mortgages (ARM) resetting to high interest rates," Lockwood writes. Inexperienced borrowers, like Vanessa and other young people, are particularly vulnerable to ARMs because they don't understand that their interest rate can wildly fluctuate throughout their contract. High interest rates prevent families from making payments on time and result in defaults, foreclosures, and ruined credit.

Like credit card companies, mortgage companies tempt clients with low starter rates. However, when the ARMs shoot upward, families begin to struggle to pay their monthly bills.

With terms like ARMs, subprime, and housing bubble, it's easy to forget that there's a human price paid in the mortgage fiasco. Predatory lenders are taking advantage of real families.

Planning Pays Off

NeighborWorks America, an organization that creates opportunities for people to live in affordable homes, posts testimonials on their website from families who have experienced foreclosure because of the subprime crisis. One such story is about Denise and Lenwood Shaver, a young couple from Columbus, Ohio.

The Shavers were thrilled to have bought their first home, a perfect place for the young couple to start their life together. Denise, a financial services tax specialist for BMW corporate headquarters, also taught history at a local community college in between working to complete her Master's thesis. Her husband, Lenwood, cared for developmentally disabled adults.

Denise gave birth to their first child within months of moving into their new home, and then a second child 11 months later. "We don't have a strong support system," Denise told NeighborWorks. "No parents nearby. For the first child, I was able to work around our schedules because Lenwood worked second shift. He would watch the baby during the day, and I'd watch the baby during the evening. When I was pregnant again, they weren't as flexible with my schedule. They wouldn't allow me to leave early enough for Lenwood to get to work on time."

A tight budget and busy work schedule caused a lot of stress in their home. At first, they fell only a little behind on their bills, but their debt accumulated over time. "Without the additional $1,300 a month in take-home pay," Denise says, "we were hit hard."

What Denise did next was the smartest avenue for anyone worried about the possibility of foreclosure: she recognized her pattern of debt and sought assistance. Lockwood and Ratzen emphasize how important it is to act preemptively like Denise: "Plan early so you can avoid the consequences."

In Denise's case, asking for help possibly saved her family

from bankruptcy. The Shavers contacted the Columbus Housing Partnership, a NeighborWorks organization, and a counselor helped them create a spending budget. Some careful planning helped the Shavers scrape by so they could make their monthly payments until Denise could get back to work after her pregnancy. While the Shavers were able to keep their home, not all families are so lucky.

Poor Evicted More

Foreclosure is a difficult time for any family, but it's particularly hard in communities of color. Two NeighborWorks studies, "Mortgage Foreclosures in Atlanta: Patterns and Policy Issues" and "Mortgage Foreclosure Trends in Los Angeles," show that foreclosures are most likely to happen in neighborhoods consisting primarily of minorities. The subprime crisis not only affects homeowners, but also renters in houses whose owners default on their mortgages.

One such renter, Adriana Diharce, 29, first learned of her foreclosure when she found an envelope taped to her front door. Adriana, her husband and their two young children would have to immediately move out of their California home. She tried to call their landlady, but the phone had been disconnected. Homeless, and unable to reclaim their deposit, she was understandably upset. "As a tenant, we have no rights, no deposit and nowhere to go."

Adriana's story is one of thousands of American families who lose their homes without ever missing a rent payment.

They have few rights even though the homeowner is the one who defaulted on a payment, not the renters themselves.

Their situation is typical of the crisis' impact on communities of color where, according to an ACORN study, African-American and Latino homeowners are more than three times as likely as whites to have a high-cost loan.

Once evicted, former tenants find they have few rights. Unless they live in a city with rent control and are covered by eviction regulations, they are at the mercy of state laws, which give evicted tenants limited recourse. And the laws don't look like they'll change anytime soon.

Bills and Remedies

In late January, the California State Senate defeated a bill sponsored by Senator Don Perata (D) of Oakland that would have required banks to give 60 days notice to tenants in foreclosed properties. The bill would have also required lenders to provide homeowners with four months' notice before mortgage payments increase by 10 percent or more.

"For folks who have been paying their rent on a regular basis, to simply be evicted without cause because the owner has been unable to maintain their mortgage payment is a real problem," said Paul Leonard, director of the California office in Oakland for the Center for Responsible Lending. "In an already flagging market, the idea that foreclosures displace renters without adequate notice creates a level of upheaval and distress that could be mitigated with more reasonable notice provisions."

In a classic example of adding insult to injury, the floundering Congressional bills offered as solutions to evicted families fuss with superficial details like the date of their eviction rather than bailouts. That's like asking a prisoner if he prefers being executed on Tuesday or Friday.

"Young couples are losing their first homes because they can't pay the mortgage. Parents are pulling their children out of college because they can't pay the bills," Senator Edward Kennedy wrote to President Bush in an open letter. "We need a simple, effective plan to stimulate the economy and also put money back in workers' pockets and give them the support they need to weather the storm."

But Kennedy and other Democrats have failed to introduce a detailed, comprehensive plan for what that support to "weather the storm" entails. Surely, it must be more than the $600 rebate check Bush is planning to mail to taxpayers.

Waiting for Solutions

The government needs to do more than issuing frivolous rebates to reverse what NYU professor Noureil Roubini calls "the worst housing bust ever." A good start would be to pass legislation that protects bankrupt tenants, even during foreclosure. I'm not talking about irresponsible borrowers. I'm talking about people that were deliberately misled by predatory lenders who offered wildly excessive ARMs, ones that low-income families have no chance of repaying.

And those pesky ARMs are definitely demon babies that need to be tossed out with the bathwater. Even the bureaucratic drones over at the House Financial Services Committee agree, and they've all managed to nod their heads in the same direction when asked if it was a good time to help maneuver borrowers out of their adjustable-rate mortgages.

Unfortunately, this agreement came in April 2007, and little has been done since then to help individuals facing eviction. Unless, of course, you count Barack Obama and Hillary Clinton squabbling over if it's fair to evict families from their homes after 90 days.

So if you are looking for deeper solutions, don't look to Washington. Politicians have been scrambling to protect the loan dealers rather than the victims of predatory lending. The government's big, shiny solution comes in the form of "Project Lifeline," a program that asks the mortgage lenders to (pretty, pretty please) wait 30 days to foreclose on houses.

Really? This is the best we can do? In a great country like America, no con artist, even one who happens to be a banker, should have the right to trick citizens into a scheme like predatory lending. Thirty days' notice isn't fair. In the case of the subprime mortgage crisis, the government must stop protecting the banks and Wall Street and start protecting American citizens.

Is This the Big One?

JEFF FAUX

April 14, 2008

OR MORE THAN A DECADE, we Americans have been living on an economic San Andreas fault—a foundation of fracturing competitiveness covered by unsustainable consumer spending with money borrowed from foreigners. A financial earthquake was inevitable. We don't know how high on the recession Richter scale the current crisis will take us, but it increasingly looks like, as they say in San Francisco, "The Big One."

Since the last Big One, the Great Depression of the 1930s, we have had eleven small to medium recessions, lasting an average of ten months. The most severe—two back-to-back downturns that began in 1979—drove price increases and the unemployment rate to double digits.

We're not at those levels yet. But the structural supports underneath our shop-till-we-drop economy are considerably weaker. For starters, we have a historic depression in the housing market. Americans' total mortgage debt now exceeds their home equity, for the first time since 1945. Housing prices have dropped 10 percent since last spring, followed by record foreclosures. Most economists expect them to drop at least another 10 percent, which could leave more than 14 million households—at least 16 percent of the total—better off if they just walked away from their homes. Prices could go even lower.

Until last year, housing prices in most places had risen rapidly since the 1990s. This enabled middle-class homeowners with stagnant wages and maxed-out credit cards to keep spending by refinancing their mortgages. The housing boom also spawned the now infamous subprime mortgage—a scheme devised by Main Street realtors and Wall Street bankers to finance home buying with loans that let the borrower buy in with little money down but carried high interest rates. The expensive payments would be made later by refinancing the mortgage as prices continued to rise. These subprimes were sold to middle-class strivers upgrading to McMansions as well as to the working poor.

The increased demand pushed housing prices further into the stratosphere—until, inevitably, they fell back to earth. When the subprime borrowers could no longer make their payments, foreclosure signs went up, lowering the value of other houses in the neighborhood. The refinancing spigot shut off, retail sales sputtered and by January the economy was shedding jobs.

But it is not the squeeze on homeowners that is giving our central bankers nightmares. It is the blowback of housing deflation on the country's massively overleveraged financial markets, which has seriously constricted the flow of credit—the lifeblood of the world's largest debtor economy.

In a typical deal, subprime mortgages were sold to investment companies, where they were commingled with prime mortgages to back up new securities that could be touted as both safe and high-yielding. This new debt paper was then peddled to investors, who used it as collateral for "margin" loans to buy yet more stocks and bonds. At each change of hands, fees and underwriting charges added to the total claims on the original shaky mortgages. The result was a frenzied bidding up of prices for a bewildering maze of arcane securities that neither buyers nor sellers could accurately value.

Giant Ponzi scheme? Not to worry, responded the Wall Street geniuses. By spreading risks among more people, the miracle of "diversity" was actually turning bad loans into good ones. Anyway, banks were buying insurance policies against default, which in turn were transformed into a set of even murkier securities called "credit default swaps" and marketed to hedge funds, pension managers and in some cases back to the banks that were being insured in the first place. At the end of 2007 the market for these swaps was estimated at $45.5 trillion—roughly twice as large as all U.S. stock markets combined.

This huge pyramid of debt was made possible by thirty years of relentless deregulation of financial markets, culminating in the 1999 repeal of the Glass-Steagall Act, which had prohibited banks from dealing in high-risk securities. In effect, Washington regulators became passive enablers to Wall Street's financial binge drinkers. When they crashed—for example, in the savings-and-loan and junk-bond debacles of the 1980s, the Long-Term Capital Management collapse of 1998 and the Enron and dotcom crashes of the early 2000s—the government cleaned up the mess with taxpayers' money and let them go back to the bar.

So here we go again. When subprime homeowners stopped paying, the prices of the mortgage-backed securities used as collateral fell. Banks demanded that their borrowers pay up or cover their margins. Panicked selling by borrowers further lowered the securities' prices, triggering more margin calls and more defaults. Massive losses piled up at places like Citigroup, Countrywide, Merrill Lynch and Morgan Stanley, and cascaded back into the insurance companies. At the end of February, the huge insurer American International Group reported the largest quarterly loss, $5 billion, since the company started in 1919.

After some delay, the Federal Reserve Board last summer started lowering interest rates on loans to the banks. But in a phrase from the bank crisis of the 1930s, it was like "pushing on a string." The bankers' problem was not that money was too expensive to lend out; it was that they were afraid they wouldn't get their money back. When they did lend, they jacked up the rates to compensate for the higher perceived risks—even to solid customers. The Port Authority of New York and New Jersey suddenly had to borrow money at 20 percent. The State of Pennsylvania couldn't finance its college student loan program. Fannie Mae, the fund created by the federal government to support perfectly sound middle-class housing, struggled to sell its bonds.

In mid-March, after anguished discussions between Federal Reserve officials and Wall Street moguls, the Fed agreed to provide $400 billion in new cash loans to banks and investment firms. Days later came the shock of eighty-five-year-old Bear Stearns going belly up. In an unprecedented deal, the Fed immediately lent JPMorgan Chase the money to buy Bear Stearns, taking suspect mortgage-backed paper as collateral. Bear's stockholders had already taken a hosing when the stock crashed. The big winners were the company's creditors and insurers, who were saved from the consequences of their bad business judgment.

We are now staring into the abyss. The Bear Stearns bailout has created a presumption of a safety net under any major stockbroker, in addition to any major bank. Rumors are that Lehman Brothers and Citigroup may be next. The Fed could handle a Lehman crash. But the collapse of Citigroup, the world's largest bank, would be catastrophic, bankrupting businesses, other banks and consumers and cutting off credit for state and local governments. And it could stretch the Fed to the limit of its resources.

There is a widespread assumption that there is no bottom to the pockets of the Federal Reserve. Not quite. The Fed has a finite amount of actual assets—mostly Treasury obligations backed by the "full faith and credit" of the government, which is a commitment to raise taxes if necessary to pay the debt. These assets total about $800 billion, some $400 billion of which have been obligated to back up loans. If the loans default, the Fed has to sell the Treasury notes in order to settle. If there are enough of these failures, the Fed could exhaust its assets. It would then have to resort to really "printing money"—issuing promissory notes not backed up by anything—or get bailed out by the Treasury, putting taxpayers further in the hole. Long before the Fed is down to the last of its stash of Treasury notes, more skittish domestic and foreign investors will flee the dollar. Interest rates would balloon and prices of oil and other imports would skyrocket. Credit would freeze, investment would plummet and tens of millions of Americans would be out on the street, with neither a job nor a roof over their heads.

Unlikely? Yes, still. Unthinkable? Not anymore. Estimates of Wall Street's losses already run well up to $500 billion. A 20 percent drop in housing prices would translate into a $4 trillion drop in the value of housing assets. A large chunk of that loss would destroy the value that underlies the mortgage-backed securities the Fed has now agreed to guarantee.

But well short of such a worst-case scenario, the country seems headed for major economic damage that will severely test whatever we have left of safety nets. It took five years from the time the recovery began in 1983 for the unemployment rate to return to pre-recession levels. Once we reach the bottom of this trough, it could be a very long time before American consumers, whose spending accounts for some 70 percent of our economy, crawl out of the debt hole and back into the shopping mall. The Japanese have still not recovered from their similar housing/debt crash in the early 1990s.

Virtually everyone who has studied Japan in the 1990s and the United States in the 1930s concludes that in both cases the government acted too late with too little in order to stop the debt dominoes from tumbling through the entire economy.

But the American political system seems as seized up as the credit markets. As the Federal Reserve tries desperately to put an overdosed Wall Street on life support, President Bush remains dizzily detached, periodically repeating his moronic mantra against government intervention in the free market. At a press conference that is impossible to parody, Treasury Secretary Henry Paulson announced the administration "plan" to safeguard the nation against a future crisis. It boiled down to a hope that the finance industry would do a better job of policing itself and that individual states would see to any new laws that might be needed. In what the *New York Times* dryly reported were his "most extensive comments to date about the credit and market problems," Paulson, formerly co-chair of the investment firm Goldman Sachs, firmly told reporters that he was not interested in finding "scapegoats." No kidding.

In response to pressure from Democrats, the White House at the end of January did reluctantly agree to a fiscal stimulus. But Bush demanded that it be limited to the only economic policy he understands: tax cuts. Democrats caved, and the government started printing up $160 billion in a one-time rebate to consumers and businesses, which will be sent out in May. Too little, too late, and likely to be spent paying down debt and buying more Chinese imports.

Senate majority leader Harry Reid has proposed a second round of stimulus—this time through public investment, putting people to work rebuilding bridges, schools and other infrastructure. But no one is talking about a level of fiscal injection needed to counterbalance the drop in consumer and business spending.

If we use the 1979–83 experience as a guide, we'd need some $600 billion to $700 billion in deficit spending. But in those days, the United States was still a creditor nation. Thanks to three decades of trade deficits, topped by the costs of the Iraq War, we now depend on foreign lenders, increasingly worried about the value of their U.S. bonds. As Lee Price, chief economist of the House Appropriations Committee, put it, "We need as big a stimulus as our foreign lenders will allow us to get away with."

To give some relief to those at the bottom of this tottering financial edifice, Barney Frank and Chris Dodd, chairs of, respectively, the House Financial Services and Senate Banking committees, are proposing updated versions of a Depression-era housing rescue program. The government would furnish $300–$400 billion to buy up existing home mortgages at prices marked down to reflect the current lower values. The plan could refinance 1–2 million homes. It may not be enough, but it probably represents the outer limit of what is possible in the twilight year of a White House whose economic competence is in the twilight zone.

Given the way Washington works, the Frank/Dodd proposal would need business support. Yet despite the fact that it would bring desperately needed trust back to the system, the capos of the Wall Street mob are unenthusiastic. Being forced to acknowledge losses on their books could toss a few more of them out of their jobs at a time when the supply of golden parachutes may be getting thin. Better to hunker down and whimper for more welfare from the Fed.

Some are already getting direct bailouts from big government. But it's not coming from the U.S. government. Foreign-government-owned "sovereign wealth funds" are now buying sizable equity shares to shore up battered firms. Citigroup, where the Saudis are already the chief stockholder, sold roughly $20 billion of itself to Abu Dhabi, Singapore and Kuwait. The Chinese just bought 10 percent of Morgan Stanley, and Merrill Lynch sold a 9 percent stake to Singapore. With oil above $100 a barrel, more of Wall Street is certain to wind up owned in the Middle East. Some members of Congress still warn that these countries are looking for political influence in America's financial heart, rather than optimizing their rate of return. They are probably right, but the nationalist fires that flared up against Dubai ownership of U.S. ports in 2006 have largely been banked. Beggars can't be choosers.

Another hope is that the Europeans, the Chinese, whoever, will take over our role as the world's consumer of last resort. As the recession slows U.S. imports, countries that have grown fat on exports to us will certainly have to shift more of their growth to their own domestic market. But to expect that the leaders of other nations would put their own economies at risk by running up trade deficits in order to save us Americans from the consequences of our own folly seems stunningly naïve.

So if this is not The Big One, it is likely to be A Big One—and a long one.

We could still get lucky, of course. Republicans facing re-election might persuade Bush to support a big fiscal stimulus and housing rescue. Home prices may miraculously stabilize. Tomorrow, bankers may wake up like Scrooge on Christmas morning and just start lending. The Chinese may start importing American-made cars …

Otto von Bismarck once remarked, "There is a Providence that protects idiots, drunkards, children and the United States of America." Let's hope it's still true.

Part Three

The Crisis Hits

▼ ▼ ▼

The Panic of 2008

EDITORS OF *THE NATION*

February 11, 2008

O N MONDAY, JANUARY 21, when the U.S. stock markets were closed for Martin Luther King Day, world markets took a bad stumble. The next morning, as our markets were about to open, the Federal Reserve took the rare step of cutting the interest rate under its direct control a deep three-quarters of a point. What was rare about the cut was not only its size— triple the quarter-point moves that were typical over the past decade—but its timing, a week ahead of a normal policy meeting at which the Fed was nearly certain to cut rates. Such inter-meeting moves are very unusual. Clearly, the cut was intended to have a dramatic psychological effect. The Fed's earlier rate cuts since last summer left the markets unimpressed and screaming for more; maybe this one will do the trick. And no doubt there's more to come.

Although real-world economic indicators have been soften-ing for well over a year, they're far from collapsing. Yes, the housing market has been heading south for the better part of two years, and the economy produced a minimal 18,000 new jobs in December. But those things alone weren't enough to cause the central bankers to push the panic button. Plainly they were worried that the turmoil that had afflicted the financial markets ever since the subprime crisis broke out last summer was threatening to do serious damage to the real economy.

The cynical interpretation of events would be that the Fed is acting to rescue its most cherished constituency, Wall Street, which has had a pretty rough go of it lately after about twenty-five years of raking it in. This isn't wholly untrue, but tragically, Wall Street holds the rest of us hostage. Were the financial markets to seize up, the economy would go down the drain. That's not always true of the stock market, which often dances to its own delusional music, but it's very true of the credit markets, because they provide crucial day-to-day funding for businesses large and small. The Fed is trying to keep that credit flowing.

It's not only our economy that's at risk. For months, it was fashionable to say that the rest of the world had "decoupled" from the United States; a recession here wouldn't necessarily affect the economies of Europe or Asia. But the idea that the rest of the world could escape the influence of the United States—which despite the erosion of its dominance over the last several decades is still responsible for about a quarter of the world's output—never made much sense, and the global stock selloff was an acknowledgment of that reality.

Just how stark is the reality? Doom-mongers are ominously predicting the worst downturn since the 1930s. Maybe. But with the Fed cutting interest rates this aggressively, and Washington almost certain to concoct a large stimulus program, a more likely outcome would be a recession followed by a year or more of stagnation. It's going to take time to work off the glut of new houses and the overhang of bad debts.

How dire things will get depends in large part on the makeup of that stimulus program. Size alone doesn't matter. If it's just tax rebates skewed to the upper brackets and business tax breaks, as the Bush administration wants, it's not going to help all that much. (Regardless of any tax cuts, why would businesses invest if the economic outlook stinks?) Money must be gotten into the hands of those most in need of it, who are also those most likely to spend it; poor and lower-middle-income Americans. And a moratorium on foreclosures is essential to minimize suffering while a longer-term solution to the housing mess is worked out. Sad to say, though, it's hard to imagine our president signing such a humane and sensible bill.

Bridge Loan to Nowhere

THOMAS FERGUSON AND ROBERT JOHNSON
September 22, 2008

I N THE MOVIE *Men in Black,* Will Smith and Tommy Lee Jones team up to save the world by resolute preventive action. By contrast, America's real-life Men in Black—Treasury Secretary Hank Paulson, Federal Reserve Chair Ben Bernanke and New York Fed President Timothy Geithner—haven't done as well lately. Ever since that classical day of reckoning, the Ides of March 2008, when the terrifying specter of chain bankruptcy and currency collapse first loomed over lower Manhattan like an attacking spaceship because of Bear Stearns, it's been downhill.

A little over a week ago, the Men in Black made a fatal mistake. They allowed the aliens to vaporize the proud old firm of Lehman Brothers. Whole fleets of spaceships then immediately began attacking AIG, Wachovia, Washington Mutual, even Morgan Stanley and Goldman Sachs. Now desperate, the Men in Black switched back to their old tactics and rescued AIG, but the damage had been done. The aliens had learned from Lehman and AIG how vulnerable Wall Street really was. Soon interbank markets everywhere in the world locked up. With financiers preferring treasuries that paid essentially nothing to every other asset in the world, huge runs started on money market funds.

In response, the Men in Black have now gone to Congress. They have put a check for $700 billion and a loaded gun on the table. Sign the check, they insist, and give us unreviewable power to buy bad assets, or take responsibility for the collapse of the whole financial system and, likely, the world economy.

In America's money-driven political system, leaders of both parties love to pretend that the sound of money talking is the voice of the people. Both presidential candidates and Democratic Congressional leaders are mostly nodding, with the Democrats adding trademarked noises about balancing off gifts to Wall Street with mortgage relief, another small economic stimulus program and perhaps some curbs on executive pay. Meantime, save for a handful of splendid exceptions, notably Gretchen Morgenson of the *New York Times*, American newspapers just keep giving their readers more reasons to keep deserting them.

Actually, there are one or two things to like in the Men in Black's latest scheme for the Mother of All Bailouts. The economic case for single-payer insurance has always been overwhelming. With all the new precedents—Bear Stearns, Fannie, Freddie, AIG, and one, two, three, many more coming—who would now dare deny the American people a chance for similar efficiencies in health insurance?

We also confess to having a soft spot for the New Deal—that remarkable moment that gives the lie to all of today's fashionable sneers about the impossibility of effective financial regulation. We just wish that the Men in Black would draw inspiration from something besides the anachronistic language of the Gold Reserve Act of 1934, which tried to make Treasury's decisions about the Exchange Stabilization Fund unreviewable by anyone else. (See the new plan's incredible Section 8, something you would think only Dick Cheney could love.)

And who can deny it? All the "Comrade Paulson" jokes should at least be good for a decent respite from Market Fundamentalism—the notion that unregulated markets automatically give you full employment and economic stability. Right now every individual financial institution is deleveraging—that is, reducing its use of borrowed money—at a terrifying pace. Financial houses are trying to recapitalize themselves by gouging depositors, borrowers, investors and credit card holders. As a group, they cannot succeed. They are collectively digging themselves into a black hole in which the gain of one is the loss of another, unless somebody from outside puts in new money.

Paulson does not exaggerate when he implies that just soldiering on and letting markets work will trigger a depression and collapse of the currency. But if it's high time for some Big Government, the Men in Black's plan is not the way to go, unless you work on Wall Street. And even if you do, there are compelling reasons to fear it.

The plan's belated focus on a systemic solution designed to reopen money and financial markets to normal transactions is exactly right. Currently there is simply too much junk out there for anyone in money markets to be sure of getting repaid if they loan to anyone else, even overnight. Everyone knows that other institutions are full of bad assets that are hugely depressed, but each sees for sure only their own desperate condition. So nobody trusts anybody.

But there is more than one way to restore trust and restart markets. Alas, not only is the plan the Men in Black are pushing the most expensive and likely to soak average Americans the most, but it is also the most likely to fail.

What Might Work

You could simply take a leaf from the New Deal and do a bank holiday. That is, send bank examiners into all the institutions—investment houses, and insurance companies and the other major players, as well as banks—to assess them. Insolvent ones are simply closed; everyone knows then that those that survive are solvent. Economic life restarts. The total cost is minimal. In the nineties, under Greenspan, the Fed ran away from its duty to oversee primary dealers in government securities. Voting it sufficient authority to do the job not just on Wall Street and the banks, but in any part of the system not covered by effective regulators would be far less expensive than the Men in Black's scheme.

Guess why Wall Street hates this one and why Bernanke (whose work on the New Deal is indeed distinguished, though many of his hypotheses have since been refuted) and Paulson do not even consider it. In all likelihood much of the Street is insolvent, which is why short-sellers were going wild until the SEC (Securities and Exchange Commission) banned them.

The government could inject capital directly into financial institutions with a reasonable prospect of survival in the long run. This was the essence of Senator Schumer's proposal that surfaced just ahead of Paulson's announcement and that triggered the rally in world financial markets. The New Deal did this, too. It used the Reconstruction Finance Corporation, which put severe terms on the banks receiving the aid. Wall Street, of course, would love the money, but not the terms. Somebody to inspect and certify the solvency of financial houses is also a requisite for this option, which, as already noted, is anathema to the Street.

The Men in Black's choice: just have the government buy the junk, giving Wall Street real money—our money—in exchange for it. Notice three points about this one: First, the lucky firms continue merrily in business. Thus far Paulson and Bernanke's plan does not even pay lip service to reforms. It is also well to remember that as the crisis hit, Paulson was at work on a preposterous scheme calling for more deregulation on grounds that New York faced competition from foreign financial markets. It is obvious where the former Goldman Sachs CEO's heart lies.

Second, there is a truly alarming likelihood that $700 billion will probably not be enough. Estimates of the total amount of junk out there vary, but the key point to hold fast to is that Bernanke, Paulson, and most financial experts have consistently underestimated the problem. Nor is there any reason to believe their forecasting is improving. Less than a fortnight ago, as Lehman was let go, the Fed was boasting that it now had a much better grip on markets than it did when Bear Stearns went down. It seems clear that even under this option, the bank inspectors had better be unleashed before much money goes out the door. Otherwise, we may well end in the worst of all possible worlds: the $700 billion is gone, but trust in the money markets remains elusive.

Third, the draft plan is silent on the prices at which assets are to be bought and, presumably later, resold. The problem of possible sweetheart deals is real and has to be addressed. Already there are reports on the web that the Treasury believes such methods are really rough-and-ready ways to get aid to firms that need it. There is also little doubt that politics colored some assets sales by the Resolution Trust Corporation, set up during George H. W. Bush's administration to dispose of debris from the S&L crisis.

Under both options 2 and 3 above, it is vital that Congress insist on reasonable terms for the public. Just as with Bear Stearns, the mere announcement of the bailout sent financial markets around the world soaring. There is absolutely no reason why some of the gains accruing both to private investors in the companies directly being bailed out and the broader market cannot be recaptured for taxpayers whose money makes it all possible.

It is easy. You can do it, for example, by taking equity in the firms you bail out and selling later. We prefer this to warrants, which are rights to buy shares at a low price that ensure a gain when they are finally exercised. Our fear is that coalitions of firms will do what Chrysler did and organize later to pressure the government not to exercise the warrants. Because there will be many of them, they are more likely to succeed.

It also makes sense to insist that firms receiving aid issue senior debt to the government with rights over all other bonds, etc., they have outstanding. That's to make sure some money comes back right from the start and that managements cannot keep all the earnings for themselves by reducing accounting profits and paying themselves more.

To recapture some of the broader market gains flowing from the injection of public money, one could place a modest new tax on interest, dividends, capital gains. "Carried interest," the ludicrous special tax break for private equity and hedge funds that not only Republicans but Senator Schumer and other Democratic Congressional leaders continue to defend, should go as part of any political deal on a bailout. It is beyond crazy to ask American workers to subsidize firms that will soon be back trying to break up their firms and throw their rescuers out of work.

And finally, obviously, it is necessary to re-regulate. Details of some reforms might require time to work out, though we see no reason they should be any more intractable than details of a bailout, which Paulson and Bernanke want to do almost overnight. Our general view is that handing out money before nailing down reforms is too dangerous; Congress should legislate at least the basics, with a promise to fix details later. If Wall Street does not like it, it does not have to accept the money.

It helps that the main reforms necessary are obvious. Compensation practices that encourage taking big risks that blow up after bonuses are paid have to go, immediately. Limits on leverage—how much financial institutions can borrow—are another no-brainer. Probably there is also need for new rules on reserve requirements across the board and restrictions on the use of insured deposits.

Above all, trading in complex derivatives—the main cause of the current disaster—has to be completely overhauled, at once. Derivatives have to be standardized and move to public exchanges that collectively guarantee them. Failure to do this will just start the whole nonsense over again. Just imagine being told a year from now that losses on credit default swaps written by firms that were bailed out under the new plan require the United States to pony up still more cash.

Congressional Options

It is fine for Democrats to hold out for mortgage relief and for another stimulus package. The best way to do the first, probably, is by reviving something like the Home Owners Loan Corporation that worked so well in the New Deal. That bought mortgages from people who were in danger of losing their

houses and converted them into obligations that they could afford to repay. This sort of bailout has the wonderful property of directing public money to the public, rather than Wall Street. But it would still bail out Wall Street, since reviving housing and stopping mortgage defaults feeds directly through to mortgage bonds values and derivatives based on them.

But no one should be fooled by Democratic talk about mortgage relief and economic stimulus. The main focus of the design of the bailout must be the bailout itself. That is the rat hole down which $700 billion and probably plenty more will soon start disappearing if Congressman Barney Frank, Senator Dodd and, of course, Senator Obama do not walk the walk instead of just talking the talk.

The situation is dire, but it is not hopeless. A flurry of discussions with other central banks and governments may soon produce claims that international agreements hem in legislators here. Congress has a straightforward counter to this and any manipulative threats of economic collapse: Turn the gun around. Move every bit as speedily as Paulson and Bernanke demand, but pass a bill that anyone can see protects the public far better than the Men in Black's proposal. If President Bush—remember him?—refuses to sign it, make it obvious to voters who's really crashing the system for private gain. All of the House and a third of the Senate are up for re-election. Enough votes can probably be found from among Republicans who would like to survive a Democratic landslide to pass something far better than the Men in Black's bridge loan to nowhere.

Crisis of a Gilded Age

DOUG HENWOOD
October 13, 2008

It looks like someday finally arrived.

FOR THE PAST TWO or three decades skeptics watched as deregulated finance got ever more reckless, as the gap between rich and poor widened to a chasm not seen since the turn of the last century, and they said, "Someday there's going to be hell to pay for all this." But despite a few nasty hiccups every few years—the 1987 stock market crash, the savings and loan debacle of the late 1980s, the Mexican and Asian financial crises of the mid-1990s, the dot-com bust of the early 2000s—somehow the economy regained its footing for another game of chicken. Has its luck finally run out?

It might seem odd to link the current financial crisis with the long-term polarization of incomes, but in fact the two are deeply connected. During the housing bubble, people borrowed heavily not only to buy houses (whose prices were rising out of reach of their incomes) but also to compensate for the weakest job and income growth of any expansion since the end of World War II. Between 2001 and 2007, homeowners withdrew almost $5 trillion in cash from their houses, either by borrowing against their equity or pocketing the proceeds of sales; such equity withdrawals, as they're called, accounted for 30

percent of the growth in consumption over that six-year period. That extra lift disguised the labor market's underlying weakness; without it, the 2001 recession might never have ended.

But that round of borrowing only extended one that had begun in the early 1980s. At first it was credit cards, but when the housing boom really got going around 2001, the mortgage market took the lead. Now households are up to their ears in debt, and the credit markets are broken.

Borrowing is only one side of the story. As incomes polarized, America's rich and the financial institutions that serve them found their portfolios bulging with cash in need of a profitable investment outlet, and one of the outlets they found was lending to those below them on the income ladder. (That's one of several places where all the cash that funded the credit card and mortgage borrowing came from.) They also poured their money into hedge funds, private equity funds and just plain old stocks and bonds. That twenty-five-year gusher of cash led to an enormous expansion in the financial markets. Total financial assets of all kinds (stocks, bonds, everything) averaged around 440 percent of GDP (gross domestic product) from the early 1950s through the late 1970s. They grew steadily, breaking 600 percent in 1990 and 1,000 percent by 2007. With a few notorious interruptions, it looked like Wall Street had entered a utopia: an eternal bull market. Regulators stopped regulating and auditors looked the other way as financial practices lost all traces of prudence. No figure embodies that negligence better than Alan Greenspan, who as chair of the Federal Reserve dropped the propensity to caution and worry characteristic of the central banking profession and instead cheered the markets onward. As he said many times in the 1990s and early 2000s, who was he, a mere mortal, to second-guess the collective wisdom of the markets? He seemed to have no sense that markets embody no collective wisdom and often act with all the careful consideration of a mob.

So while the proximate cause, as the lawyers say, of the current financial crisis is the bursting of the housing bubble and the souring of so much of the mortgage debt that financed it, that's really only part of a much larger story. And while it's inevitable that the government is going to have to spend hundreds of billions to repair the damage over the next few years, there's a lot more that needs to be done over the longer term.

This is the point where it's irresistibly tempting to call for a re-regulation of finance. And that is sorely needed. But we also need to remember why finance, like many other areas of economic life, was deregulated starting in the 1970s. From the point of view of the elite, corporate profits were too low, workers were too demanding and the hand of government was too heavy. Deregulation was part of a broad assault to make the economy more "flexible," which translated into stagnant to declining wages and rising job insecurity for most Americans. And the medicine worked, from the elites' point of view. Corporate profitability rose dramatically from the early 1980s until sometime last year. The polarization of incomes wasn't an unwanted side effect of the medicine—it was part of the cure.

Although we're hearing a lot now about how the Reagan era is over and the era of big government is back, an expanded government isn't likely to do much more than rescue a failing financial system (in addition to the more familiar pursuits of waging war and jailing people). Nothing more humane will be pursued without a far more energized populace than we have. After this financial crisis and the likely bailout, it looks impossible to go back to the status quo ante—but we don't seem ready to move on to something appealingly new yet, either.

Henry Paulson's Shell Game

JOSEPH E. STIGLITZ
September 26, 2008

THE CHAMPAGNE BOTTLE CORKS were popping as Treasury Secretary Henry Paulson announced his trillion-dollar bailout for the banks, buying up their toxic mortgages. To a skeptic, Paulson's proposal looks like another of those shell games that Wall Street has honed to a fine art. Wall Street has always made money by slicing, dicing and recombining risk. This "cure" is another one of these rearrangements: somehow, by stripping out the bad assets from the banks and paying fair market value for them, the value of the banks will soar.

There is, however, an alternative explanation for Wall Street's celebration: the banks realized that they were about to get a free ride at taxpayers' expense. No private firm was willing to buy these toxic mortgages at what the seller thought was a reasonable price; they finally had found a sucker who would take them off their hands   called the American taxpayer.

The administration attempts to assure us that they will protect the American people by insisting on buying the mortgages at the lowest price at auction. Evidently, Paulson didn't learn the lessons of the information asymmetry that played such a large role in getting us into this mess. The banks will pass on their lousiest mortgages. Paulson may try to assure us that we will hire the best and brightest of Wall Street to make sure that this doesn't happen. (Wall Street firms are already licking their lips at the prospect of a new source of revenues: fees from the U.S. Treasury.) But even Wall Street's best and brightest do not exactly have a credible record in asset valuation; if they had done better, we wouldn't be where we are. And that assumes that they are really working for the American people, not their long-term employers in financial markets. Even if they do use some fancy mathematical model to value different mortgages, those in Wall Street have long made money by gaming against these models. We will then wind up not with the absolutely lousiest mortgages, but with those in which Treasury's models most underpriced risk. Either way, we the taxpayers lose, and Wall Street gains.

And for what? In the S&L bailout, taxpayers were already on the hook, with their deposit guarantee. Part of the question then was how to minimize taxpayers' exposure. But not so this time. The objective of the bailout should not be to protect the banks' shareholders, or even their creditors, who facilitated this bad lending. The objective should be to maintain the flow of credit, especially to mortgages. But wasn't that what the Fannie Mae/Freddie Mac bailout was supposed to assure us?

There are four fundamental problems with our financial system, and the Paulson proposal addresses only one. The first is that the financial institutions have all these toxic products—which they created—and since no one trusts anyone about their value, no one is willing to lend to anyone else. The Paulson approach solves this by passing the risk to us, the taxpayer—and for no return. The second problem is that there is a big and increasing hole in bank balance sheets—banks lent money to people beyond their ability to repay—and no financial alchemy will fix that. If, as Paulson claims, banks get paid fairly for their lousy mortgages and the complex products in which they are embedded, the hole in their balance sheet will remain. What is needed is a transparent equity injection, not the nontransparent ruse that the administration is proposing.

The third problem is that our economy has been supercharged by a housing bubble which has now burst. The best experts believe that prices still have a way to fall before they return to normal, and that means there will be more foreclosures. No amount of talking up the market is going to change that. The hidden agenda here may be taking large amounts of real estate off the market—and letting it deteriorate at taxpayers' expense.

The fourth problem is a lack of trust, a credibility gap. Regrettably, the way the entire financial crisis has been handled has only made that gap larger.

Paulson and others in Wall Street are claiming that the bailout is necessary and that we are in deep trouble. Not long ago, they were telling us that we had turned a corner. The administration even turned down an effective stimulus package last February—one that would have included increased unemployment benefits and aid to states and localities   and they still say we don't need another stimulus. To be frank, the administration has a credibility and trust gap as big as that of Wall Street. If the crisis was as severe as they claim, why didn't they propose a more credible plan? With lack of oversight and transparency the cause of the current problem, how could they make a proposal so short in both? If a quick consensus is required, why not include provisions to stop the source of bleeding, to aid the millions of Americans that are losing their homes? Why not spend as much on them as on Wall Street? Do they still believe in trickle-down economics, when for the past eight years money has been trickling up to the wizards of Wall Street? Why not enact bankruptcy reform, to help Americans write down the value of the mortgage on their overvalued home? No one benefits from these costly foreclosures.

The administration is once again holding a gun at our head, saying, "My way or the highway." We have been bamboozled before by this tactic. We should not let it happen to us again. There are alternatives. Warren Buffet showed the way, in providing equity to Goldman Sachs. The Scandinavian countries showed the way, almost two decades ago. By issuing preferred shares with warrants (options), one reduces the public's downside risk and insures that they participate in some of the upside potential. This approach is not only proven, it provides both incentives and wherewithal to resume lending. It furthermore avoids the hopeless task of trying to value millions of complex mortgages and even more complex products in which they are embedded, and it deals with the "lemons" problem—the government getting stuck with the worst or most overpriced assets.

Finally, we need to impose a special financial sector tax to pay for the bailouts conducted so far. We also need to create a reserve fund so that poor taxpayers won't have to be called upon again to finance Wall Street's foolishness.

If we design the right bailout, it won't lead to an increase in our long-term debt—we might even make a profit. But if we implement the wrong strategy, there is a serious risk that our national debt—already overburdened from a failed war and eight years of fiscal profligacy—will soar, and future living standards will be compromised. The president seemed to think that his new shell game will arrest the decline in house prices, and we won't be faced holding a lot of bad mortgages. I hope he's right, but I wouldn't count on it: it's not what most housing experts say. The president's economic credentials are hardly stellar. Our national debt has already climbed from $5.7 trillion to over $9 trillion in eight years, and the deficits for 2008 and 2009—not including the bailouts—are expected to reach new heights. There is no such thing as a free war—and no such thing as a free bailout. The bill will be paid, in one way or another.

Perhaps by the time this article is published, the administration and Congress will have reached an agreement. No politician wants to be accused of being responsible for the next Great Depression by blocking key legislation. By all accounts, the compromise will be far better than the bill originally proposed by Paulson but still far short of what I have outlined should be done. No one expects them to address the underlying causes of the problem: the spirit of excessive deregulation that the Bush administration so promoted. Almost surely, there will be plenty of work to be done by the next president and the next Congress. It would be better if we got it right the first time, but that is expecting too much of this president and his administration.

View from Asia

WALDEN BELLO

September 24, 2008

Manila

M ANY ASIANS ABSORB what is happening in Wall Street with a combination of déjà vu, skepticism and "I-told-you-so."

For many, the Wall Street crisis is a replay, though on a much larger scale, of the 1997 Asian financial crisis, which brought down the red-hot "tiger economies" of the East. The shocking absence of Wall Street regulation brings back awful memories of the elimination of capital controls by East Asian governments, which were under pressure from the International Monetary Fund and the U.S. Treasury Department. That move triggered a tsunami of speculative capital onto Asian markets that sharply receded after sky-high land and stock prices came tumbling down.

Treasury Secretary Paulson's proposed massive bailout of Wall Street's tarnished titans reminds people here of the billions the I.M.F. hustled up after '97 in the name of assisting them—money that was used instead to rescue foreign investors.

So Asian governments and financial players are skeptical about Washington's talk of re-regulating the financial sector, and, although their central banks and sovereign wealth funds are flush with cash, they're wary about being drawn into the Wall Street maelstrom. Among East Asian official funds, only Singapore's Temasek and the China Investment Corporation have stepped up to the plate. Temasek pumped over $4 billion into Merrill Lynch a few months ago, but only after driving a hard bargain. CIC invested $5 billion in Morgan Stanley last December but refused the troubled investment bank's recent desperate plea to increase its share of the firm. Initially seen as a potential savior, the Korean Development Bank turned down the overtures of Lehman Brothers a week before the latter's historic collapse into bankruptcy.

Trillions of dollars of Asian public and private money are invested in U.S. firms and property, with the five biggest Asian holders accounting for over half of all foreign investment in U.S. government debt instruments. Funds from Asia have become a key prop of U.S. government spending and the middle-class consumption that have become the driver of the American economy. With so much of Asia's wealth relying on the stability of the U.S. economy, there is not likely to be any precipitate move to abandon Wall Street securities and U.S. Treasury bills.

At home, however, there are growing worries, and consumer advocates, NGOs and academics are demanding more transparency about how much the local banking system is exposed to Wall Street's toxic assets. In the Philippines, there are calls from civil society groups for the banning of derivatives trading, the return of capital controls and the renegotiation of the country's massive foreign debt now that the international banks are in a weak position.

There is, moreover, resignation throughout Asia about the inevitability of a deep U.S. recession and its likely massive impact on the East: the United States is China's top export destination, while China imports raw materials and intermediate goods from Japan, Korea and Southeast Asia to shape into the products it sends to the United States. Despite some talk a few months ago about the possibility that the economic fate of Asia could be "decoupled" from that of the United States, most observers now see these economies as members of a chain gang shackled to one another, at least in the short and medium term.

Greater regional integration is now seen widely as a healthy antidote to a global integration that has run out of control. Some elements of regional economic cooperation are now in place, notably the so-called "ASEAN Plus Three" formation, which unites the Association of Southeast Asian Nations with China, Korea and Japan in a mechanism to facilitate bilateral exchanges of funds in the event of a financial crisis. Eventually this arrangement could become a full-blown regional monetary fund.

On the other hand, NGOs and social movements, while in theory supportive of integration, distrust a process monopolized by governing elites they view as unaccountable. Active participation of civil society, they insist, must be central to the crafting of such regional formations.

Born-Again Democracy

WILLIAM GREIDER

October 20, 2008

O UR COUNTRY is at a rare and dangerous juncture. The old
order is crumbling, and virtually all the centers of power
that govern us have been discredited by events. The president
is irrelevant, weak and unbelievable, even to his own party. The
Democratic majority controlling Congress is stalled by its own
shortcomings. The treasury secretary, given his arrogant approach to the financial crisis, is not to be trusted as a steward of
the public interest. Nor are the conservative Federal Reserve
and its chairman. The private power of Wall Street is utterly
disgraced and desperate.

This condition of vulnerability is sure to prevail for at least
the next three months, until a new president and new Congress
take office. In the meantime, the governing elites are clinging to
the old order, trying to salvage it by delivering massive amounts
of relief from taxpayers to the failing financial institutions. The
American people correctly see this approach as a historic swindle that rewards the villains at the expense of the victims. A
Nevada real estate broker asked the *Washington Post*, "Instead
of having a bailout, why don't we have indictments?"

Indictments can wait, along with fundamental reforms. Right
now the country needs to confront the fire raging through the
financial system and engulfing people and productive assets in

the real economy. Aroused and angry, the public, for a change, can play a decisive role in the political arena, as it did when the House rejected the bailout package. That shock to the system was valuable therapy. People can drive politicians to begin facing reality and to develop a more forceful strategy for national recovery, an approach that serves the country as a whole and has a far better chance of succeeding. The sooner our leaders recognize that the old order is gone, the sooner Americans can begin reconstructing a more viable and equitable economy.

The calamitous unwinding of financial institutions in recent months has an ominous resemblance to events that unfolded after the stock market crash of 1929, when three years of recurring waves of bank failures and economic contraction led to massive suffering. The government, led by the Federal Reserve, was scandalously derelict during that crisis. This time Washington has reacted more aggressively but still hasn't found a strategy to stabilize finance or reverse the gathering recession.

Another total collapse like the one in the 1930s may still be avoided if politics changes direction. We do have some factors in our favor. First, our living standard is abundant by comparison, despite our indebtedness to foreign nations. Second, the New Deal created economic mechanisms that remain in place as automatic stabilizers, like federal deposit insurance to prevent disastrous runs on banks like the ones that wiped out more than 10,000 back then.

Given the political paralysis, people have to find their own way. Corny as it sounds, the necessary first step is honesty—getting a clear understanding of what we are facing and what can be done, then forcing our views and ideas on the governing circles in both parties. The bitter tragedy of our era is that the hard lessons Americans learned during the crisis of the New Deal years have been tossed aside—either repealed or systematically subverted—by the present generation of governing elites. Democratic partisans who claim an aura of innocence are falsifying the past. For the last generation, Democrats have colluded with conservatives in the destruction of New Deal law and principle. And Democrats do not yet have a clear idea of how to restore those lost lessons and update them for our present predicament.

Understanding the situation begins by recognizing the real crisis—the great wound to the nation that Treasury Secretary Paulson and his supporters have obscured with their alarm-bell rhetoric. The United States has collectively suffered a massive loss of wealth—capital in the financial system as well as savings in the real economy of families and producers. With the collapse of Wall Street's phony valuations, financial capital disappeared like air from a deflating balloon. Banks are endangered because they have lost $1 trillion or maybe twice that. Therefore the banking industry will shrink considerably. We are witnessing that bloody spectacle right now—failing firms and forced mergers, either propped up by government or taken over by private investors like Warren Buffett.

When Japan went through a low-grade depression during the 1990s after its financial bubble burst, something like twenty-one major banks were reduced to four. The U.S. system is shrinking in similar fashion, but much faster. This inspires recurring panic among investors, creditors and shareholders, but a smaller financial system will eventually be good for the country—more focused on the real purpose of banking, which is to channel capital investment into the economy. In recent years financiers have instead amassed speculative fortunes by peddling exotic debt instruments.

Paulson's solution was to relieve bankers of their rotten assets—primarily mortgage securities—and then replenish their lost capital. He did not explain this clearly, because he knows even $700 billion is not enough to save them all. So his extraordinary powers would put him or his successor in the role of savior and Grim Reaper, the titan who picks and chooses which banks will survive and which must die. But even if he chose wisely, it would not solve the basic problem. The financial system is going to shrink no matter what; under Paulson's plan, the public would be stuck with all its costly mistakes.

The other half of the nation's great loss of wealth belongs to the people—ordinary working people, mostly, who have borrowed heavily in order to sustain their faltering standard of living under pressure from flat or falling incomes. Given the bubble of inflated housing prices, people borrowed most easily from their own savings—the equity they had accumulated in their homes. When housing prices collapsed, economist Dean Baker estimates, their loss of wealth was $4 trillion to $5 trillion. Three decades ago, American homeowners held 70 percent equity in their homes. Today it has fallen below 50 percent. Many families have spent their retirement savings and are still working.

Just as the financial system is doomed to become smaller, so must millions undergo a painful fall in their standard of living. Many already have. There is no obvious way around this, but if they face the facts, people can begin to focus on what is possible and then pressure government to undertake remedies to mitigate the pain and avoid the worst. Right now, everyone is scared, hunkering down.

Only government has the leverage to "get the money moving again," as New Dealers used to say. No other sector or interest is equipped to raise the financing. Government can borrow money from people afraid to spend and wealth-holding institutions afraid to lend, then pump it into real economic activity. It can issue cheap loans if the banking system won't. It can forgive debts or relax the terms if that puts people back to work and keeps them in their homes. As economist James Galbraith suggests, it can hand off the money to state and local governments and make sure they spend it. All this is elementary Keynesian economics, the doctrine taught by the New Deal era. I restate it in plain English because even the Democratic Party seems to have forgotten the basics, having become obsessively fearful of large budget deficits (except when powerful interests want the money). Average Americans need to start saving again, and business and banking will not begin to reinvest in the economy until they see that government is leading the way.

Washington must assert its full emergency powers and tackle two things at once: manage the gradual downsizing of the financial system in an orderly fashion that sustains lending, and revive production and employment by force-feeding activities of many kinds. This cannot be a voluntary program that simply invites bankers to participate on their terms. The government must impose emergency regulatory controls to keep finance in step with the nation's overall goals. If bankers resist these terms, they should be cut off, isolated from the public's lifesaving assistance.

These are not idle suggestions. The nation is now in the grip of dynamic political change, and this will not stop with the decision on Paulson's grandiose bailout. Presuming the bailout prevails in Congress, Paulson will be handing out public billions to Wall Street players in the next few months. The political counterforce for genuine public-spirited solutions should be pushing back right away. Activists and intellectuals, public citizens and heavyweight financial players, even some members of Congress are already at work on the details. If Congress reconvenes for a lame-duck session, you will see some of these measures surface for public debate and popular agitation.

The essence of this action will borrow ideas and models from the New Deal and update them to fit our present circumstances. This not simple nostalgia. It is a clearheaded recognition that the public interest has not been served and the crisis will not recede until it is. Here are five concepts for recovery and reconstruction that are in circulation. If we are lucky, these proposals will redefine the next presidency, whoever wins.

1. Stop the easy-money bailout. Instead of buying rotten assets from Wall Street firms with no strings attached, the government should examine their books and decide which banks can be saved with direct infusions of capital in exchange for public ownership—roughly on the terms Warren Buffett got when he aided Goldman Sachs (preferred shares and guaranteed dividends). The failing institutions should get regulatory euthanasia. This approach gives the government direct control over the survivors and ensures that the public is protected from egregious loss. The model is the Reconstruction Finance Corporation of the 1930s, which recapitalized banks and corporations under stern supervision.

2. Help the folks who are hurting—directly. A homeownership corporation patterned after the New Deal original would have the money and the flexible authority to supervise "workouts" for millions of failing families. This is what bankers do for corporations when they get in over their head. Government can do the same for indebted households: stop the liquidation, stretch out default dates and arrange manageable terms. This is not a bleeding-heart gesture—keeping families in their homes is economic stimulus, and it halts the decay of neighborhoods.

3. Get serious about economic stimulus. We need a recovery program five or six times larger than the pitiful $60 billion proposed by Democratic leaders. These billions should go for the familiar list of neglected priorities—fixing bridges and schools—but should also jump-start the green agenda for alternative fuels and restoration of ruined ecosystems. The government should subsidize the new industries of our age, just as New Deal spending financed the modern development of aircraft, petrochemicals, steelmaking and other key industries in the 1930s.

4. Re-regulate the bad actors and indict the criminals. Start by restoring the law against usury—the predatory lending practices that ruin weak and defenseless borrowers. Government cannot wait for a relaxed debate about restoring regulations. We need newly designed controls over the financiers and well-defined public obligations imposed not only on banking but also on hedge funds and private equity firms. These cannot be discretionary rules. If the money guys don't like them, they should get out of the business. Paulson's Wall Street colleagues are already mobilizing lobbyists for this fight, but they may discover that Washington has been changed by events. The easygoing deference to Big Money seems suddenly out of fashion.

5. Create a new brain for government management of the economy. The crisis and the halting decision-making by the Treasury and the Federal Reserve—not to mention the secrecy and special deal-making on behalf of financial interests—make it clear that deep reform is required. I would start with a special reconstruction and recovery agency, empowered to lead policy and oversee banking regulators and the economic stimulus. The Federal Reserve's so-called independence is an antique concession to the big banks and doesn't make any sense. Monetary policy and fiscal policy must be balanced and decided in the same process. That rational approach might have stopped the Fed from the biases and dereliction that led to this crisis.

These ideas and many others are in gestation. They will reach fruition when politicians and other leaders swallow their bruised egos and rethink their supine posture, arm in arm with Wall Street. That looks improbable at the moment. But voters can help them change their minds.

The Suicide Solution

BARBARA EHRENREICH

July 28, 2008

A FEW DAYS BEFORE Congress passed its housing bill, Carlene Balderrama of Taunton, Massachusetts, found her own solution to the housing crisis. Just a little over two hours in advance of the time her mortgage company, PHH Corporation—may its name live in infamy—was to auction off her home, Balderrama killed herself with her husband's rifle.

This is not the kind of response to hard times that James Grant had in mind when he wrote his July 19 *Wall Street Journal* essay titled "Why No Outrage?" "One might infer from the lack of popular anger," the famed Wall Street contrarian wrote, "that the credit crisis was God's fault rather than the doing of the bankers and the rating agencies and the government's snoozing watchdogs." For contrast, he cites the spirited response to the depression of the 1890s, when lawyer/agitator Mary Lease stirred crowds with the message that "We want the accursed foreclosure system wiped out. ... We will stand by our homes and stay by our firesides by force if necessary."

Grant could have found even more bracing examples of resistance in the 1930s, when farmers and tenants used mob power—and sometimes firearms—to fight foreclosures and evictions. For more on that, I consulted Frances Fox Piven, coauthor of the classic text *Poor People's Movements: Why They Succeed, How They Fail,* who told me that in the early 1930s a number of cities were so shaken by the resistance that they declared moratoriums on further evictions. A 1931 riot by Chicago tenants who had fallen behind on their rent, for example, had left three dead and three police officers injured.

According to Piven, these actions were often spontaneous. A group of unemployed men would get word of a scheduled eviction and march through the streets, gathering crowds as they went. Arriving at the site of the eviction, they would move the furniture back into the apartment and stay around to protect the threatened tenants. In one instance in Detroit, it took 100 cops to evict a single family. Also in Detroit, Piven said, "two families protected their apartments by shooting their landlord and were acquitted by a sympathetic jury."

What a difference eighty years makes. When the police and the auctioneers arrived at Balderrama's house, the family gun had already been used—on the victim of foreclosure herself. I don't know how "worthy" a debtor she was—the family had been through bankruptcies before, though probably not as a result of Caribbean vacations and closets full of designer clothes. It was an adjustable rate mortgage that did them in, and Balderrama, who managed the family's finances, had apparently been unwilling to tell her husband that their ever-rising monthly mortgage payments were eating up his earnings as a plumber.

Suicide is becoming an increasingly popular response to debt. James Scurlock's brilliant documentary, *Maxed Out,* features the families of two college students who killed themselves after being overwhelmed by credit card debt. "All the people we talked to had considered suicide at least once," Scurlock told a gathering of the National Association of Consumer Bankruptcy

Attorneys in 2006. According to the *Los Angeles Times,* lawyers in the audience backed him up, "describing clients who showed up at their offices with cyanide, or threatened, 'If you don't help me, I've got a gun in my car.'"

India may be the trendsetter here, with an estimated 150,000 debt-ridden farmers succumbing to suicide since 1997. With guns in short supply in rural India, the desperate farmers have taken to drinking the pesticides meant for their crops.

Dry your eyes, already: death is an effective remedy for debt, along with anything else that may be bothering you too. And try to think of it too from a lofty, corner-office perspective: if you can't pay your debts or afford to play your role as a consumer, and if, in addition—like an ever-rising number of Americans— you're no longer needed at the workplace, then there's no further point to your existence. I'm not saying that the creditors, the bankers and the mortgage companies actually want you dead, but in a culture where one's credit rating is routinely held up as a three-digit measure of personal self-worth, the correct response to insoluble debt is, in fact, "Just shoot me!"

The alternative is to value yourself more than any amount of money and turn the guns, metaphorically speaking, in the other direction. It wasn't God, or some abstract economic climate change, that caused the credit crisis. Actual humans— often masked as financial institutions—did that (and you can find a convenient list of names in Nomi Prins's article in the July 2008 issue of *Mother Jones.*) Most of them, except for a tiny few facing trials, are still high rollers, fattening themselves on the blood and tears of ordinary debtors. I know it's so 1930s, but may I suggest a march on Wall Street?

Great Depression II

NICHOLAS VON HOFFMAN
September 18, 2008

FOR MILDRED, a professional woman around sixty years of age, Great Depression II has started. I am going to have to work the rest of my life, she said. I can't retire.

She is not a rich woman, and her retirement investments have been decimated by the perpendicular drop in the stock market. Despite a lifetime of working and saving, like a thrifty squirrel burying acorns in the backyard, she's now broke.

One of the places she buried her acorns was AIG, thinking it would be hard to find a more conservative, rock-solid place to put her retirement money. She bought AIG preferred shares, that is, shares that are guaranteed to pay dividends and are thus ideal for retirement.

What none of the experts let the investors know was that somewhere along the path, AIG had stopped being rock-solid. Before Mildred knew it, the government had bought AIG and wiped out the stockholders. She, along with others, read in the papers that AIG's new owners will not be paying preferred stockholders their promised dividends.

It may be necessary for the government to take over control and ownership of these very large concerns with tens of thousands of stockholders, but the procedure is not unlike an oncologist administering chemotherapy. The doctor intends to knock out the cancer cells, but a lot of other innocent cells go down with the bad ones.

It would help if John McCain, Barack Obama and the other politicians careening around America would give a thought to Mildred when they come to the part in their stump speeches where they denounce Wall Street speculators. There are Wall Street speculators, lots of them, and the smart ones are doing very well cashing in on the enveloping depression, but they do not own most of the stocks in the hands of non-speculators like Mildred.

According to the Securities Industry Association, over half the households of America—something like 57 million families—own stocks directly or through mutual funds. McCain and Obama might bear in mind that this block of 100 million or so Americans are the very heart of the middle classes they both cannot praise enough.

By necessity, Mildred has cut back on her spending. We can assume millions more in the same situation are cutting back on theirs. Other millions who have seen the value of their houses drop have been doing the same. Even though they were not intending to sell their houses or cash in their mutual funds or their 401(k)s, they now feel poorer and less secure.

Although inflation is getting almost no public attention at the moment, it does not need publicity to carry on its economically subversive work. As prices go up and wages do not, people—particularly lower income people—buy less. They have no choice.

In sum, the less that is bought, the lower the demand for goods and services and the only thing that goes up on the graphs is unemployment. As the construction industries, among our largest employers, go down the toilet, unemployment rises.

Fear—Franklin D. Roosevelt's nameless, unreasoning, unjustified terror—is also at work here. It is driving countless people to take what money they have left out of money market funds, cash in stocks at a loss and withdraw money from savings accounts to put it in government notes which, for practical purposes, pay no interest. Money stuck away in government notes and bonds is unproductive money, money that will not be spent to generate wealth. Stagnant money makes for a scum-pond economy and fewer jobs.

Fear has made it next to impossible to borrow for anything— working capital for one's business, for new ventures, for investment in new equipment. Bankers who a couple of years ago were out on the street corners begging people to take the money off their hands will not cough up a car loan.

Banks are now so scared of getting stuck, they will not lend to each other. Well they might be, for even after recent spectacular bankruptcies and takeovers unresolved debts and unfathomable obligations still overhang the society.

Neither Mildred nor the captains of industry and the masters of the financial universe are spending, let alone lending. If this freeze continues there is no avoiding it—Great Depression II will begin to resemble Great Depression I, when one-third of a nation was out of work and on the dole.

We're All Minskyites Now

ROBERT POLLIN

November 17, 2008

A S THE MOST SEVERE financial crisis since the 1930s Depression has unfolded over the past eighteen months, the ideas of the late economist Hyman Minsky have suddenly come into fashion. In the summer of 2007, the *Wall Street Journal* ran a front-page article describing the emerging crisis as the financial market's "Minsky moment." His ideas have since been featured in the *Financial Times*, *Business Week* and the *New Yorker*, among many other outlets. Minsky, who spent most of his academic career at Washington University in St. Louis and remained professionally active until his death in 1996, deserves the recognition. He was his generation's most insightful analyst of financial markets and the causes of financial crises.

Even so, most mainstream economists have shunned his work because it emerged out of a dissident left Keynesian tradition known in economists' circles as post-Keynesianism. Minsky's writings, and the post-Keynesian tradition more generally, are highly critical of free-market capitalism and its defenders in the economics profession—among them Milton Friedman and other Nobel Prize–winning economists who for a generation have claimed to "prove," usually through elaborate mathematical models, that unregulated markets are inherently rational, stable and fair. For Friedmanites, regulations are harmful most of the time.

Minsky, by contrast, explained throughout his voluminous writings that unregulated markets will always produce instability and crises. He alternately termed his approach "the financial instability hypothesis" and "the Wall Street paradigm."

For Minsky, the key to understanding financial instability is to trace the shifts that occur in investors' psychology as the economy moves out of a period of crisis and recession (or depression) and into a phase of rising profits and growth. Coming out of a crisis, investors will tend to be cautious, since many of them will have been clobbered during the just-ended recession. For example, they will hold large cash reserves as a cushion to protect against future crises.

But as the economy emerges from its slump and profits rise, investors' expectations become increasingly positive. They become eager to pursue risky ideas such as securitized subprime mortgage loans. They also become more willing to let their cash reserves dwindle, since idle cash earns no profits, while purchasing speculative vehicles like subprime mortgage securities that can produce returns of 10 percent or higher.

But these moves also mean that investors are weakening their defenses against the next downturn. This is why, in Minsky's view, economic upswings, proceeding without regulations, inevitably encourage speculative excesses in which financial bubbles emerge. Minsky explained that in an unregulated environment, the only way to stop bubbles is to let them burst. Financial markets then fall into a crisis, and a recession or depression ensues.

Here we reach one of Minsky's crucial insights—that financial crises and recessions actually serve a purpose in the operations of a free-market economy, even while they wreak havoc with people's lives, including those of tens of millions of innocents who never invest a dime on Wall Street. Minsky's point is that without crises, a free-market economy has no way of discouraging investors' natural proclivities toward ever greater risks in pursuit of ever higher profits.

However, in the wake of the calamitous Great Depression, Keynesian economists tried to design measures that could supplant financial crises as the system's "natural" regulator. This was the context in which the post World War II system of big government capitalism was created. The package included two basic elements: regulations designed to limit speculation and channel financial resources into socially useful investments, such as single-family housing; and government bailout operations to prevent 1930s style depressions when crises broke out anyway.

Minsky argues that the system of regulations and the bailout operations were largely successful. That is why from the end of World War II to the mid-1970s, markets here and abroad were much more stable than in any previous historical period. But even during the New Deal years, financial market titans were fighting vehemently to eliminate, or at least defang, the regulations. By the 1970s, almost all politicians—Democrats and Republicans alike—had become compliant. The regulations were initially weakened, then abolished altogether, under the strong guidance of, among others, Federal Reserve chair Alan Greenspan, Republican Senator Phil Gramm and Clinton Treasury Secretary Robert Rubin.

For Minsky, the consequences were predictable. Consider

the scorecard over the twenty years before the current disaster: a stock market crash in 1987; the savings-and-loan crisis and bailout in 1989–90; the "emerging markets" crisis of 1997–98— which brought down, among others, Long-Term Capital Management, the super–hedge fund led by two Nobel laureates specializing in finance—and the bursting of the dot-com market bubble in 2001. Each of these crises could easily have produced a 1930s-style collapse in the absence of full-scale government bailout operations.

Here we come to another of Minsky's major insights—that in the absence of a complementary regulatory system, the effectiveness of bailouts will diminish over time. This is because bailouts, just like financial crises, are double-edged. They prevent depressions, but they also limit the costs to speculators of their financial excesses. As soon as the next economic expansion begins gathering strength, speculators will therefore pursue profit opportunities more or less as they had during the previous cycle. This is the pattern that has brought us to our current situation—a massive global crisis, being countered by an equally massive bailout of thus far limited effectiveness.

Minsky's Wall Street paradigm did not address all the afflictions of free-market capitalism. In particular, his model neglects the problems that arise from the vast disparities of income, wealth and power that are just as endemic to free-market capitalism as are its tendencies toward financial instability, even though he fully recognized that these problems exist.

Yet Minsky's approach still provides the most powerful lens for understanding the roots of financial instability and developing an effective regulatory system.

Minsky understood that his advocacy of comprehensive financial regulations made no sense whatsoever within the prevailing professional orthodoxy of free-market cheerleading. In his 1986 magnum opus, *Stabilizing an Unstable Economy*, he concluded that "the policy failures since the mid-1960s are related to the banality of orthodox economic analysis. ... Only an economics that is critical of capitalism can be a guide to successful policy for capitalism."

The Bailout:
Bush's Final Pillage

NAOMI KLEIN
November 17, 2008

I N THE FINAL DAYS of the election, many Republicans seem to have given up the fight for power. But that doesn't mean they are relaxing. If you want to see real Republican elbow grease, check out the energy going into chucking great chunks of the $700 billion bailout out the door. At a recent Senate Banking Committee hearing, Republican Senator Bob Corker was fixated on this task, and with a clear deadline in mind: inauguration. "How much of it do you think may be actually spent by January 20 or so?" Corker asked Neel Kashkari, the 35-year-old former banker in charge of the bailout.

When European colonialists realized that they had no choice but to hand over power to the indigenous citizens, they would often turn their attention to stripping the local treasury of its gold and grabbing valuable livestock. If they were really nasty, like the Portuguese in Mozambique in the mid-1970s, they poured concrete down the elevator shafts.

The Bush gang prefers bureaucratic instruments: "distressed asset" auctions and the "equity purchase program." But make no mistake: the goal is the same as it was for the defeated Portuguese—a final frantic looting of the public wealth before they hand over the keys to the safe.

How else to make sense of the bizarre decisions that have governed the allocation of the bailout money? When the Bush administration announced it would be injecting $250 billion into America's banks in exchange for equity, the plan was widely referred to as "partial nationalization"—a radical measure required to get the banks lending again. In fact, there has been no nationalization, partial or otherwise. Taxpayers have gained no meaningful control, which is why the banks can spend their windfall as they wish (on bonuses, mergers, savings …) and the government is reduced to pleading that they use a portion of it for loans.

What, then, is the real purpose of the bailout? I fear it is something much more ambitious than a one-off gift to big business—that this bailout has been designed to keep pillaging the Treasury for years to come. Remember, the main concern among big market players, particularly banks, is not the lack of credit but their battered share prices. Investors have lost confidence in the banks' honesty, and with good reason. This is where Treasury's equity pays off big time.

By purchasing stakes in these institutions, Treasury is sending a signal to the market that they are a safe bet. Why safe? Because the government won't be able to afford to let them fail. If these companies get themselves into trouble, investors can assume that the government will keep finding more cash, since allowing them to go down would mean losing its initial equity investments (just look at AIG). That tethering of the public interest to private companies is the real purpose of the bailout plan: Treasury Secretary Henry Paulson is handing all the companies that are admitted to the program—a number potentially in the thousands—an implicit Treasury Department guarantee. To skittish investors looking for safe places to park their money, these equity deals will be even more comforting than a Triple-A rating from Moody's.

Insurance like that is priceless. But for the banks, the best part is that the government is paying them—in some cases billions of dollars—to accept its seal of approval. For taxpayers, on the other hand, this entire plan is extremely risky, and may well cost significantly more than Paulson's original idea of buying up $700 billion in toxic debts. Now taxpayers aren't just on the hook for the debts but, arguably, for the fate of every corporation that sells them equity.

Interestingly, Fannie Mae and Freddie Mac both enjoyed this kind of unspoken guarantee. For decades the market understood that, since these private players were enmeshed with the government, Uncle Sam would always save the day. It was the worst of all worlds. Not only were profits privatized while risks were socialized but the implicit government backing created powerful incentives for reckless investments.

Now, with the new equity purchase program, Paulson has taken the discredited Fannie and Freddie model and applied it to a huge swath of the private banking industry. And once again, there is no reason to shy away from risky bets—especially since Treasury has not required the banks to give up high-risk financial instruments in exchange for taxpayer dollars.

To further boost confidence, the federal government has also unveiled unlimited public guarantees for many bank deposit accounts. Oh, and as if this wasn't enough, Treasury has been encouraging the banks to merge with one another, ensuring that the only institutions left standing will be "too big to fail." In three different ways, the market is being told loud and clear that Washington will not allow the country's financial institutions to bear the consequences of their behavior. This may well be Bush's most creative innovation: no-risk capitalism.

There is a glimmer of hope. In answer to Senator Corker's question, Treasury is indeed having trouble dispersing the bailout funds. It has requested about $350 billion of the $700 billion, but most of this hasn't yet made it out the door. Meanwhile, every day it becomes clearer that the bailout was sold on false pretenses. It was never about getting loans flowing. It was always about turning the state into a giant insurance agency for Wall Street—a safety net for the people who need it least, subsidized by the people who need it most.

This grotesque duplicity is an opportunity. Whoever wins the election on November 4 will have enormous moral authority. It can be used to call for a freeze on the dispersal of bailout funds—not after the inauguration, but right away. All deals should be renegotiated immediately, this time with the public getting the guarantees.

It is risky, of course, to interrupt the bailout. The market won't like it. Nothing could be riskier, however, than allowing the Bush gang their parting gift to big business—the gift that will keep on taking.

Part Four

The Road to Recovery

▼ ▼ ▼

How to Fix
Our Broken Economy

JEFFREY MADRICK

October 22, 2007

THE AMERICAN ECONOMY is broken. And it's not likely that the Democrats, even if they do as well as expected in the 2008 elections, are going to fix it. Of course, there's no chance that the Republicans will either, wedded as they are to endless tax cuts.

The experience of the past decade makes clear the need for a sharply new way of thinking about the economy. The subprime mortgage crisis, although dangerous, is not the issue. It's not even the rising prospect of recession and lost jobs. The real problem is that even when the financial times have seemed to be healthy, the economy was not. Since the 2001 recession gross domestic product is up, profits are at record levels and unemployment is low—but wages, capital investment and, now, productivity are weak. Without these, there is little on which to build an economic future.

Wages for the typical male are actually down since 2001. The fabulous accrual of private fortunes comes at a time when a typical household's income is lower than it was in 1999, despite the many working spouses. And while subdued wages have enabled companies to generate soaring profits, capital investment in equipment and computer software has in recent years been significantly lower as a proportion of GDP than it was in the late 1990s.

Productivity should be the biggest worry, but it gets the least attention. After growing robustly for a few years, productivity growth since 2003 is as low as it was before the Internet boom. Productivity, defined as the output the nation can produce per hour of work, is the nation's source of wealth. If it doesn't rise rapidly, there is no chance workers on average will see their standard of living rise.

Finally, the value of the dollar is significantly lower, and the trade deficit, though improving, will remain a problem. A lower dollar makes exports more competitive, but even with this dollar, rebalancing the economy will not be easy. After years of living with a high dollar, manufacturers don't have the capacity or trained workforce to make many of the products the rest of the world wants.

Tinkering with the safety net, placing a few restrictions in trade agreements or pressuring the Chinese to raise the value of their currency will not fix matters. What America needs is a set of policies that will make it a high-wage nation again, no longer dependent on ever increasing consumer debt and work hours to make ends meet. It must once again invest adequately in the public goods and services required to compete in the new century, including early education, transportation infrastructure, energy conservation and healthcare reform. The mainstream economic model on which most Democrats have relied since Bill Clinton's presidency will not deliver this. Here are a few of the key precepts of the outmoded mainstream model—hardly an agenda for our times.

Wage growth must be moderate. Every time wages have gone up more than moderately since the 1980s, Wall Street and Washington worry, and this has long included the Democrats. Fearing inflation, the Federal Reserve clamps down rapidly if wages begin to increase the way they once did—with overwhelming support from both parties. The one exception was the late 1990s, when the Fed allowed a wage rise in anticipation of rapidly rising productivity to offset it.

All this didn't start with the newest wave of job offshoring. As Isabel Sawhill of the Brookings Institution and John Morton of the Pew Charitable Trusts recently reported, a typical male in his 30s makes less today, after inflation, than his father did a generation ago. MIT economists Frank Levy and Peter Temin are the latest of many who have shown that even for men with college degrees, wages have not been keeping up with productivity since sometime in the 1970s.

Low taxes mean fast growth. "Case Closed: Tax cuts mean growth," wrote former Tennessee Senator and GOP presidential hopeful Fred Thompson in the *Wall Street Journal* in April. But most Democrats are hardly champions of tax increases either. Both parties emphasize that by minimizing government regulation and social spending, market incentives will stimulate productive investment. Moreover, they see low wages as a way to deal effectively with overseas competition. House Democrats, for example, are considering lowering corporate income taxes.

Balancing the budget increases savings. Mainstream Democrats and Republicans alike believe savings are the key to economic growth and that the most direct path to more savings is to reduce budget deficits. It's a page right out of pre-Depression economic theory. Since the early 1980s, when massive deficits became the norm, budget balancing has become a self-destructive rallying cry of the Democratic Party. By contrast, some Republicans, like Thompson, will give up savings for lower taxes and an ever lower ceiling on government spending, thereby "starving the beast." Surveys find that Americans who identify as Democrats are more concerned with the size of the federal deficits than are Republicans, a reversal from two decades ago. But the best way to raise savings is by growing incomes.

Public investment is not as important as a balanced budget. Republicans in general are distrustful of public investment. But when it comes to choosing between a budget deficit and investment in infrastructure, early education systems or basic research, most Democrats choose a balanced budget. This has left the nation bereft of the most critical foundation for the economic future.

Do Democrats really believe America can succeed in the coming century without high-quality, universal early education? Do they believe the nation will be satisfied with a rate of college attendance that is now exceeded in other rich nations? Do they believe we can get by with roads and bridges that professionals grade a C or D?

Some proponents of the savings model still believe the Clinton boom was proof that it worked. The tax hikes of 1993, they argue, cut deficits and increased savings. In fact, the Clinton boom was led by government stimulus of demand, a good old Keynesian tactic. Other factors, of course, also contributed, including the remarkable fall in computer-chip prices and the rise of a new crop of innovative mass-market corporate giants. But government stimulus was supplied by the Federal Reserve under Alan Greenspan, who kept interest rates low in the late 1990s, in part to calm the fragile financial markets during the international crises of 1997 and '98. In addition, consumers and businesses spent lavishly, supported by borrowing against the rising value of stocks and their homes.

This can't last. Building a nation on credit rather than higher wages has led to record levels of debt, compared with income; dependence on a high dollar to attract foreign capital (thereby undermining manufacturing at home); and the current subprime mortgage crisis. And families can't work many more hours than they do now.

Policy-makers need a better way to think about the economy, and there is one. It is a model grounded in history and based on what economists call demand-led growth theory. It partly harks back to John Maynard Keynes, who during the Great Depression argued that inadequate demand for goods and services is a primary cause of economic stagnation: When economies run at less than full employment of their capacities, it is because of a lack of buying power. Raising savings can, in fact, lead to stagnation because it reduces purchase of goods or services. Keynes argued that even if the government runs at a deficit, it is imperative to stimulate buying power.

Another argument for maintaining buying power is that increases in demand do not merely help to fully use otherwise underused resources; they can also increase an economy's productivity in just the way Adam Smith suggested. High demand enhances productivity by making it possible to exploit economies of scale. The division of labor can result in lower costs by producing more volume, but this is only worthwhile if you can sell many more products.

Contemporary demand-theory economists in Europe, Britain and the United States have added new wrinkles: growing output stimulates more investment, and more investment creates new ideas and other spillover consequences that can induce still greater investment. The increased production and investment also results in "learning by doing," another important source of increased productivity: you learn more about how to produce efficiently, in other words, as you do more producing.

This way of thinking about economic policy has broad consequences. It means higher wages are not just a cost of business; they are exactly what Henry Ford talked about when he justified paying workers up to $5 a day, well more than the going rate. He had to be sure someone could buy his cars. Demand-led theory points out that if wages rise, they can stimulate productivity, reducing pressure on business to raise prices. Given this dynamic, Federal Reserve policy can take greater risks of higher short-term inflation. Today's seemingly low unemployment rate, as unlikely as it may appear, can be pushed still lower.

Such a theory means that federal policies to promote higher wages have an additional justification: economic growth. Higher minimum wages, support of living wages and laws more favorable to unionized labor may actually improve productivity and benefit us all rather than being a cost to society.

When one also considers the potential social and fiscal returns from public investment, the Democratic determination to balance the budget makes no sense. There is overwhelming evidence that the benefits of public investment in some cases generate enough additional income and cost savings that the resulting revenues cover most of, or even more than, the initial cost. The most promising are studies of early education programs that have made their participants better workers, better citizens and probably more fulfilled people. An important new model developed by William Dickens and Charles Baschnagel at the Brookings Institution assesses the fiscal returns that will be produced by a high-quality universal early education program. Over time, the cautious researchers find, the returns in higher government taxes and reduced welfare expenditures will more than pay for the programs.

The Congressional Budget Office should similarly score the potential returns of public investment in transportation, energy conservation and research projects. It typically regards such outlays as costs with no future tax benefits. Thus, a $100 billion expenditure may in fact be only $50 billion over time, as tax returns rise because of an improved economy. In some cases, that $100 billion outlay may be wiped away entirely.

Healthcare reform fits into this category. A new, efficient healthcare system, many claim, will pay for itself over time through reduced administrative expense and healthier people who require less expensive care. Still, even in the best of circumstances, there will be substantial initial outlays. With the support of demand-led theory, Democrats can tolerate such deficits in the short run. Without it, serious healthcare reform, despite the encouraging proposals of some Democratic presidential candidates, will remain a pipe dream.

There are two final components of this approach to economic policy. The first has to do with globalization. The objective of trade pacts should not be to protect American workers per se but to bring to the rest of the world the progressive revolution in living standards that U.S. factory workers started to enjoy a century ago. Higher minimum wages, protection against labor abuses, adequate healthcare and a decent environment will help develop domestic markets in these nations, which will in turn stimulate their productivity growth and make them less dependent on exporting to the United States. Meanwhile, Americans will compete on a more level playing field and find export markets for their goods.

The other final component is the re-regulation of finance. Our financial system now operates under a set of domestic incentives that strongly favor short-term profits, from which CEOs personally benefit. Some in Congress, notably Representative Barney Frank, are taking up this cause. Addressing these issues should be an integral part of a new economic model, including requirements for more transparent reporting (including on hedge funds and other private investment vehicles), greater shareholder power and more restrictions on how executives are compensated. The system also favors debt. Closer oversight of credit standards is required.

Similarly, the international flow of hot capital has upended theories about the system of floating exchange rates. The fact that America's dollar stays high despite a huge trade deficit is not self-correcting. As Robert Wade of the London School of Economics argues, some intelligent combination of semi-pegged currencies and capital-flow restraint would go miles toward rebalancing the international economy.

The mainstream Democratic model is at best outdated; at worst, it never worked. Wages can surely rise too rapidly and contribute to destabilizing inflation, as occurred in the 1970s. Inflation can be embedded in the expectations of labor and consumers, making it intractable. Very high inflation will distort the economy. Budget deficits can be too high. But we are a long way from such an economy. Policy-makers are fighting the last war. The wage share of the nation's income has fallen sharply since rising in the late 1990s. Inflation is at rock bottom and inflationary expectations are weak. Labor unions, which in the 1970s helped push wages high, are now too weak to bargain for a fair share. The budget deficit is low.

And so are taxes, for that matter. No economist has ever made a defensible case that high taxes impede economic growth in the long run. Joel Slemrod of the University of Michigan methodically analyzed studies on high-tax and low-tax countries and found that tax rates did not affect growth. Nancy Stokey of the University of Chicago and Sergio Rebelo of Northwestern University note that the long rise in the income tax since 1913 has "produced no noticeable effect on the average growth rate of the economy."

Let's also keep in mind that until twenty-five years ago America generally paid the highest wages in the world. Government was often an equal if sometimes too reluctant partner in the economy. In a time of wide-eyed confidence in the power of private enterprise, whose dynamic energies are vital and will remain remarkable, Americans should remember that government guaranteed access to land in early America, built canals, established free primary schools and later high schools, started agricultural universities, subsidized railroads, sanitized cities, protected workers, established a central bank, built highways and generously helped the elderly.

When America has been at its best, it has been willing to experiment rather than retreat. Current mainstream thinking has ushered in a self-defeating age of limits. It will take both government and business to break the yoke that unnecessarily burdens us.

Ending Plutocracy:
A 12-Step Program

SARAH ANDERSON AND SAM PIZZIGATI

June 30, 2008

AMERICA's FIRST Gilded Age didn't merely end. Progressives had to fight to end it. Our forebears did battle, decade after decade, for proposals that dared to "soak the rich."

How quaint that phrase now seems. Progressives today do talk about making the superrich pay their "fair tax share," but we no longer dare imagine an America without the superrich.

We have become addicted to a politics that ignores the power of the fabulously wealthy to define—and distort—our nation's political agenda.

How can we end this addiction? In the 12-step spirit of dependency-busters everywhere, we offer a dozen policy approaches that can help slice America's superwealthy down to democratic size. To help us rebuild our plutocracy-busting self-confidence, we begin with the somewhat more winnable.

Step 1. Admit we are powerless unless we learn more about how concentrated our nation's wealth has become.

In 1907 Joseph Pulitzer ended his publishing career with a farewell that urged readers to forever beware "predatory plutocracy." He had started that career, years earlier, exposing wealthy tax dodgers. Disclosure has been a prime weapon in the progressive arsenal ever since.

- Require government contractors to reveal how much their executives make. The Securities and Exchange Commission requires publicly traded companies to reveal how much their top five executives are making. But privately held companies face no such mandate, and the CEO of private security giant Blackwater last fall refused to divulge how much he has pocketed from his company's contracts in Iraq. A bill now before Congress, the Government Contractor Accountability Act, would force companies like Blackwater to disclose their top executive pay.
- Require corporations to report CEO-worker pay gaps. CEOs now take in, as a share of corporate earnings, twice

as much as they walked off with just a decade ago. The labor share of national income, meanwhile, has shrunk to record lows. Which companies are shoving the most cash up the corporate flowchart? If corporations were required to document annually the gap between their highest- and lowest-paid employees, we would know.

- Require the superrich to make their tax returns public. In 1934 early New Dealers enacted legislation that made the incomes of wealthy people—and the taxes they pay—a matter of public record. But the superrich quickly launched a fervid PR campaign that attacked the statute as an open invitation to kidnappers. In an America still reeling from the infamous Lindbergh baby snatching, that claim gave lawmakers a convenient cover for repealing this tax sunshine mandate. In 2005 America's top-earning 400 paid a paltry 18.2 percent of their income in federal tax. It's time to let the sunshine back in.

Step 2. Trust in a power greater than CEOs and their buddies. The top one-hundredth of 1 percent of America's taxpayers have seen their collective income quadruple, after inflation, over the past two decades. Corporate executives account for about a fifth of that income. How have CEOs engineered their awesome take-homes? They essentially pay themselves. They sit on one another's corporate boards and rubber-stamp executive pay plans that come from consultants who know where their bread is buttered. Democratizing corporate governance could help end this enabling.

- Give shareholders a "say on pay." The House of Representatives voted last year to give shareholders the right to vote on executive compensation. But these votes would be advisory only, and such nonbinding votes—in Britain, for instance—haven't done much to break executive pay spirals. Still, the prospect of shareholder no votes could dampen the willingness of corporate boards to keep signing blank checks. The Senate has so far stalled on "say on pay."

- End Kremlin-style corporate board elections. To really rein in CEO pay, shareholders need more than an advisory say on pay. They need a say on who sits on corporate boards. Corporate board elections currently sport all the democratic trimmings of Leonid Brezhnev's Supreme Soviet, complete with fixed slates. In 2003 the SEC proposed giving shareholders a halfway meaningful right to vote for alternative candidates. But fierce opposition from the Business Roundtable, the nation's leading CEO club, nyeted this attempt at corporate perestroika.

- Give all stakeholders a real corporate voice. Shareholders, suitably empowered, could help check executive excess. But workers and their communities have just as much stake in CEO pay decisions as shareholders—because over-the-top pay plans give CEOs an incentive to pump up short-term bottom lines at the expense of long-haul enterprise success. Mandating worker and community representation on corporate boards could institutionalize a voice for all corporate stakeholders.

Step 3. Don't let the tax code enable executive excess.
Corporate boards don't deserve all the blame for excessive executive compensation. Lawmakers have been enablers, too. They've littered the tax code with provisions that encourage outsized rewards at the top of the corporate ladder. Progressives ought to be launching an "anti-littering" campaign.

- Eliminate stock-option accounting sleight-of-hand. Corporations can legally claim tax deductions for executive stock options that run up to ten times higher than the cost of these options that corporations record in their annual financial statements. In 2005, just-released IRS figures show, the gap between what executive options cost corporations and what corporations deducted from their taxes for these options hit $61 billion. Senator Carl Levin has introduced legislation that would shut this loophole and raise billions annually in new tax revenue.

- End bankruptcy bonanzas. In 2005 Congress banned companies in bankruptcy proceedings from giving executives retention and severance bonuses that run over ten times the bonus that workers receive. But the law doesn't limit "performance-based" bonuses, and corporations are sailing through this loophole. Calpine, a California energy company, exited bankruptcy last winter with a workforce cut by nearly a third. The company's CEO exited with a $10.9 million bonus.

- Cap tax-free "deferred pay." Of Fortune's top 1,000 U.S. companies, 90 percent have set up deferred-pay accounts to let top executives shield unlimited amounts of compensation from taxes. Target CEO Robert Ulrich, for example, held $133.5 million in his deferred-pay account at the end of 2006. By contrast, the cubicle crowd faces strict limits on how much income can be deferred via 401(k) plans— $15,500 is the max for most workers. Corporate lobbyists last year squashed a Senate effort that would have placed a modest $1 million cap on executive pay deferrals.

Step 4. Insist on a searching IRS inventory of super-wealthy wallets.

Today's IRS agents, OMB Watch reported earlier this year, are actually spending more time auditing poor taxpayers than rich ones. Progressives ought to be demanding an IRS that zeroes in on the awesomely affluent.

- Shut down offshore income hideaways. A University of Michigan study estimates that the superrich are dodging as much as $50 billion per year in federal taxes by stashing income overseas. Arbitrary time limits on IRS investigations help make recovering these lost billions next to impossible.
- End charitable giveaway scams. Wealthy Americans are routinely overvaluing the artwork they donate to museums—and the IRS remains too understaffed to stop them. America's rich, overall, claim about $1 billion a year in tax write-offs for donated artwork. Let's stop subsidizing art museum vanity wings.
- Put the kibosh on wealth warehousing at elite alma maters. Superrich alums are saving beaucoup bucks in taxes by pouring enormous wealth into elite private

universities. Harvard's endowment last year hit $34.6 billion—at a time when public colleges are cutting programs and hiking tuitions. Elite endowments pay a mere 2 percent excise tax on their investment earnings. They should pay at twice that rate—and even higher if they don't spend, on education, at least 5 percent of their endowment value a year.

Step 5. Clamp down on hedge-fund kingpins.
Last year fifty hedge-fund managers took home more than $210 million each. Perhaps even more amazing: hedge-fund office receptionists pay more of their incomes in taxes than their bosses. How is that possible? A good bit of hedge-fund-manager income comes as a cut of the profits the funds generate. Our financial royals can claim this cut as a capital gain, a neat maneuver that chops their tax rate from 35 to 15 percent. Last year an attempt to shut this hedge- and private-equity-fund loophole died in the Senate.

Step 6. Make amends to those who truly earn their income.
We could skip Step 5 if we simply taxed "earned income"—the money people make from actual labor—at the same rate as the "unearned income" that comes from sitting back and letting money do all the heavy lifting. America's richest regularly realize vast amounts of this unearned income, mostly through dividends and capital gains from trading stocks, bonds and other forms of property. On these unearned billions, they pay taxes at a 15 percent rate, less than half the 35 percent top rate on ordinary earned income.

Step 7. Treat outsized pay as a defect of corporate character.
Our tax law lets corporations claim reasonable business expenses as tax deductions. But what's reasonable? Corporations can deduct as "reasonable" whatever they shell out in excessive executive pay, so long as they label that excess a reward for "performance." Representative Barbara Lee's Income Equity Act, a bill introduced last year, would cap the executive pay that corporations can deduct at twenty-five times the pay of a company's lowest-paid workers. State senators Paul Pinsky and Richard Madaleno have introduced similar legislation in Maryland.

Step 8. Awake to the simplicity of tax surcharges.
Debating the ins and outs of the tax code can take time. In the past, progressives used a shortcut to hike taxes on the financially fortunate: the surcharge, a simple add-on to the tax owed under existing law. Last year Representative Charlie Rangel proposed a 4 percent surtax on couples' income over $200,000 and a 4.6 percent surcharge on income over $500,000, hikes that would raise $832 billion over ten years. Commentator Nicholas von Hoffman has urged a somewhat edgier surcharge, a special "Victory Over Terror" levy that would subject incomes over $5 million to a 20 percent extra charge that would expire only "when the war on terror is won or declared over."

Step 9. Seek a more progressive reckoning with the dearly departed.
In 2001 the first Bush tax cut included a phaseout of the estate tax, our nation's only levy on inherited wealth. But after 2010, unless Congress acts, the estate tax on America's largest be-

quests will revert to pre-W levels. Estate tax foes, to prevent that, want estate tax rates slashed to mere nuisance status. If they succeed, the last three decades of excess in corporate America will turn into a skyscraper-high foundation for a new aristocracy that would have the wealth—and power—to frustrate progressive social change for generations to come. Representative Jim McDermott has a better idea. He's promoting legislation that would place a 55 percent estate tax on fortunes greater than $10 million.

Step 10. Restore sanity to the taxation of wealth.

Typical American families have little net worth outside the value of their homes. The superwealthy, even those with multiple mansions, hold the vast bulk of their wealth in financial investments. Normal property taxes leave this financial wealth untaxed. The result: average Americans pay a tax on their wealth; rich Americans don't. About a dozen European nations sidestep this double standard by levying a small annual tax on all wealth holdings. In the United States, economist Edward Wolff has calculated, a wealth tax that exempted the first $250,000 of household wealth, then imposed a graduated rate that topped off at 0.8 percent on fortunes over $5 million, would raise about $60 billion a year.

Step 11. Leverage the power of the public purse.

Our tax dollars, by law, do not go to companies that increase racial or gender inequality. We deny government contracts to firms that discriminate, in their employment practices, by race or gender. So why should we let our tax dollars go to firms that increase economic inequality? Hundreds of billions of taxpayer dollars are flowing annually to companies that pay their CEOs more for a day's work than their workers make in a year.

One antidote: we could deny federal contracts or subsidies to companies that pay their top executives more than twenty-five times what their lowest-paid workers receive. One bill pending in Congress, the Patriot Corporations of America Act, steps in this direction. The bill would extend tax breaks and federal contracting preferences to companies that meet benchmarks for good corporate behavior. Among the benchmarks: not compensating any executive at more than "10,000 percent"—100 times—the income of the company's lowest-paid full-timer.

Step 12. Admit to ourselves that maybe Ike had it right.

In Eisenhower's America income over $400,000—the equivalent of less than $3 million today—faced a top marginal tax rate of 91 percent. Our current top rate: 35 percent. In 2004, after exploiting loopholes, taxpayers who took home more than $5 million paid an average 21.9 percent of their incomes in federal tax. In 1954 the federal tax bite on taxpayers with comparable incomes averaged 54.5 percent.

How much revenue could be raised by a significant tax hike on America's highest incomes? If the top rate was raised to 50 percent on all income between $5 million and $10 million and 70 percent on income above $10 million, federal revenues would jump $105 billion—and the nation's richest 0.1 percent would still be paying less in taxes than they did under Ike.

A century ago, progressives never actually agreed on any one set of proposals to end rule by the rich. They vigorously—and constantly—debated competing proposals. That debate needs restarting. We hope this list helps.

We also need to recognize that blueprints for social change don't go anywhere without social changers, without organized pressure from below. In America's first great triumph over plutocracy, that pressure came mainly from a resurgent labor movement. To repeat that success, labor once again needs to be surging, one big reason initiatives that aim to help unions organize—like the Employee Free Choice Act campaign—have a key role to play in any plutocracy-busting offensive.

Can such an offensive succeed? Why not? Our forebears faced a plutocracy more entrenched than ours. They beat that plutocracy back. Our turn.

Trust but Verify

JAMES K. GALBRAITH AND
WILLIAM K. BLACK
October 13, 2008

"THESE ARE THE DAYS of miracles and wonders." The market has collapsed! Only the government can save us now! Thirty years of cant have evaporated. Suddenly, we're all in it together—Henry Paulson and Ben Bernanke in the lead, Congress pulling like postpartisan galley slaves, George W. Bush lying low and looking, no doubt fervently, for the exits.

Something must be done—but on what terms? Treasury proposes to spend $700 billion to buy mortgage-backed securities, accountable to no one. Paulson asks for trust. But has he earned it? Remember, he started out in office gutting the Sarbanes-Oxley Act; he tried to cripple the SEC and recently relied on Morgan Stanley—not a disinterested party—for advice on the nationalization of Fannie Mae and Freddie Mac. Therefore "trust but verify," as Ronald Reagan would (and did) say.

Congress must impose conditions to protect the public, the national interest and, not least, the interests of the next administration. Herewith a short list:

1. Disclosure clause. Treasury should have immediate and complete access to information about portfolios, counterparties, the internal valuation methods used by financial firms, their proprietary models and the history of adjustments made to those models to recognize or conceal losses as the crisis unfolded.

2. Pricing clause. Treasury should establish a transparent mechanism to establish a before-the-bailout fair market value for mortgage-backed securities, set limits on the premium paid over that value and require that financial institutions value their full portfolios at the sale price. In other words, concealment of losses— "accounting forbearance"—should be prohibited.

3. Fraud clause. Securities purchased should be reviewed, and those found to be based on fraudulent appraisals, inadequate documentation, or predatory and other abusive practices should be kicked back to the lenders at a penalty rate.

4. Enforcement clause. Treasury should be required to establish a framework for investigations and criminal referrals and to prove that it is in aggressive use. Participating firms should be required to investigate and document past frauds, establish internal anti-fraud controls and make criminal referrals as necessary. The FBI and assistant U.S. Attorneys should get "blank check" authorization to pursue the crimes behind this debacle.

5. Arbitrage clause. One big danger of Paulson's plan is that non-U.S. institutions, hedge funds and others will seize the chance to sell their bad holdings to eligible U.S. institutions, replenishing the swamp just as the Treasury seeks to drain it. All U.S. financial institutions should be required to provide baseline information on their mortgage-backed securities and other eligible holdings as of September 15.

6. Transparency clause. Treasury operations under this plan, including communications and consultation with outside advisers, should be transparent to Congress, which should get whatever information it wants, at regular intervals. No exceptions.

7. Crony clause. This program must be run by people who are free of conflicts of interest. To ensure this the Treasury should require full financial disclosure for anyone hired to administer the program, and impose rules to enforce a strict conflict code. Special note to Congress: John McCain personifies the crony system. Do not pass a bill that would give him, as president, unfettered control over how this program is run.

8. Modification and disposal clause. As foreclosures mount, Treasury will end up with physical properties, which degrade rapidly if not sold or rented and occupied. To prevent this, an agency should be established to rapidly modify mortgage contracts; manage rental conversions; and lease, sell or demolish vacated homes. The agency can be run as draft boards were in wartime, by citizens in each community under federal guidelines.

Is this all? No, it's only a start. Other measures must follow, including regulatory reform, mortgage relief, revenue sharing to protect state and local public spending as property tax revenues tank, support for public capital investment and job creation. But this is the agenda for the next administration.

Getting to that next administration is the job for the American people.

King George and Comrade Paulson

RALPH NADER

October 13, 2008

MANY YEARS AGO my father asked his children in a dinner-table conversation, "Why will capitalism always survive?" His answer: "Because socialism will always be used to save it."

The cause of the financial markets meltdown is simple: powerful greed fanned by fraud and reckless risk transfers. Wall Street wanted something for nothing. This fairy tale was written by an army of Wall Street lobbyists who tore down regulations and safeguards meant to protect savers and shareholders.

The financial black belts who made billions from this Ponzi scheme deserve the brunt of law enforcement. But deregulation meant there was very little law, much less enforcement. Instead, the socialist superman has swept down to New York City from Washington to bail out casino capitalism on Wall Street, which is spewing forth ever more kryptonite.

Every time Congress has acted in haste, it has led to a boondoggle, from the $3 billion synthetic fuels legislation of 1980 to the Iraq War resolution of 2002. Without public hearings, without safeguards, accountability and Congressional oversight, without comprehensive regulation and shareholder governance, King George and Comrade Paulson's $700 billion blank check of cash for trash will be the goliath of domestic panic legislation.

Slow down, Hank!

- Taxpayers must get prudent participation for taking the risk of bailing out Wall Street (the bill for which is edging up to $1.6 trillion), ideally in the form of stock warrants.
- Homeowners and neighborhoods must be protected by passing a law with a sunset clause allowing below-median-value homeowners facing foreclosure the right to rent-to-own their homes at fair-market-value rates.
- Conflicts of interest must be reduced by taking away the power of auditor and credit-rating-agency selection from companies and placing it in the hands of the Securities and Exchange Commission, to be administered on random assignment.
- Accountability must be restored to financial markets by introducing covered bonds for the majority of mortgage products as they do in Western Europe, which prevents originators of mortgages from passing the buck.

- And before the taxpayer gambles on bailing out Wall Street, we need to implement restraints on Wall Street's dangerous habit of gambling with other people's money. This should start with a securities-speculation tax and effective margin requirements to refocus the financial markets on their proper function.

A Big Government Bailout

HOWARD ZINN
October 27, 2008

IT IS SAD TO SEE both major parties agree to spend $700 billion of taxpayer money to bail out huge financial institutions that are notable for two characteristics: incompetence and greed. There is a much better solution to the financial crisis. But it would require discarding what has been conventional wisdom for too long: that government intervention in the economy ("big government") must be avoided like the plague, because the "free market" can be depended on to guide the economy toward growth and justice. Surely the sight of Wall Street begging for government aid is almost comic in light of its long devotion to a "free market" unregulated by government.

Let's face a historical truth: we have never had a free market. We have always had government intervention in the economy, and indeed that intervention has been welcomed by the captains of finance and industry. These titans of wealth hypocritically warned against "big government" but only when government threatened to regulate their activities or when it contemplated passing some of the nation's wealth on to the neediest people. They had no quarrel with big government when it served their needs.

It started way back when the founding fathers met in Philadelphia in 1787 to draft the Constitution. The year before, they had seen armed rebellions of farmers in western Massachusetts (Shays's Rebellion), where farms were being seized for nonpayment of taxes. Thousands of farmers surrounded the courthouses and refused to allow their farms to be auctioned off. The founders' correspondence at this time makes clear their worries about such uprisings getting out of hand. General Henry Knox wrote to George Washington, warning that the ordinary soldier who fought in the Revolution thought that by contributing to the defeat of England he deserved an equal share of the wealth of the country, that "the property of the United States ... ought to be the common property of all."

In framing the Constitution, the founders created "big government" powerful enough to put down the rebellions of farmers, to return escaped slaves to their masters and to put down Indian resistance when settlers moved westward. The first big bailout was the decision of the new government to redeem for full value the almost worthless bonds held by speculators.

From the start, in the first sessions of the first Congress, the government interfered with the free market by establishing tariffs to subsidize manufacturers and by becoming a partner with private banks in establishing a national bank. This role of big government supporting the interests of the business classes has continued all through the nation's history. Thus, in the nineteenth century the government subsidized canals and the merchant marine. In the decades before and during the Civil War, the government gave away some 100 million acres of land to the railroads, along with considerable loans to keep the railroad interests in business. The 10,000 Chinese and 3,000 Irish who worked on the transcontinental railroad got no free land and no loans, only long hours, little pay, accidents and sickness.

The principle of government helping big business and refusing government largesse to the poor was bipartisan, upheld by Republicans and Democrats. President Grover Cleveland, a Democrat, vetoed a bill to give $10,000 to Texas farmers to help them buy seed grain during a drought, saying, "Federal aid in such cases encourages the expectation of paternal care on the part of the government and weakens the sturdiness of our national character." But that same year, he used the gold surplus to pay wealthy bondholders $28 above the value of each bond—a gift of $5 million.

Cleveland was enunciating the principle of rugged individualism—that we must make our fortunes on our own, without help from the government. In his 1931 *Harper's* essay "The Myth of Rugged American Individualism," historian Charles Beard carefully cataloged fifteen instances of the government intervening in the economy for the benefit of big business. Beard wrote, "For forty years or more there has not been a President, Republican or Democrat, who has not talked against government interference and then supported measures adding more interference to the huge collection already accumulated."

After World War II the aircraft industry had to be saved by infusions of government money. Then came the oil depletion allowances for the oil companies and the huge bailout for the Chrysler Corporation. In the 1980s the government bailed out the savings and loan industry with hundreds of billions of dollars, and the Cato Institute reports that in 2006 needy corporations like Boeing, Xerox, Motorola, Dow Chemical and General Electric received $92 billion in corporate welfare.

A simple and powerful alternative would be to take that huge sum of money, $700 billion, and give it directly to the people who need it. Let the government declare a moratorium on foreclosures and help homeowners pay off their mortgages. Create a federal jobs program to guarantee work to people who want and need jobs.

We have a historic and successful precedent. The government in the early days of the New Deal put millions of people to work rebuilding the nation's infrastructure. Hundreds of thousands of young people, instead of joining the army to escape poverty, joined the Civil Conservation Corps, which built bridges and highways and cleaned up harbors and rivers. Thousands of artists, musicians and writers were employed by the WPA's arts programs to paint murals, produce plays, write symphonies. The New Deal (defying the cries of "socialism") established Social Security, which, along with the GI Bill, became a model for what government could do to help its people.

That can be carried further, with "health security"—free healthcare for all, administered by the government, paid for from our Treasury, bypassing the insurance companies and the other privateers of the health industry. All that will take more than $700 billion. But the money is there: in the $600 billion for the military budget, once we decide we will not be a war-making nation anymore, and in the bloated bank accounts of the superrich, once we bring them down to ordinary-rich size by taxing vigorously their income and their wealth.

When the cry goes up, whether from Republicans or Democrats, that this must not be done because it is "big government," the citizens should just laugh. And then agitate and organize on behalf of what the Declaration of Independence promised: that it is the responsibility of government to ensure the equal right of all to "Life, Liberty, and the pursuit of Happiness."

This is a golden opportunity for Obama to distance himself cleanly from McCain as well as the fossilized Democratic Party leaders, giving life to his slogan of change and thereby sweeping into office. And if he doesn't act, it will be up to the people, as it always has been, to raise a shout that will be heard around the world—and compel the politicians to listen.

Water the Roots

REV. JESSE L. JACKSON

September 24, 2008

WITH BILLIONS OF taxpayer dollars being used to bail out banks and big corporations, the public must focus on the question, What do the people get from the investment of our tax money into these bailouts? They must be included in the benefits. Two-thirds of U.S. economic activity is driven by consumers. When working Americans suffer, everyone suffers.

How did we get here? Borrowers were steered into predatory mortgage loans with grossly escalating interest rates that they could not afford. They still can't. The pain of homeowners has now spread throughout the economy.

We must challenge plans that bail out the rich, put out the poor and put down the middle class. We can't just bail out Wall Street and ignore Main Street. The bailout must be bottom up, not just top down. The poor—the unemployed poor, the working poor and the fixed-income poor—must benefit from the investment of their tax dollars. Any "solution" or remedy must be judged by how it affects "the least of these."

The oversight committees and the overseers must come off the payroll of Wall Street. They cannot eat from the same trough and retain any credibility as regulators. If the owners pay the referees and umpires, the integrity of the game will be corrupted, leaving all outcomes suspect.

We must freeze multimillion-dollar golden parachute retirement payouts to fired executives who "led" their companies down a failed road. There must be a cap on executive pay and compensation.

We must freeze foreclosures and restructure and modify the loans; we must protect the home equity of people defrauded and victimized by the subprime lending schemes.

Urban policy must be included in the bailout: we must reinvest in America and put Americans back to work. If billions of taxpayer dollars can go to bail out the banks, funds must also go to build new infrastructure, schools and roads as well as to incentives to stop plant closures. Investment must be made to provide healthcare for all Americans. In this way, we not only do the right thing; we do the smart thing to create lasting economic growth.

In these economic times, we must invest in job creation—green jobs and public works jobs. We must water and feed the roots. Confidence cannot be restored from the top. When big banks lend to businesses while consumers remain doubtful and afraid to spend, businesses can't sell and businesses can't repay.

America Needs a New New Deal

KATRINA VANDEN HEUVEL AND
ERIC SCHLOSSER

September 27, 2008

THE BUSH ADMINISTRATION has proposed the most expensive government spending plan in American history, allocating as much as $700 billion to a Wall Street bailout. The proposal was attacked by members of both parties, who immediately began negotiations to find an alternative. The Bush plan was not only a political blunder; it was also a complete repudiation of the administration's own economic policies. It could not be justified by any of the core beliefs governing free enterprise and the free market.

As with the decision to invade Iraq, the administration sought to commit the federal government to massive spending without a clear exit strategy. Most important, it drew upon the New Deal's legacy of government intervention in the marketplace—without any of the New Deal's fundamental concern for the well-being of ordinary Americans.

This year happens to be the 75th anniversary of the New Deal, a revolution in governmental philosophy that began with the Emergency Banking Act of 1933. That first piece of New Deal legislation was a hurried response to the worst banking crisis in U.S. history—until now.

President Franklin Delano Roosevelt outlined the problem clearly in his first fireside chat, a week after taking office. "We had a bad banking situation," Roosevelt said. "Some of our bankers had shown themselves either incompetent or dishonest in the handling of people's funds. They had used the money entrusted to them in speculations and unwise loans. ... It was the government's job to straighten out this situation and do it as quickly as possible."

President Roosevelt's banking plan ended the panic. But it did much more than that. In Roosevelt's words, it "reorganized, simplified, and made more fair and just our monetary system."

Compare those aims and that achievement with what the Bush administration proposed. Having championed the free market, small government and deregulation for years, the administration asked taxpayers to assume the costs of Wall Street's poor investments—while allowing Wall Street to hold on to the good ones.

The size and scale of the Bush administration's proposal are mind-boggling. During the New Deal, the Roosevelt administration spent about $250 billion (in today's dollars) on public-works projects, building about 8,000 parks, 40,000 public buildings, 72,000 schools and 80,000 bridges. The entire cost of all the New Deal programs (in today's dollars) was about $500 billion. The secretary of the Treasury now wants to spend perhaps twice that amount, simply to prevent a financial collapse.

Of course, something must be done—and quickly. "Government intervention is not only warranted," President George W. Bush said last week. "It is essential." With those nine words, he contradicted the governing philosophy of the Republican Party for the past thirty years.

According to President Roosevelt, the New Deal had three fundamental aims: relief, reform and reconstruction. On Wednesday night, President Bush described his far more expensive but far less inclusive spending plan as merely a "rescue effort." Mr. Bush's proposal—to hand over $700 billion to Wall Street banks without any Congressional oversight, without any means to prevent conflicts of interest, and without any measures to help ordinary Americans—was disgraceful.

What we really need is a new New Deal: a systematic approach to the financial and economic problems of the United States.

Firstly, we need relief for ordinary Americans. At the moment, four million households are behind on their mortgage payments and facing foreclosure. Some estimates suggest that an additional two million may face eviction next year.

On Wednesday in the *Wall Street Journal*, Senator Hillary Clinton called for a revival of the Home Owner's Loan Corporation (HOLC). Organized in the early months of the New Deal, the HOLC avoided widespread foreclosures by purchasing troubled mortgages from banks and then reissuing them with more favorable terms. It proved a tremendous success—for homeowners, taxpayers and banks.

A new HOLC should be created immediately, and with the power to keep people in their homes.

As winter approaches, millions of families will need help keeping those homes warm. During the past year, the cost of heating oil has increased about 30 percent. Meanwhile, the Bush administration is now trying to cut funding for the Low Income Energy Assistance Program. Instead of cutting, the federal government should more than double the current budget of $2.6 billion. That is awfully small change on Wall Street these days.

Second, we need reform. In recent years, one federal regulatory agency after another has been handed over to the industries they were created to regulate. It should come as no surprise that during the Bush administration the United States has witnessed the largest recall of contaminated beef in its history, thousands of deaths from unsafe prescription drugs, and one of our worst financial meltdowns.

Advocates of the free market must confront the fact that both the Great Depression and the current financial chaos were preceded by years of laissez-faire economic policies. Strictly enforced regulations not only protect consumers, they protect companies that behave ethically from those that don't. The sale of tainted baby food in China demonstrates, once again, that when industries are allowed to police themselves, there's absolutely no limit on what they'll do for money.

Third, we need reconstruction, not only of America's physical infrastructure, but also of its society. Today close to 50 million Americans lack health insurance. About 40 percent of the nation's adult population is facing medical debts or having difficulty paying medical bills. A universal healthcare system would help American families, while cutting the nation's long-term healthcare costs. And a large-scale federal investment in renewable energy and public-works projects would build the foundation for a strong 21st century economy.

Contrary to the myth of the free market, direct government intervention has played a central role throughout American economic history, subsidizing the growth of the railroad, automobile, aerospace and computer industries, among others. It will take well-planned government investment to break our dependence on foreign oil and create millions of new Green jobs.

The events of the past month have proven, beyond any doubt, that the federal government must actively address America's great social and economic problems. That necessity was recognized by Franklin Delano Roosevelt during the 1930s—and by his cousin, President Theodore Roosevelt, a generation earlier.

The opposing view, promoted by President Bush until recently, is now as bankrupt as one of our leading investment banks. A Wall Street bailout plan that relies upon the mechanisms of the New Deal, while betraying its underlying spirit, should be rejected. Federal relief should not be aimed at the top and somehow expected to trickle down.

A new New Deal wouldn't require another alphabet soup of federal agencies, micromanaging every aspect of the economy. It would simply ensure that federal spending is driven by the needs of every American. Anything less than this—any proposal that rewards those who created the problem and penalizes those who can least afford it—is a raw deal.

What Do We Want?
An Emergency Town Hall

FEATURING WILLIAM GREIDER,
FRANCIS FOX PIVEN, DOUG HENWOOD,
ARUN GUPTA & NAOMI KLEIN

MODERATED BY CHRISTOPHER HAYES

October 10, 2008

FOR THE U.S. FINANCIAL MARKETS, October 2008 was the cruelest month. Despite a $700 billion bailout passed by the U.S. Congress at the urging of U.S. Treasury Secretary Henry Paulson, stocks suffered their greatest losses since 1987. The earthquake on Wall Street sent tremors through the "real economy," as credit markets froze up and consumers, watching their 401Ks evaporate and property values plummet, were gripped with fear. The fear was all the worse because it was laced with confusion: Why hadn't federal regulators reined in this risky speculation? How could this have been allowed to happen? What should be done now?

On the left, the tumult inspired fear and confusion as well, but also a sense of new possibilities. On October 10, 2008, *The Nation* convened an emergency town hall in response to the crisis at the Brecht Forum in New York City. The panel of leading progressive intellectuals and activists debated the complex roots of the meltdown and put forward a range of bold, radical solutions. Moderated by *Nation* Washington editor Christopher Hayes, the panel featured national correspondent William Greider, famed author of the classic book on the Fed, *Secrets of the Temple;* Frances Fox Piven, longtime poor people's activist and author of many books, including *The Breaking of the American Social Compact;* contributing editor Doug Henwood, author of *Wall Street;* Arun Gupta, activist and editor of the *Indypendent* newspaper; and columnist Naomi Klein, author of the bestseller, *The Shock Doctrine: The Rise of Disaster Capitalism.* Following is an edited transcript of their discussion.

Chris Hayes: There are a lot of technical questions about this crisis that I don't think we're going to be able to resolve tonight: what's a credit default swap and how does it work, for example. But the key two political questions a lot of us are asking are: how do we fit what is happening now into our political understanding, into our power analysis—what has led us to the moment we're in politically? And second is the old organizer question, which is, what are our demands—what do we want? When Hank Paulson and Ben Bernanke came to the Hill, it was clear what they wanted. It's clear what Morgan Stanley wanted. It's clear what a lot of people want out of what's going on now. And one question I think that all of us are trying to kind of parse through is what do we want, what do we want to happen.

Bill Greider: I've been standing on a street corner with a big placard for 20, 25 years like those bag ladies we all know, and the placard says "the end is nigh, repent." And it was cold and lonely out there for a number of years writing about the disorders of the Federal Reserve, and monetary policy, and the financial system, and the economy, and globalization and so forth and so on.

I did have a premonition that a reckoning was ahead. I wrote my book, *Come Home America, the Rise and Fall and Redeeming Promise of Our Country,* in the expectation that these forces bearing down on our country were going to reach a point where they had to be recognized because they were rolling us up, one way or another.

In that spirit, I'm not gloating, I'm feeling kind of sad for the country, frankly, because there were a lot of us in different ways trying to explain in our quiet little voices that this system was destabilized and headed for something awful. And as we all know, the media in America don't want to say that until the blood is in the streets, and so that's where we are.

What excites me, and I hope excites all of you, is that we're in a very rare moment of history where a dynamic has taken hold that changes everything. That breaks all of the ideological barriers and practical political barriers and is a serious crisis for the nation and also the world. But it is also a liberating moment. You could see that for yourselves just watching the newspapers, 10 days ago, two weeks ago, when Brother Paulson put on the table his very arrogant proposal to bail out his colleagues in the Wall Street club, and perhaps a few others, and literally said, Take it or leave it: this is what we need to stop this crisis.

And Congress choked a little bit, but basically caved, particularly the Democratic party, without questioning for a moment whether it made any sense or whether it would work, or what the equities were. And they passed it on a Friday and on Monday the stock markets of the world just blew it away. And it was an extraordinary thing to see, because all of the editorials and the hand wringing invested in Paulson's genius suddenly just disappeared.

... Our perception should be this is a rare opening, the old order is crumbling. The politics right now is the fight of the old order represented not just by Wall Street, but other interests, to cling to their diminishing power. And up to now, they have been assisted and supported in that by both political parties and most so-called "responsibles," but that, too, is changing rapidly.

So you have to put aside the reflexive despair that people on the left usually experience, and look at it as a dynamic process that we can influence. And put big ideas, fundamental conceptions of American society and economy on the table as loudly as possible and to speak with confidence. There is a beginning of a consciousness in at least some of the politicians that they're in that situation and they don't know what to do about it, but they're stumbling around trying to get act two together. And this is the moment when we talk about the society we want to help create, in the most ambitious terms. I'm not being a pie-eyed optimist, I understand all the reasons why that may well fail, but this is a moment of history people rarely, rarely get, and we got it, and we should try to make the most of it.

Frances Fox Piven: Like Bill Greider, I think that there are a lot of unknowns, there are a lot of things I don't know, that we all don't know. We don't know how deep the financial crisis is, we don't know how much it will spread to what's called the real economy. We don't know whether the government interventions that presumably are designed to stabilize the financial markets or to jumpstart the financial markets will work, and we also don't know whether Wall Street is taking over government through those interventions or whether government is taking over Wall Street. We don't know whether it's merely another bailout—we've had quite a few, on this rollercoaster ride that we've been through as a result of the financialization of the American economy.

And we aren't quite clear about whether the government interventions, the bailouts, simply mean more redistribution of American wealth upward and more scapegoating of the poor for the crisis. For example, the Community Reinvestment Act is being blamed—mortgage lending to poor people is blamed for the collapse in the markets.

I don't want to talk about those things. I want to talk, rather, about the long-standing belief on the left that economic crisis, although it's terrible, it's tragic, also generates new political possibilities.

Whenever we say that or remember that, we're really thinking about the Great Depression. That's our model because the Great Depression generated a lot of economic insecurity and real hardship, but that was combined with a virtual total discrediting of the economic ruling class. Because the economy had failed, and when the economy failed, we finally got a candidate, FDR, who railed against the economic royalists in his speeches. It was just rhetoric at that stage, but we also got a Congress that hauled these people before Congressional committees and machine-gunned them with questions, and it had a huge impact on the political culture of the country.

For a moment, a big moment actually, maybe a 10-, 15-, 20-year moment, people were not in the grip of the ideas of the economic ruling class. Maybe something like that will happen now. It's already the case that the press, and the Congress, has moved away from this sort of idiotic worship of the Delphic statements of Alan Greenspan. Remember that? It wasn't that long ago. But now they're really angry about the terms of the bailout, for example.

And did you read the story about the Chicago sheriff who said he wasn't going to evict anybody who defaulted on their mortgages? That's what happens in this kind of crisis because everything—who's right, who's wrong, the way the world is—is up for grabs.

So when the reigning ideas are questioned like this, deep economic reform becomes possible. And I want to say how specifically that happens. It's not just by us prattling up here. There is an election coming up in just a few weeks. In the Great

Depression, people had to wait three years for an election. Barack Obama is bringing out lots of new voters, young voters, minority voters. It's also the case that the Republicans will try to steal the election on a huge scale. On a huge scale. The kind of vote suppression, voter caging, voter challenges, the destruction of voter registrations and ballots is going to be unbelievable. But maybe, because the Barack team is pretty smart and shrewd about this sort of thing, just maybe he'll pull it off. But if he pulls it off, if we have a new president on January 1, that I think has got to be only the beginning of the period of transformation, not the end.

In the New Deal, if that's our model, it wasn't FDR winning in 1932 that led to significant economic social and political change in the country. It was that FDR and his rhetoric, rhetoric designed to win elections, gave people a sense that they mattered, that they had influence, that they had hope. He created a climate that helped to encourage the great social movements of the 1930s. From the movement of the unemployed, to the farmers movements, to the movement of the aged, and especially, of course, the labor movement. Those movements created a lot of social disorder, but they also created a lot of instability in the electoral system. And because they did, FDR responded to the demands of the movements.

Bill Greider said we should talk big, we should think big, we should think about how to reorganize the economy, we should think about the end of empire perhaps. And I think we should think about those things, but I don't think we should overlook the more homely reforms that people will respond to. Reforms like restoring unions in the United States, restoring the social welfare system in the United States—reversing the cutbacks, restructuring those programs.

We don't want a national health system that gives everything to the providers, we want to rein in the providers in our national healthcare system. We want good income support systems, a decent retirement system, and we want to regulate the unregulated economy.

In other words, if we really are in the middle of a new period of possibility, we should also be willing, not only to think big, but to take it one step at a time, building the institutional arrangements that empower ordinary Americans, and stand as walls, as levies, restraining the next episode of market plunder if it comes.

Doug Henwood: Is the end nigh? I don't know. I just want to remind people that we've been here many times before, and securities fraud and financial panics are as American as apple pie. So I don't know just how different the present moment is from the many that have happened in the past. But I do want to talk about how we got to this particular moment and how we might get out of here, and what it all means.

A long-term issue is the tremendous polarization of income that's gone on in the last 30 years or so, which means that lower and middle class people have to borrow to maintain the semblance of a middle class standard of living, but then the rich also have plenty of spare money that they need to invest profitably. Lending it to those below them in the income ladder was a great outlet, at least until many of them started defaulting. That is one of the long-term issues behind the present crisis we're in.

But the proximate cause, as they say in law, is that we had a housing bubble. And as is always the case with bubbles, you can't have a good bubble without easy credit and lots of it. And so the bust really now has two dimensions: the effects on household finances—people owe money on houses that are falling in value—and on the other side, the financial system is holding an awful lot of loans that are now sour. So we've got two sides to the problem that are combining to produce a gigantic crisis.

But, and this is important, it's not just a matter of simple loans on the financial side. There's a big change. Banks no longer hold loans to maturity—they package them, securitize them, sell them to institutional investors, so they get distributed all over the place. And not only that, but Wall Street took those loans and sliced them and diced them and assembled them to lovely gratins of all kinds, baked into single dishes. Some of the layers are very fine loans, some of the layers are middle quality loans, and some of them are really sour loans.

And the problem is that nobody knows what mix is in which dishes. And so everyone is very, very afraid. As a result, the credit system has largely frozen up. Nobody wants to do business with banks because they're afraid they won't see their money again. So the interbank lending market has virtually ceased to exist.

Now this may sound abstract, but it actually is very, very important. Financial markets sometimes dance to their own tune, and the stock market has an especially tangential relationship with reality, but the credit markets are very important to the real world. Let me just list a couple of ways that's true.

First of all, consumer households borrow a lot, even in better times they would be borrowing to pay for cars, credit cards, mortgages to buy houses. I was actually shocked to discover to-day that the mortgage volume was over $1 trillion during 2005, the peak of the housing bubble, and the second quarter of this year it's down to $80 billion at its annual rate. That's a decline of 95 percent in mortgage lending, so something very, very dramatic has happened in that market.

Businesses also need to borrow, not just recklessly, but also to finance day-to-day activity; retailers need to buy inventory, manufacturers need to buy raw materials. Large companies borrow in the commercial paper market, unsecured short-term debt. That market is completely frozen up. And even longer term bank, commercial and industrial lending, which had picked up some of the slack when the commercial paper market imploded, is also beginning to shrink. So business lending, which is the lifeblood of day-to-day economic activity, is really seizing up.

And then finally, the federal government is borrowing very heavily and having no problem selling its bonds so far, but states like Massachusetts and California are finding it very difficult to borrow—even just routine short-term borrowing is difficult. Governments get tax payments, big, quarterly tax payments, big annual tax payments, and then they have to borrow to tide them over between those large lumps of receipts. And the states are having a hard time doing that borrowing now. County and city governments are having similar problems, and we're likely to see the largest municipal bankruptcy in American history very soon, in the county in Alabama where Birmingham is, which will I think be about twice the size of the Orange County bankruptcy of about 10 years ago. So this is having real world effects. And when governments can't borrow they have to cut services and lay people off. So this is very, very real stuff here.

Now this is a credit crunch, so it's not about the price of credit, the interest rate, but the availability of it. I've heard several responses to this, and let me just deal with a couple of them.

I've heard several people say it's a hoax. No, it's not: the credit freeze is not like WMDs in Iraq, it's visible in real stats that are quoted daily, weekly, or even quoted in real time in Bloomberg terminals around the world. People say it's their problem, but it's ours, too, for the reasons I just outlined.

Some people say let it all fall down. I say that's not politics, that's nihilism. There is a temptation to echo what Edmund Wilson said after the '29 crash, one couldn't help but be exhilarated at the sudden, unexpected collapse of that stupid, gigantic fraud. But the unemployment rate hit 25 percent in 1933. I don't think we want to see a rerun of that. Or maybe some people do, but not me.

Other people have said that the bailout package is the wrong approach, what we need is debt relief, infrastructure spending, green jobs. All those things are very, very good, and I want to see them, too, but they are very slow, very complicated, and sad to say, there is not all that much popular support for them right now. That may change, but it's not a walk in the woods getting that kind of program enacted.

Another complaint is that the bailout is a giveaway to the bankers. Yes, that's true to some degree, but without it we're all cooked. We can change that maybe someday if we have a better government.

And the latest complaint is that it hasn't worked. It's only been in existence for a week and they haven't spent any money yet, and these things take years to work through, so we should be a little more patient than that.

But we can do it better, and let me start with the realistic ways and then ascend toward the dreamy.

First of all, equity infusions—that is, the government should buy stock in the banks rather than asset purchases. A study by some I.M.F. economists that looked at scores of banking crises around the world found that equity infusions, recapitalizing the banks, are a much more effective way of dealing with this than buying bad assets and trying to sell them.

Then, financing it: Yes, it's a giveaway to the bankers now, but there is plenty of money at the top of the society. The top 10 percent of the population has 45 percent of the income, the top 1 percent about 16 percent. The top 1 percent has about $2 trillion in income, and we don't have to take it all at once, but we can take bits of it over the course of several years.

Debt relief. The I.M.F. study also showed that debt relief is an important part of getting out of any kind of financial crisis, so this is an instance in which economic efficiency and social justice coincide. So that is an important demand to make.

Re-regulate the financial system. Yes, we need to do that but it is very hard to think about exactly how to do that. The financial system is so sprawling, and complicated, and global, and interconnected that we can't even begin to think about that.

That's a project that is going to take a long time, but it has to be done so we don't have a rerun of this nonsense 5 or 10 years down the road.

On the equity issue, Paulson is likely to take a passive stake. Just two weeks ago we weren't even talking about the government taking equity interest in banks and buying stock, injecting capital directly into the banks. Now we are and it is likely to happen perhaps as soon as next week. We may be nationalizing the banks the week after next, who knows.

But Paulson wants this to be a passive stake, non-voting shares. Why is that? And this is where my dreaming really begins. If we are going to nationalize the banks, why not control them, as well, and not just give them a blank check to run things as they were. Or short of that, why not regulate them like utilities, or the way we used to regulate utilities before the preposterous experiment in utility deregulation began?

Out of the wreckage we could create all kinds of new economic development institutions, nonprofit, cooperative, locally owned, whatever. We can create institutions that provide low cost financial services for people now who are fleeced by check cashing services and payday lenders. So there are a lot of possibilities, we just have to start thinking about these things. And we need to think about the details: these ideas are very vague and need some flesh on those bones.

And finally, just a few words on the politics at the moment. People are talking about the end of neoliberalism. Maybe so, but I see a lot more continuity between neoliberalism and the 400 years of capitalism that went before it than some people do. But that aside, there is an idea, popular among the left, right, and center, that neoliberalism means that the state got out of the economy. The state never got out of the economy, markets are not the state of nature, they need to be established and maintained by state power. The nature of that state and what it does is what matters.

The more benign functions of the state have been taken out—like supporting people, the kinds of things that Frances Piven was talking about—but the more malignant kinds of functions, the policing functions, have been expanded, and, of course, the bailout functions have been greatly expanded.

There is an ideological opening. You can say that markets are not self-regulating and they tend to eat themselves if left to their own devices. And with the state getting so explicitly involved in rescuing the mess that finance brought on itself and us, there is an opportunity to push things in a better direction. But we're pretty weak right now and I'm really not all that sure who we are. So we have to think about what kinds of demands we can make, because who are we?

Arun Gupta: We are in a severe economic crisis that requires dramatic action. It's gone from the U.S. to global, the pathogen has jumped from the financial sector to the rest of the economy. And right now the only institutions that can do anything about it are governments. So there has to be some sort of concerted action, not just by the U.S., but now globally. And our role is to make sure that whatever policies are enacted are democratic, transparent, and accountable.

This market failure and the need for systemic government interventions mean that our work is largely done on an ideological level, in terms of arguing for the necessity of, say, something like a green new deal, or single payor national healthcare. That's because it's hard to argue against these things on free-market principles when you have this massive intervention in the economy.

This crisis is the culmination of 30 years of laissez-faire economics, that is, neoliberalism. The monoculture economy: and that's what we have across the world, and if we think of it as a monoculture, then the pathogens spread through the system rapidly, and that's why stock markets around the world are declining, particularly the integrated ones, the industrialized countries.

But without a mass-based dynamic opposition with a clear vision, agenda and strategy, the neoliberal model will just reassert itself. And it is already reasserting itself. The Paulson plan is essentially for self-regulation, which is how we got into this mess in the first place.

The U.S. is reportedly turning to the I.M.F. for consultation. Iceland is going hat in hand to the I.M.F. for a loan, and what they'll get in return is a severe austerity program.

Especially scary at the local and state level, such as in New York State, is all this talk about selling off assets or at least leasing them out for 99 years, like toll roads, like lotteries. This is a hallmark of the neoliberal model, where our assets are going to be sold off to corporations for a quick infusion of cash to cover some budget shortfall.

What we need is a polyculture economy. Without it we'll be vulnerable to other global contagions, and without diverse economic structures, whatever regulatory frameworks are put in place will just be undermined and overturned down the road. Right now there is a huge opening for left and anti-capitalists and we can actually talk a good bit about what we're demanding. But I don't think it's that hard to come up with detailed programmatic proposals. What is much more difficult, and this is something for all of us to really think about because the left does not like to think about it, is organization and ideology.

I've been in a lot of meetings and discussions in the last few weeks around organizing against the Wall Street bailout plan, and it comes up time and again. People don't want to confront the need for organization and the need to have a clear ideology because once you do that, it leads to political battles. And that is not necessarily a bad thing, but without an ideology, something to counter the neoliberal ideology, we can't really say what we're for, we can't say who the agent of change is, we don't have anything to organize around. So I think that is really one of the biggest tasks ahead. ...

Naomi Klein: As Doug Henwood said, crises are not new, and we may be in uncharted territory but we have experienced these bursting bubbles before. I want to talk about two recent crises that have something to teach us. One of them is the Asian financial crisis in 1997–98, and the other is the Argentina economic meltdown in December 2001.

In *The Shock Doctrine*, I have a chapter about the Asian financial crisis. It's called "Let it Burn," and the reason why it's called that is because the very same banks that have been so anxious to get bailouts from U.S. taxpayers at the time were saying that what Asia needed—this is a quote—"what Asia needs is more pain." Because, of course, Citibank, Goldman, Morgan Stanley, went into Asia after the crisis reached bottom and bought up the crown jewels of the Asian tiger economies.

What I want to read you from the book is something Alan Greenspan said at the time. He said that what he thought was being witnessed with the Asian financial crisis was "a very dramatic event towards a consensus of the type of market system which we have in this country," this country being America. In other words, Greenspan thought that the crisis was a lesson being taught to the Asian tigers for daring to protect their national industry. And, of course, the I.M.F. imposed structural adjustment programs that forced them to lower those barriers, which allowed the very Wall Street firms at the center of this crisis to go in and engage in what the *New York Times Magazine* at the time called "the world's biggest going out of business sale."

Michel Camdessus, the head of the I.M.F. at the time, agreed. He saw the crisis as Asia being reborn into American style free markets. He said economic models are not eternal. There are times when they are useful and other times when they become outdated and must be abandoned. Once again, he saw it as a lesson.

Maybe it's time for progressives to think of themselves as a sort of people's I.M.F. Look at the way the I.M.F. responded to that crisis: clearly the model was broken, and the response should not just be to bail it out, but to change it into the proper model. We could see this moment in similar terms, but in more democratic terms, which is to say we now have evidence that this market model is broken. And clearly what is needed is some dramatic structural adjustment in the USA. So let's play I.M.F.

In Argentina they did try to use the 2001 crisis to push through more structural adjustment, but the problem, and the reason why this didn't work in Argentina, was that just a few months earlier the I.M.F. had been holding up Argentina as the model student. And they had already privatized everything. I mean they came up with a list of more things they should privatize, but it was just the ports, because that was all that was left— they had privatized everything.

But also, the country itself had been very much indoctrinated in the idea that they were the model student, that they had followed the rules. And so it was much harder to sell the idea that you needed more neoliberal structural adjustment. Instead what you had was a popular uprising and a revolt against the entire expert class. The slogan then in the streets is a really good slogan for this moment: "Que se vayan todos," all of them must go. This was the period where they went through five presidents in three weeks, but it wasn't just the politicians, it was the pundits, it was the economists. And because they had boasted so much about the miracle of Argentina, they found themselves really bereft of the usual tools.

Now I think the United States in this moment is experiencing something a little bit similar in the sense that there is this consensus, and Barack Obama has turned his election campaign into a kind of referendum on Friedmanite economic policies. But whether or not he is actually going to follow through on this critique depends very much on the forces that we're talking about in this room.

I want to talk about some short-term structural adjustments, the kind of pressure that can be placed on Obama right now.

Bob Rubin, Larry Summers, have got to go. This is really crucial. These guys are advising Obama on a day-to-day basis.

When he wants to say that he has great people surrounding him, he talks about Bob Rubin. And that fantastic piece in the *New York Times*, which I never thought I would read, questioning the Greenspan legacy, was very effective in pairing Rubin with Greenspan at every turn in creating the crisis we have now.

So we have a real opening right now. If MoveOn wasn't MoveOn, they would be using their networks to say that these guys should be exiled, that they broke it, and that does not give them the right to feed on the remains.

We saw the two political campaigns actually issuing a joint statement about the bailout, much to their shame. How about pushing the political campaigns, which are both running on these platforms of getting the special interests and the lobbyists out of Washington (which, as we know, is complete bullshit), to get the lobbyists out of the bailout discussions? They are swarming in on this right now, trying to have a say that they should not have in who is eligible for the bailout. And they are also resisting progressive change within the context of the bailout. These are the people who created the crisis we're in. There should be a blanket ban on lobbying on anything having to do with the bailout.

… One of the things that's incredible that's happening now is they're handing out no bid contracts to the very companies that created this mess.

The new frontier for disaster capitalism—this expanding economy going from Iraq to Hurricane Katrina, and just feeding off the next disaster—is capitalism. Okay, it's cleaning up after capitalism. It's a $700 billion industry, and expanding.

One last point, to think big, because I've been thinking small here. We know that this crisis is being transferred from Wall Street to Washington. All of these bad debts that are now exploding on the public books are going to be used by the right to argue that whoever the next president is, they can't afford to keep their campaign promises. Think of this as Republican insurance against an Obama presidency. Everything he's saying, Yes, we can; no, you can't. You can't because we just dumped this huge crisis on your lap, and Obama is already capitulating. He's already said, Well, maybe I can afford some things like green energy and so on, we'll have to phase them in.

Here's a big idea. I've been calling for the nationalization of Exxon. Because I think if nationalization is on the table, let's go big, let's not just nationalize junk, let's nationalize the biggest corporate criminals of them all, the people who have left us with the biggest crisis that we actually face, which is climate change. And now we're going to hear that we actually can't afford the investments to get us to address this crisis, to change course, that addressing climate change is a luxury we can no longer afford.

This is the fight we have to win. But actually, we can't nationalize them, because how would you tell the difference between a nationalized oil company and what you have right now? So we need to internationalize them. There needs to be an international trust and these huge profits won by the oil and gas industry have to be the money that we use to create a sustainable economy. I know there are a lot of legal arguments we need to win to get from A to B, but that's a big idea I'll just throw out there.

The Global Perspective

WILL HUTTON

November 19, 2008

O N NOVEMBER 15, the most important economic summit process for a generation began. The leaders of the major industrialized countries, China, Russia, Brazil and India along with the heads of the I.M.F., UN, World Bank and EU, met to discuss how to first reform, and then govern, the international financial system. Summit aims do not get any more ambitious.

Fundamental questions are being raised about how capitalism is to be organized and globalization is to be governed. No longer can the U.S. argue that this is something for others to worry about and that it will dictate terms; America's financial system is broken along with the wider international framework. Repairing them is vital and cannot be done in isolation. But a lame-duck Bush administration and an Obama transition team anxious not to make too many commitments too early in an area full of quicksand are hardly an auspicious backdrop. However, urgency about finding some common goals and shared principles for reform are an imperative. The EU has forced the pace by declaring that the summiteers should come up with answers by the end of next February. The Obama team is compelled to engage.

Nonetheless, it is an ambitious deadline. It took nearly two years of discussion before there was sufficient agreement to attempt the 1944 Bretton Woods Conference in New Hampshire that famously established the post-war international financial system and to which the current summit process is being compared. But shared awareness that the system is broken and that the world risks a credit-crunch-induced global depression is concentrating minds wonderfully.

Where to start? The architects of Bretton Woods I knew they had to avoid the beggar-my-neighbor policies of the 1930s—economic autarchy and hyper-militarization—and that if the U.S. and Britain could clinch a deal, then everybody else would have to follow. Even then it was a struggle. The question then, as now, is how much are governments prepared to pool economic sovereignty and accept fiscal disciplines in order to produce the greater global public good? The American answer was not much. The U.S. only agreed to the I.M.F. managing a system of fixed exchange rates if in effect the U.S. ran it. The dream of creating a system of global financial governance was passed up. Realpolitik had triumphed.

The system then only lasted as long as the Americans thought the benefits of running it outweighed the costs. When in 1971 the Nixon administration was faced with the choice of increasing taxes to finance the Vietnam War or abandoning the Bretton Woods fixed-exchange-rate system that delivered predictability and less risk in international financial relationships, it had no hesitation. The markets would do the job instead— and if other governments did not like the new risks, tough.

For a long time, it looked as though private markets could step into the breach—recycling first petrodollars in the 1970s and then Asian dollars back into the global system. Floating exchange rates were volatile, but instruments like markets in future exchange rates emerged to manage new risks. There might be serious ruptures, like the 1980s Latin American debt crisis or the 1990s Asian financial crisis when private markets took fright, but basically governments could step away from global economic management. The U.S. could have guns, butter and allow its great multinationals and banks to expand abroad willy-nilly—and the markets would manage the implications spontaneously, finding the capital the U.S. needed with no constraint on either its government or financial system.

Now we know they cannot. The crises of trust and out-of-control speculation that wrecked Latin America and Asia has now attacked the system's core in the U.S. and Europe. The system proved unworkable. In good times uncontrollable flows of private lending justified by the delusion that risks were diversifiable and insurable created massive asset price bubbles. In bad times nearly $3 trillion of loan losses have overwhelmed the capital of the Western banking system. Vicious tsunamis of speculation in a $360 trillion global financial derivatives market, allegedly hedging risk, mean that everything—currencies, interest rates, share and commodity prices—swings unstably, irrationally and incredibly fast, beyond the capacity of actors in the real economy to react. The system is devouring itself.

Emergency action has stopped the collapse of Western banks, but now there is a dual challenge. We must design a new system while trying to make sure that the disastrous legacy of the broken system does not drag the world into depression. And unlike 1944, there are many more interests to be brokered into a common position. The U.S. is still not willing to pool sovereignty, and still not coming to terms with new realities.

Britain will pool sovereignty, but not to the degree that it will join the euro or become part of a European regulatory regime. Europeans, led by President Sarkozy, want an attack on laissez-faire finance, to restrict sovereign wealth fund activity and propose systemic regulation. China wants to contribute as little as possible while being free to rig its currency to promote its exports. OPEC countries and Russia want the freedom to invest their $2 trillion of sovereign wealth funds where they choose. Japan wants to stop the yen from becoming wildly uncompetitive. Less developed countries want more voice and more money, but accept no responsibility for managing the system.

All have a different conception of how to do capitalism. All jockey for individual advantage. All want somebody else to make sacrifices for the common global good. Meanwhile most financiers remain in a state of denial about what has happened—resenting government support and desperately hoping that they can get back to the freewheeling old days as soon as possible. Change must be minimal. The auguries for agreement do not seem great.

Yet there are contrary forces. Policy-makers are terrified. For the first time, it is apparent to America's political and financial elite, if not the country at large, that the U.S. can no longer square the circle of simultaneously mounting expensive foreign wars and domestic booms by freely borrowing other countries' dollars. The consequent debt and volatility has broken the U.S.'s own financial system. The country is now in a similar position to Mexico in 1981 or South Korea in 1998—facing tough economic adjustment because forces outside its control will not allow it to live above its means. There is an emergent consensus in Europe and Asia—which the Obama administration is likely to join—that accepts that governments have got to organize the world financial system so there is less systemic risk, like exchange-rate volatility, risk of national bankruptcies or uncontrollable lending. Moreover, governments must also ensure that the market mechanisms devised to handle risk—like the derivatives markets and the capital base of the banking system—are better managed. There is no alternative. Only once this has been achieved can banks return to their core mission—lending to businesses and households all around the world.

The starting point is the I.M.F. For all its weaknesses it is at least a functioning institution on which the world can build. It needs to be beefed up massively. We now live in a world in which private capital flows run into trillions of dollars; yet the I.M.F. has only $250 billion of lending power. It needs up to a trillion dollars—as does the World Bank. British Prime Minister Gordon Brown has won Saudi commitment to replenish the I.M.F.'s coffers, and begun to get some real momentum. Obama must assume a leadership position and ensure both institutions are given the financial muscle they need. Nor need he worry too much about calls for enlarged voting rights from China, India, Brazil, Russia and the less developed world. Until they can contribute convertible currency to the I.M.F. and World Bank like the dollar, euro and yen, they cannot be at the heart of the system.

Obama should try to organize his emergency economic stimulus package in the U.S. in tandem with efforts by the Europeans, Japanese and Chinese. It will be much more effective if it is coordinated internationally. He should be uncompromising about the need to end the destabilizing role of tax havens as sources of dodgy lending and tax evasion—a position on which he has staked out ground before his election. Many are under British jurisdiction, and he should combine with France's President Sarkozy—rotating head of the EU until Christmas—to insist that Britain join with the rest of the world to constrain if not eliminate an important source of financial destabilization.

I would like the U.S. to consider going back to Bretton Woods basics—unfashionable though it may seem. It was not just Lyndon B. Johnson who opened the way to the Republicans' "Southern Strategy" and nearly 40 years of conservative dominance: It was also Nixon's abandonment of government-led economic disciplines through his suspension of Bretton Woods fixed exchange rates. Obama should propose the end of floating exchange rates and argue for a system of managed rates between the euro, dollar and yen to bring back more predictability into the system. The American, EU and Japanese governments would undertake, as in Bretton Woods I, whatever economic action is needed to maintain stability between their exchange rates. There would also be explicit rules on exchange rate rigging—a more effective way of tackling the China issue than threatening it with tariffs.

Then there is improving the financial system's own risk-handling mechanisms. Obama should attack the British position. Prime Minister Gordon Brown advocates more effective cross-border financial regulation, but not so much as to endanger the City of London's standing as home of minimal regulation—in a race to the bottom with New York. This has to change. Obama should pick up the Financial Stability Forum's proposal that global trade in financial derivatives be organized in licensed exchanges. If London wants the current casino, let the bulk of the trade be organized out of New York. But more importantly, the U.S. should insist that there be an international college of financial regulators which it will host, fund and coordinate.

And the U.S. should eschew protectionism. Keynes argued, and I agree, that when financial freedoms induce crises in the real economy—as they always will because free finance poses an existential threat to the real economy—the wrong solution is to attack trade flows while leaving finance largely free. The relationship should be the other way round: control, regulate and manage finance in order to permit a more stable real economy and the free trade that succors it.

There is a Bretton Woods II deal to be done. The EU, Americans and Japanese accept the need to strengthen the I.M.F. There is also a head of steam behind the case for organizing the financial derivatives markets into global exchanges, and for heavily influencing the price at which these gambling chips change hands. There will be action on bonuses for bank staff that are far too high.

But this is only a fraction of what is necessary. We need a paradigm shift toward a greater acceptance of global principles, rules and governance by both banks and governments. We need global rules on the terms and means by which banks are recapitalized and how they are bailed out of their bad loans. Banks need to accept that the world has changed. We need global rules on hedge funds, tax havens and derivative trading. And we need Western governments to lead in de-risking the system by declaring their willingness to manage the values of their currencies in predictable zones. This is what we need. Obama, if he is to be a great reforming president, needs to combine his reforming zeal at home with no less zeal abroad to ensure we get it.

How to End the Recession

ROBERT POLLIN
November 24, 2008

THE ECONOMY NEEDS a shot of public investment—and if it's green, the payoff will be greatest.

The collapse on Wall Street is now decimating Main Street, Ocean Parkway, Mountain View Drive and I-80. Since January the economy has shed 760,000 jobs. In September alone, monthly mass layoff claims for unemployment insurance jumped by 34 percent. General Electric, General Motors, Chrysler, Yahoo! and Xerox have all announced major layoffs, along with the humbled financial titans Goldman Sachs and Bank of America. Fully one-quarter of all businesses in the United States are planning to cut payroll over the next year. State governments are facing a tax revenue shortfall of roughly $100 billion in the next fiscal year, 15 percent of their overall budgets. Because states have rules requiring balanced budgets, they are staring at major budget cuts and layoffs. The fact that the economy's overall gross domestic product (GDP) shrank between July and September—the first such decline since the

September 2001 terrorist attacks—only confirms the realities on the ground facing workers, households, businesses and the public sector.

The recession is certainly here, so the question now is how to diminish its length and severity. A large-scale federal government stimulus program is the only action that can possibly do the job.

So far, our leaders in Washington have dithered. Treasury Secretary Henry Paulson and Federal Reserve chair Ben Bernanke continue improvising with financial rescue plans, committing eye-popping sums of money in the process. Paulson's original program for the Treasury to commit $700 billion in taxpayers' money to purchase "toxic" loans—the mortgage-backed securities held by the private banks that are in default or arrears—was at least partially shelved in favor of direct government purchases of major ownership stakes in the banks. But neither of Paulson's strategies has thus far helped to stabilize the situation, with global stock and currency markets gyrating wildly and investors dumping risky business loans in favor of safe Treasury bonds. The crisis has even hit the previously staid world of money market mutual funds, where the fainthearted once could park their savings safely in exchange for low returns. Money market fund holders have been panic-selling since mid-September, dumping $500 billion worth of these accounts.

To stanch a money market fund collapse, Bernanke announced on October 21 that, on top of the Paulson bailout plan, the Fed stands ready to purchase $540 billion in certificates of deposit and private business loans from the money market funds. This action is in addition to two previous initiatives committing the Fed to buy up, as needed, business loans from failing banks. Until this crisis, the Fed had conducted monetary policy almost exclusively through the purchase and sale of Treasury bonds, rarely buying directly the debts of private businesses or banks. But the pre-crisis rules of monetary policy are out the window.

Even if some combination of Treasury and Federal Reserve actions begins to stabilize financial markets in the coming weeks, this will not, by itself, reverse the deepening crisis in the nonfinancial economy. A rise in unemployment to the range of 8 to 9 percent—upward of 14 million people without work—is becoming an increasingly likely scenario over the next year.

President-elect Obama as well as most members of the newly elected Democratic-controlled Congress seem to recognize the urgency of such a large-scale stimulus program above and beyond any financial bailout program. Even Bernanke, whose term of office continues through January 2010, has offered his endorsement. But despite the near consensus, questions remain, including: How should the stimulus funds be spent? How large does the stimulus need to be? Where do we find the money to pay for it?

A Green Public-Investment Stimulus

Recessions create widespread human suffering. Minimizing the suffering has to be the top priority in fighting the recession. This means expanding unemployment benefits and food stamps to counteract the income losses of unemployed workers and the poor. By stabilizing the pocketbooks of distressed households, these measures also help people pay their mortgages and pump money into consumer markets.

Beyond this, the stimulus program should be designed to meet three additional criteria. First, we have to generate the largest possible employment boost for a given level of new government spending. Second, the spending targets should be in areas that strengthen the economy in the long run, not just through a short-term money injection. And finally, despite the recession, we do not have the luxury of delaying the fight against global warming.

To further all these goals we need a green public-investment stimulus. It would defend state-level health and education projects against budget cuts; finance long-delayed upgrades for our roads, bridges, railroads and water management systems; and underwrite investments in energy efficiency—including building retrofits and public transportation—as well as new wind, solar, geothermal and biomass technologies.

This kind of stimulus would generate many more jobs—eighteen per $1 million in spending—than would programs to increase spending on the military and the oil industry (e.g., new military surges in Iraq or Afghanistan combined with "Drill, baby, drill"), which would generate only about 7.5 jobs for every $1 million spent. There are two reasons for the green program's advantage. The first factor is higher "labor intensity" of spending—that is, more money is being spent on hiring people and less on machines, supplies and consuming energy. This becomes obvious if we imagine hiring teachers, nurses and bus drivers versus drilling for oil off the coasts of Florida, California and Alaska. The second factor is the "domestic content" of spending—how much money is staying within the U.S. economy, as opposed to buying imports or spending abroad. When we build a bridge in Minneapolis, upgrade the levee system in New Orleans or retrofit public buildings and private homes to raise their energy efficiency, virtually every dollar is spent within our economy. By contrast, only 80 cents of every dollar spent in the oil industry remains in the United States. The figure is still lower with the military budget.

What about another round of across-the-board tax rebates, such as the program the Bush administration and the Democratic Congress implemented in April? A case could be made for this in light of the financial stresses middle-class families are facing. However, even if we assume that the middle-class households will spend all the money refunded to them, the net increase in employment will be about fourteen jobs per $1 million spent—about 20 percent less than the green public-investment program (the main reason for this weaker impact is the lower domestic content of average household consumption). Also, it isn't likely that the households would spend all their rebate money. Just as with April's rebate program, households would channel a large share of the money into paying off debts.

The Matter of Size

This is no time to be timid. The stimulus program last April totaled $150 billion, including $100 billion in household rebates and the rest in business tax breaks. This initiative did encourage some job growth, though as we have seen, the impact would have been larger had the same money been channeled toward a green public-investment stimulus. But any job benefits were negated by the countervailing forces of the collapsed housing bubble, the financial crisis and the spike in oil prices. The resulting recession is now before us. This argues for a significantly larger stimulus than the one enacted in April. But how much larger?

One way to approach the question is to consider the last time the economy faced a recession of similar severity, which was in 1980–82, during Ronald Reagan's first term as president. In 1982 gross domestic product contracted by 1.9 percent, the most severe one-year drop in GDP since World War II. Unemployment rose to 9.7 percent that year, which was, again, the highest figure since the 1930s.

The Reagan administration responded with a massive stimulus program, even though its alleged free-market devotees never acknowledged as much. They preferred calling their program of military expansion and tax cuts for the rich "supply-side economics." Whatever the label, this combination generated an increase in the federal deficit of about two percentage points relative to the size of the economy at that time. In 1983 GDP rose sharply by 4.5 percent. In 1984 GDP growth accelerated to 7.2 percent, with Reagan declaring the return to "morning in America." Unemployment fell back to 7.5 percent.

In today's economy, an economic stimulus equivalent to the 1983 Reagan program would amount to about $300 billion in spending—roughly double the size of April's stimulus program, though in line with the high-end figures being proposed in

Congress. A stimulus of this size could create nearly 6 million jobs, offsetting the job-shedding forces of the recession.

Of course, the green public-investment stimulus will be much more effective as a jobs program than the Reagan agenda of militarism and upper-income tax cuts. This suggests that an initiative costing somewhat less than $300 billion could be adequate to fight the job losses. But because the green public-investment stimulus is also designed to produce long-term benefits to the economy, there is little danger that we would spend too much. Since all these investments are needed to fight global warming and improve overall productivity, the sooner we move forward, the better. Moreover, under today's weak job market conditions, we will not run short of qualified workers.

How to Pay for All This?

Let's add up the figures I have tossed around. These include the $700 billion bank rescue operation being engineered by the Treasury, the $540 billion with which Fed chair Bernanke has pledged to bail out the money market mutual funds, along with unspecified additional billions to buy unwanted business debts held by banks. On top of these, I am proposing $300 billion for a second fiscal stimulus beyond last April's $150 billion program. At a certain point, it is fair to wonder whether we are still dealing with real dollars as opposed to Monopoly money.

In fact, the whole program remains within the realm of affordability, albeit approaching its upper bounds. But major adjustments from the current management approach are needed. In particular, the Federal Reserve has to continue exerting control over the Treasury on all bailout operations. That is, we need more initiatives like Bernanke's $540 billion program to stabilize the money market mutual funds and less Treasury fumbling with taxpayers' money to buy either the private banks' bad assets or ownership shares in the banks.

We need to recognize openly what has largely been an unspoken fact about these bailout operations: that the Federal Reserve has the power to create dollars at will, while the Treasury finances its operations either through tax revenues or borrowed funds (which means using taxpayer money at some later time to pay back its debts with interest). The Fed does not literally run printing presses when it decides to inject more money into the economy, but its normal activity of writing checks to private banks to buy the banks' Treasury bonds amounts to the same thing. When the banks receive their checks from the Fed, they have more cash on hand than they did before they sold their Treasury bonds to the Fed. Especially during crises, there is no reason for the Fed to restrain itself from making good use (though of course not overuse) of this dollar-creating power.

The Fed is also supposed to be the chief regulator of the financial system. Now is the time to make up for Alan Greenspan's confessed failures over twenty years in this role. In exchange for the Fed protecting the private financial institutions from collapse, Bernanke must insist that the banks begin lending money again to support productive investments, while prohibiting them from yet another return to high-rolling speculation. Special measures are also needed to keep people in their homes.

The Deficit Looms

When the economy began slowing this year, the fiscal deficit more than doubled, from $162 billion to $389 billion. We cannot know for certain how much the deficit will expand. It could rise to $800 billion, $1 trillion or even somewhat higher, depending on how the bailout operations are managed. Of course, it would be utterly self-defeating for the United States to run a reckless fiscal policy, no matter how pressing the need to fight the financial crisis and recession. But in the current crisis conditions, even a $1 trillion deficit need not be reckless.

Let's return to the Reagan experience for perspective. In 1983 the Reagan deficits peaked at 6 percent of the economy's GDP. With GDP now around $14.4 trillion, a $1 trillion deficit would represent about 7 percent of GDP, one percentage point higher than the 1983 figure.

Of course, the global financial system has undergone dramatic changes since the 1980s, so direct comparisons with the Reagan deficits are not entirely valid. One change is that government debt is increasingly owned by foreign governments and private investors. This means that interest payments on that debt flow increasingly from the coffers of the Treasury to foreign owners of Treasury bonds.

At the same time, as one feature of the crisis, Treasury bonds are, and will remain for some time, the safest and most desirable financial instrument in the global financial system. U.S. and foreign investors are clamoring to purchase Treasuries as opposed to buying stocks, bonds issued by private companies or derivatives. This is pushing down the interest rates on Treasuries. For example, on October 15, 2007, a three-year Treasury bond paid out 4.25 percent in interest, whereas this past October 15, the interest payment had fallen to 1.9 percent. By contrast, a BAA corporate bond paid 6.6 percent in interest one year ago but has risen this year to 9 percent. As long as the private financial markets remain gripped by instability and fear, the Treasury will be able to borrow at negligible interest rates. Because of this, allowing the deficit to rise even as high as 7 percent of GDP does not represent a burden on the Treasury greater than what accompanied the Reagan deficits.

There is, then, no reason to tread lightly in fighting the recession, with all its attendant dangers and misery. Indeed, severe misery and danger will certainly rise as long as timidity— the path of least resistance—establishes the boundaries of acceptable action. The incoming Obama administration can take decisive steps now to defend people's livelihoods and to reconstruct a viable financial system, productive infrastructure and job market on the foundation of a clean-energy economy.

In Praise of a Rocky Transition

NAOMI KLEIN

December 1, 2008

T HE MORE DETAILS EMERGE, the clearer it becomes that Washington's handling of the Wall Street bail-out is not merely incompetent. It is borderline criminal.

In a moment of high panic in late September, the U.S. Treasury unilaterally pushed through a radical change in how bank mergers are taxed—a change long sought by the industry. Despite the fact that this move will deprive the government of as much as $140 billion in tax revenue, lawmakers found out only after the fact. According to the *Washington Post,* more than a dozen tax attorneys agree that "Treasury had no authority to issue the [tax change] notice."

Of equally dubious legality are the equity deals Treasury has negotiated with many of the country's banks. According to Congressman Barney Frank, one of the architects of the legislation that enables the deals, "Any use of these funds for any purpose other than lending—for bonuses, for severance pay, for dividends, for acquisitions of other institutions, etc.—is a violation of the act." Yet this is exactly how the funds are being used.

Then there is the nearly $2 trillion the Federal Reserve has handed out in emergency loans. Incredibly, the Fed will not reveal which corporations have received these loans or what it has accepted as collateral. *Bloomberg News* believes that this secrecy violates the law and has filed a federal suit demanding full disclosure.

Despite all of this potential lawlessness, the Democrats are either openly defending the administration or refusing to intervene. "There is only one president at a time," we hear from Barack Obama. That's true. But every sweetheart deal the lame-duck Bush administration makes threatens to hobble Obama's ability to make good on his promise of change. To cite just one example, the $140 billion in missing tax revenue is almost the same sum as Obama's renewable-energy program. Obama owes it to the people who elected him to call this what it is: an attempt to undermine the electoral process by stealth.

Yes, there is only one president at a time, but that president needed the support of powerful Democrats, including Obama, to get the bail-out passed. Now that it is clear that the Bush administration is violating the terms to which both parties agreed, the Democrats have not just the right but a grave responsibility to intervene forcefully.

I suspect that the real reason the Democrats are so far failing to act has less to do with presidential protocol than with fear: fear that the stock market, which has the temperament of an overindulged two-year-old, will throw one of its world-shaking tantrums. Disclosing the truth about who is receiving federal loans, we are told, could cause the cranky market to bet against those banks. Question the legality of equity deals, and the same thing will happen. Challenge the $140 billion tax giveaway, and mergers could fall through. "None of us wants to be blamed for ruining these mergers and creating a new Great Depression," explained one unnamed Congressional aide.

More than that, the Democrats, including Obama, appear to believe that the need to soothe the market should govern all key economic decisions in the transition period. Which is why, just days after a euphoric victory for "change," the mantra abruptly shifted to "smooth transition" and "continuity."

Take Obama's pick for chief of staff. Despite the Republican braying about his partisanship, Rahm Emanuel, the House Democrat who received the most donations from the financial sector, sends an unmistakably reassuring message to Wall Street. When asked on *This Week with George Stephanopoulos* whether Obama would be moving quickly to increase taxes on the wealthy, as promised, Emanuel pointedly did not answer the question.

This same market-coddling logic should, we are told, guide Obama's selection of Treasury secretary. Fox News's Stuart Varney explained that Larry Summers, who held the post under Clinton, and former Fed chair Paul Volcker would both "give great confidence to the market." We learned from MSNBC's Joe Scarborough that Summers is the man "the Street would like the most."

Let's be clear about why. "The Street" would cheer a Summers appointment for the same reason the rest of us should fear it: because traders will assume that Summers, champion of financial deregulation under Clinton, will offer a transition from Henry Paulson so smooth we will barely know it happened. Someone like FDIC chair Sheila Bair, on the other hand, would spark fear on the Street—for all the right reasons.

One thing we know for certain is that the market will react violently to any signal that there is a new sheriff in town who will impose serious regulation, invest in people and cut off the free money for corporations. In short, the markets can be relied on to vote in precisely the opposite way that Americans have just voted. (A recent *USA Today*/Gallup poll found that 60 percent of Americans strongly favor "stricter regulations on financial institutions," while just 21 percent support aid to financial companies.)

There is no way to reconcile the public's vote for change with the market's foot-stomping for more of the same. Any and all moves to change course will be met with short-term market shocks. The good news is that once it is clear that the new rules will be applied across the board and with fairness, the market will stabilize and adjust. Furthermore, the timing for this turbulence has never been better. Over the past three months, we've been shocked so frequently that market stability would come as more of a surprise. That gives Obama a window to disregard the calls for a seamless transition and do the hard stuff first. Few will be able to blame him for a crisis that clearly predates him, or fault him for honoring the clearly expressed wishes of the electorate. The longer he waits, however, the more memories fade.

When transferring power from a functional, trustworthy regime, everyone favors a smooth transition. When exiting an era marked by criminality and bankrupt ideology, a little rockiness at the start would be a very good sign.

Acknowledgments

The Nation's editorial team reacted swiftly to the financial collapse, working together to produce the stellar coverage that is represented in this collection. Executive Editor Betsy Reed oversaw the compilation of the articles and edited many of the pieces when they originally appeared in the magazine, as did Managing Editor Roane Carey and Associate Editor Richard Kim, who lent their insight and historical knowledge to the final selection.

Special thanks also to Victor Navasky, Karen Rothmyer and Richard Lingeman, the originating editors behind other articles collected here; William Greider and Christopher Hayes for editorial advice; to Hamilton Fish, Taya Kitman and The Nation Institute for essential support; to Ruth Baldwin, Carl Bromley and Jayati Vora at Nation Books; and to John Sherer, Robert Kimzey and Christine Marra at the Perseus Books Group, who worked round the clock to produce this book in record time.

In countless ways the crucial work of *The Nation*'s staff is exhibited here. Joan Connell, *The Nation*'s Web editor, brought in the online-only content, Mark Sorkin deftly copyedited the articles, and *The Nation*'s talented interns ensured that all our facts were accurately reported.

And finally, special thanks to our contributors, many of whom are longtime writers for *The Nation,* and without whom this book could not exist.

About the Contributors

Laura K. Abel is deputy director of the Justice Program at the Brennan Center for Justice at New York University, where she has worked since 1999.

Sarah Anderson is the global economy project director of the Institute for Policy Studies in Washington, D.C., and author, with John Cavanagh, of the report *Lessons of European Integration for the Americas*.

Dean Baker is the co-director of the Center for Economic and Policy Research. He is a frequent guest on NPR, Marketplace, CNN, CNBC and more. He is the author of several books, including *The United States Since 1980*.

Walden Bello, professor of sociology at the University of the Philippines, is the author of *Dilemmas of Domination*. He is a senior analyst at Focus on the Global South, a program of Chulalongkorn University's Social Research Institute, president of the Freedom from Debt Coalition, and a fellow of the Transnational Institute.

William K. Black is an associate professor of Economics and Law at the University of Missouri-Kansas City School of Law and the executive director of the Institute for Fraud Prevention. He is the author of *The Best Way to Rob a Bank Is to Own One*.

Barbara Ehrenreich, the bestselling author of *Nickel and Dimed*, is the winner of the 2004 Puffin/Nation Prize. Her latest book is *This Land Is Their Land: Reports from a Divided Nation*.

Frances Fox Piven is on the faculty of the Graduate Center of the City University of New York. She is the author, most recently, of *Challenging Authority: How Ordinary People Change America*.

Arun Gupta has been a writer and editor for the *Indypendent* since 2000. Gupta has written extensively about the Iraq War and is a frequent guest on "Democracy Now!" with Amy Goodman. He is currently working on a book about the history of the war.

Jeff Faux was the founder of, and is now distinguished fellow at, the Economic Policy Institute. His latest book is *The Global Class War*. He is currently working on a new book about America's future.

Thomas Ferguson, a contributing editor of *The Nation*, is professor of political science at the University of Massachusetts, Boston. He is the author of *Golden Rule: The Investment The-*

ory of Party Competition and *The Logic of Money-Driven Political Systems*.

Thomas Frank, a founding editor of the *Baffler* and the author of *What's the Matter with Kansas*. His latest book is *The Wrecking Crew: How Conservatives Rule*.

Steve Fraser is working on a book about the two gilded ages. A TomDispatch regular and co-director of the American Empire Project series at Metropolitan Books, he is the author of, among other works, the recently published *Wall Street: America's Dream Palace*.

James K. Galbraith is author of *The Predator State: How Conservatives Abandoned the Free Market and Why Liberals Should Too*. He teaches at the University of Texas at Austin.

William Greider, a prominent political journalist and author, has been a reporter for more than 35 years. He is the national affairs correspondent for *The Nation*. Over the past two decades, he has persistently challenged mainstream thinking on economics. Greider's new book is *Come Home, America: The Rise and Fall (and Redeeming Promise) of Our Country*, to be published by Rodale in March 2009.

Christopher Hayes is *The Nation's* Washington editor and a fellow at the New America Foundation. He has written for the

American Prospect, the *New Republic,* the *Washington Monthly,* the *Guardian* and the *Chicago Reader.*

Doug Henwood, who edits the *Left Business Observer,* is working on a study of the current American ruling class. He has been the host of "Behind the News," a radio show on WBAI, since 1996, and is the author of three books including *After the New Economy.*

Nicholas von Hoffman is the author of *A Devil's Dictionary of Business,* now in paperback. He is the author of 13 books, including *Hoax,* and a frequent contributor to thenation.com.

Will Hutton is the author of many books including *The Writing on the Wall: Why We Must Embrace China as a Partner or Face It as an Enemy* and *A Declaration of Interdependence: Why America Should Join the World.* Hutton is chief executive of the Work Foundation and columnist for the *Observer* (London), where he was editor, then editor-in-chief for four years.

Rev. Jesse L. Jackson, founder and president of the Rainbow/PUSH Coalition, is one of the United States' foremost civil rights, religious and political activists. He is the author of two books: *Keep Hope Alive* and *Straight from the Heart.*

Robert Johnson currently sits on the Board of Directors of the Economic Policy Institute and the Institute for America's Future. In 2007–2008, he was an executive producer of the Oscar-winning documentary, *Taxi to the Dark Side*. Previously, he was a managing director at Soros Fund Management and served as Chief Economist of the U.S. Senate Banking Committee.

Allison Kilkenny is a radio host and political humorist, a fancy way of saying writer. She is a regular contributor to The Huffington Post, the Beast, 236.com, AlterNet.org, and *Wiretap* magazine. She is a regular guest on SIRIUS radio.

Naomi Klein is an award-winning journalist, syndicated columnist and author of the international and *New York Times* bestsellers *The Shock Doctrine: The Rise of Disaster Capitalism* and *No Logo*. She is a columnist at *The Nation* and the *Guardian*.

Jeffrey Madrick, editor of *Challenge Magazine*, is visiting professor of humanities at Cooper Union and director of policy research at the Schwartz Center for Economic Policy Analysis at the New School. He is the author of, most recently, *Why Economies Grow*.

Walter Mosley is the author of two series of mysteries, literary fiction, science fiction, and political philosophy. He has been the recipient of many awards and honors including a Grammy Award for his liner notes accompanying *Richard Pryor—And It's Deep Too!* and the Sundance Institute Risk-Takers Award for 2004. He has also been honored by TransAfrica Forum, was a recipient of the prestigious Anisfield Wolf Award, and served as editor for *The Best American Short Stories of 2003*.

Bobbi Murray lives in Los Angeles and writes frequently on economic justice issues. She has written for *The Nation*, *Los Angeles Magazine*, the *LA Times*, *LA Weekly*, AlterNet and others.

Ralph Nader, the longtime consumer advocate, was an independent candidate for president in 2008. He has been named by *Time* magazine as one of the 100 Most Influential Americans in the Twentieth Century.

Garrett Ordower is an investigative journalist based in New York. His work has appeared in *The Nation*, Chicago's *Daily Herald* and the *Beacon News*.

Sam Pizzigati is an associate fellow at the Washington, D.C.-based Institute for Policy Studies and edits *Too Much*, an online weekly on excess and inequality.

Robert Pollin is a professor of economics and co-director of the Political Economy Research Institute at the University of Massachusetts. His books include, most recently, *A Measure of Fairness* and *An Employment-Targeted Economic Program for Kenya*.

Nomi Prins is a senior fellow at Demos, a nonpartisan public policy think tank. Before becoming a journalist, she served as a managing director for Goldman Sachs in New York. She is the author of *Other People's Money: The Corporate Mugging of*

America and *Jacked: How "Conservatives" Are Picking Your Pocket.*

Robert Sherrill, a frequent and longtime contributor to *The Nation*, was formerly a reporter for *The Washington Post.* He has authored numerous books on politics and society, including *Why They Call It Politics: A Guide to America's Government.*

Jordan Stancil teaches history and international relations at the Institute of Political Studies (Sciences Po) in Paris. He has written for *The Nation*, *The New Republic* and *The Michigan Daily* online.

Joseph E. Stiglitz is University Professor at Columbia University. He received the Nobel Prize in Economics in 2001 for research on the economics of information. Most recently, he is the co-author, with Linda Bilmes, of *The Three Trillion Dollar War: The True Costs of the Iraq Conflict.*

Eric Schlosser is the author of two bestsellers: *Fast Food Nation* and *Reefer Madness.* He is a correspondent for *Atlantic Monthly* and has written for *Rolling Stone, Vanity Fair* and *The New Yorker.* He has received a National Magazine Award and a Sidney Hillman Foundation Award for reporting.

Katrina vanden Heuvel has been *The Nation*'s editor since 1995 and publisher since 2005. She is the co-editor of *Taking Back America—And Taking Down the Radical Right* and editor of *The Dictionary of Republicanisms.* She is a frequent commentator on American and international politics on MSNBC, CNN and PBS. Her articles have appeared in the *Washington Post,* the *Los Angeles Times,* the *New York Times* and the *Boston Globe.*

Kai Wright, a writer in Brooklyn, New York, is the author of *Drifting Toward Love: Black, Brown, Gay* and *Coming of Age on the Streets of New York.* He is a columnist for TheRoot.com.

Howard Zinn is the author of *A People's History of the United States, A Power Governments Cannot Suppress* and most recently, *A People's History of American Empire.*

NOBODY OWNS.
THE NATION.
THAT'S WHY
SO MANY
SOMEBODIES
READ IT.

The Nation

Why Conferences Fail by Harold J. Laski

If the Supreme Court
Overrules Roosevelt

by Paul Y. Anderson

Lippmann: Obfuscator

Third Article by Amos Pinchot

SUBSCRIBE NOW
WWW.READERNATION.COM
800-333-8536

"The Nation, as we all know,
has often represented minority
opinion and mighty unpopular
minority opinion at that."
—Franklin D. Roosevelt (1940)

FDR was a longtime Nation reader.